GATEWAYS TO GOD

Pete shares with us not only profound insights into the Word, but also his heart and becomes a great friend in the journey through the gateways of God.

Juras Grincevicius, Vineyard Ministries, Lithuania

A good and helpful book: sound, intelligent and challenging. Pete Lowman understands his Bible and its place in the modern world as well as in the believer's heart. He reads the Bible as a man of his times.

Peter Lewis, Senior Pastor of Cornerstone Evangelical Church, Nottingham.

GATEWAYS TO GOD

Seeking Spiritual Depth in a Postmodern World

Pete Lowman

Christian Focus

ISBN 1-85792-657-9

© Peter Lowman 2001

Published in 2001
by
Christian Focus Publications
Geanies House, Fearn
Ross-shire, IV20 1TW, UK

www.christianfocus.com

Printed and bound by
Guernsey Press, Guernsey

Cover Design by Owen Daily

Contents

Prologue:

A Spirituality for the Twenty-First Century

We're drinking tea in a flat in Moscow. Suddenly my colleague says: What is spiritual depth?

It is a question that has bothered many of us – at least once we've been Christians a few years. We've heard a fair number of sermons, read books, begun to learn. But now we start to have a sense of repetitiveness: we've heard a lot of this before. So what next? Where now?

What does it really mean to go on with God? Is there, indeed, somewhere to go – or should we pay our spiritual taxes on Sundays but give our real energies to the secular? How can we develop spiritual depth?

And this same question arises in our longing to serve God. A team of us have been working with Christian student movements in Russia, Belarus and the Baltics. It's been an enormous joy and privilege to give our lives in the service of these countries, to seek to cultivate something lasting for the growth of the Church there. And we have seen God's power at work. Particularly in the early days after communism, many, many students turned to Christ.

But now my colleague was asking: What is that 'depth' which we should seek to foster in our friends? Some of those conversions didn't last. Jesus warned us about seed that falls on rocky places, putting down no roots – where someone 'receives the word with joy', but *'because he has no root* he lasts only a short time... When trouble comes, he quickly falls away.' We've watched it happen. Pressures and ethical challenges erode the commitment to holiness; or a young believer finds an attractive lover, who sadly has no faith. We look around, and see friends, once so keen, no longer showing much spiritual life. Well, it's a tough culture, and our hopes have to be realistic. Yet if these things happen too often, our work becomes, literally, fruitless. And so the question haunts us, as it must anyone who longs to build something that lasts: How do we foster those 'roots'? What is spiritual depth?

The question hangs over churches in Britain too. Our services used to be accused of dullness. So we have worked really hard to make them attractive. Now, perhaps, we face the opposite problem: cheery everyday-ness that slides into shallowness. We walk out of the church door on Sunday knowing our kids have enjoyed themselves ('Dad, did you see the puppets?'); but for us there was little to feed on, little or nothing deep.

Is being 'happy-clappy' the problem? That's how the media have stereotyped us in recent years, along with 'fearsome fundamentalists'. We shouldn't be too alarmed at either; both are preferable to the old 'drippy vicar' image. Actually, the use of 'fearsome fundamentalist' often reflects alarm that practical Christianity is winning a hearing; while beneath the 'happy-clappy' jibe may lie envy at churches that show real joy. Yet the stereotype does signal a danger. The problem of shallow triviality can be a real one. And we have to solve it if Sunday is to be more than a 'pit-stop': if it is to give an encounter with God profound enough to help us put him first throughout the week.

There is a hunger in our 'postmodern' culture, where everything is dazzling surface, contrived image, packaged shallowness; where, with the death of truth, profundity has become inaccessible. There is a hunger for a rediscovery of 'spirituality' – whatever that is. If the Church cannot meet this hunger, no one can (though people will go on searching in all kinds of unhealthy places). But first we need some answers ourselves. What is spiritual depth?

Doorways to depth

Various responses can be heard today. 'You want to go further as a Christian? – Why, you should go to Bible college.' And for many it works. God has blessed them with that particular cast of mind, and as they study, the doctrines become tongued with flame; they are coming to know God himself better, rather than merely discussing ideas about him. For others, it isn't so. The enriched understanding is a valuable tool, the mind is better equipped for service. But in the end there remains a sense of drought; all the articles read and notes written may not give a sense of deepened spirituality.

From another quarter comes a different response: Spiritual depth means acquiring more gifts, more blessings, more experiences in the Spirit. And God often uses these contexts, so that we meet him in a new depth of reality. But again, with the quest for one new wave of blessing after another, there can come a sense of repetitiveness – what South African student worker Bill Houston called 'the search for spiritual kicks, for the next exciting meeting where it's all at'. The process continues from climax to climax, conference to conference; but, somehow, God himself goes missing.

What is spiritual depth? From one angle, it is what Watchman Nee calls 'developing a history with God' – we have walked with God, listened to him and talked with him, seen the reality of his presence and power in us. As in a marriage, deep relationship is grounded in years of experiences shared (both good and difficult), conversations enjoyed, things seen and accomplished together. Not far removed from this is Paul's deep longing: 'I want to know Christ, and the power of his resurrection, and the fellowship of sharing in his sufferings.'[1]

Put it another way: depth of spirituality is a life that utterly fulfils what Christ called the two great commandments: flooded by the Spirit with continual passion to love the Lord with all our heart, soul, mind and strength, and our neighbour as ourselves. Growth in prayer, in devoted holiness, in worship, service, fellowship and evangelism will all find their place here. The weakness with this phrasing, however, might be its focus on what should flow out from us, rather than what, through grace, must flow in to get us started.

This book takes its theme from an insight, shared with me by an older believer, that has been enormously helpful. If we really want to 'know' God, if we want continual growth and depth, then we must have a vision of God that continually broadens. And that comes, he said, from continually **pioneering** in God's Word. What is 'pioneering'? It means exploring, in faith, the areas of the Bible that are unfamiliar to us; learning more and more of what the Spirit has embedded in them to show us the glory of God and the meaning of his will; then turning that into worship, prayer and action.

Pioneering offers us a challenge: maybe our spirituality runs out of steam because we lack faith in the God of Scripture! The Bible is so long, we suspect, because it was put together by over-enthusiastic archangels; really, some Epistles and prophets could have been omitted. A slimline Bible, the length of a *Reader's Digest*, should give us all we need to know. And often our knowledge of the Bible becomes a 'Greatest Hits' compilation. We have our favourite sections of the Gospels and Acts; the occasional chapter in the Epistles; some stories from the old testament; and maybe a handful of psalms... Yet faith tells us that God has prepared a far fuller diet, to give us a rounded grasp of what he is like. We impoverish ourselves if we don't open each doorway into his glory that he's chosen to give us. We *need* the unique insights we receive from chewing on 1 John, Job or Isaiah. ('I never thought there was so much in it!', as someone said delightedly to me.) Pioneering, in company with the Spirit, is essential if we want an ever-deepening spirituality: 'ever further and deeper, into the heart of God'.

This is obvious when we remember what God is like. A Creator God of Love is not a static God. Love is always on the move, always reaching out, always expressing itself afresh. The Church is likewise always on the move: ever pioneering, carrying God's love and truth from frontier to unreached frontier, Jerusalem to Judea then on to Samaria and the ends of the earth. That's what it's like to partner with God. Ever-deepening participation in his eternal adventure – whether our personal 'frontier' is a faraway people group, or a house down the street untouched by God's love – is a fundamental aspect of 'depth'. Life with this kind of God means moving onward with him, always more to be done in partnership with him, more to be seen in companionship with him.

The same principle marks our deepening knowledge of God. We shall never know exhaustively the deeds, the love, the glorious character of the infinite God of eternity. We speak scathingly of the 'quest for novelty', but it is not entirely wrong. To minds wearied by our culture's stresses, some variety may be essential. As we approach God, our minds are like a child's bucket seeking to empty the ocean; millennia will not suffice for us to grasp each diverse aspect of his infinity. God has far more to reveal than our consciousness can ever grasp.

We see that in the design of the Book he has given us. From one point of view, it is breathtakingly simple: a six-year-old can receive from it intuitions so powerful that they lead to a life-changing experience of salvation. On the other hand, it is long, and at times obscure. Some passages do not yield their meaning on the first, or even the fifth, reading. The combination is masterly. The Bible has enough on its surface for the simplest would-be disciple, yet is so designed that in eighty years we will never exhaust all it has for us. The more we master one set of insights, from one group of books maybe, the more we find our fading memories need refreshing with the glory of what we were feeding on a year previously. (Surely that's what we experience when, say, we return to the Gospels after a period in the old testament. Or when we think, 'Three years ago Philippians was exhilarating, but now I've forgotten why.')

It is this pioneering process that will keep us rooted in the most pressured times. Spurts of spiritual growth often come in a time of special outreach, or the communal experience of a conference. But the depth that survives drought or hurricane comes through years of storing up in our hearts (like Mary[2]) insight upon insight of the ways and the glory of God.

Engaging our hearts

But spirituality isn't merely reading the Bible. If indeed the 'chief end of man is to glorify God and enjoy him forever', then there is a vital further step: responding to what we have seen in specific worship, and specific intercession. Those two aspects are indispensable to the whole experience.

And it is at this point that pioneering, Bible-grounded spirituality is an experiential spirituality. Obviously experience isn't our goal, otherwise we turn it into an idol; encountering experience becomes our secret hope, rather than encountering God. But as we learn to worship God with passion for what he shows us in each new step of pioneering, the sense of glory will find its way to us, in the Spirit's own time. It is as we deliberately respond to what God has spoken, in praise, then in prayer, that our pioneering ceases to be academic, and becomes relational.

It has to be deliberate. The postmodern world knows no depth: it rushes us as passive consumers from shallow experience to shallow experience. Postmodern Christians likewise can drift from stimulus to stimulus, from one powerful meeting to another. But if we become mere spectators, consumers, it is worship-as-fix: shimmering surface, but with little depth or profundity. One of two grim consequences can follow. Either our faith shrinks totally to the recurrent stimulus of Sunday mornings; or there comes a point when we feel we've seen it all, and need a new faith altogether. ('Moving from evangelicalism to Orthodoxy, and then on to yoga,' as a Russian colleague put it.) True spirituality isn't a passive consumption of stimulants. It sets out actively to interact with God: to discern the fuel for today's worship in what God has spoken, then to express a response worthy of him – being sure that, somewhere along the line, God himself will warm our hearts.

It is like a romantic relationship. In the early months, everything about the beloved may be dazzling, irresistibly stimulating; we can't sleep, we're off our food (remember?). Later comes a more mature stage, growing now through conscious choice. We know each other better (though never totally, thank God!); the marriage deepens as we choose to spend time, choose to perceive our partner's beauty, choose to feel, choose to respond with 'I love you!' That in turn somehow cleanses our perceptions; and sooner or later it draws out a reaction! But if we don't learn these things, we face the same grim consequences as in the previous paragraph. If we don't grow beyond waiting for stimulus, then the marriage can come to seem tepid, and we are in danger of falling for the instant thrill of a miniskirt down the road. But the result won't be real relationship, merely the shallowness of the one-night stand. Or, our marriage can drift until it is merely a matter of custom. It is not divorce, but we're missing out on joy, and missing out on love.

So too with spirituality. We can choose to pass beyond the passive waiting for stimulus. We choose to invest the effort, to cultivate the perception of what is glorious and worthy of worship in what we read; choose to respond with something of the passion God deserves, in prayer and in adoration. And as we do so, in God's good time his grace impacts us; the love of God catches fire.

The heart of this book, then, is a challenge to pioneer; to be committed to exploring, by faith in the Spirit of revelation, the stretches of the Bible with which we are not yet familiar; and then to turning them into prayer and worship, and sharing what we've seen with others. Pioneering means finding, and passing through, more and more of the gateways provided by the Spirit into the glory of God. Solid roots, depth in the knowledge of God, breadth in understanding his will and his world – a spirituality rich enough and rooted enough for the twenty-first century: these things will assuredly follow.

Pioneering is personal

The Word of God is a living Word; what God speaks through it to each of us is a message he designs for us individually. He knows what passages we will read in any given month; he will have truths there that fit the needs he knows we will face at that time. The Bible certainly isn't a horoscope (finding 'Do not go to Egypt' in our Bible reading isn't the way to fix our holiday). But surely God knows, and prepares, the principles and insights we need in any given month. In that sense, in our Bible reading God speaks to us as specifically and directly as when we respond to him in prayer.

In one respect, what any believer receives in encountering God's Word is individual, unique. Because the Bible is *true*, biblical doctrines are universal facts; biblical historical statements are objective realities; biblical commands are universally authoritative. But no two believers' grasp of all Scripture's applications and priorities will ever be identical, because what God prioritizes to reveal to us is what we, individually, have most needed to hear. So none of us has 'seen it all'; and there will always be more truth for each of us to learn. Even purely human writers – Shakespeare, Conrad, Eliot – give rise to ever-expanding rereadings, such is the richness of their books. From his far richer, 'living' Word, God will go on speaking: as one of the Pilgrim Fathers put it, humbly, 'God has yet more light to break forth from his holy Word.'

That, for me, has been a joy of working in an international and transdenominational Christian movement. My own culture and denomination gave me a set of 'glasses' well-equipped to see some things in Scripture – and ill-equipped for others. When I began to mix with believers from other evangelical backgrounds, I found there were things they saw, things that thrilled them, that I would not have noticed. Studying in Wales, for example, meant meeting a certain kind of Calvinist for the first time. And as we argued into the night, I was never convinced by their framework – but they permanently enriched my grasp of God with insights, visions, that I might never have otherwise seen. C.S.Lewis extols the reading of books from other centuries for this reason: and the same enrichment occurs as we expose ourselves to teachers from other cultures. Chinese Bible teachers have opened vast windows to God in my own spiritual life. Because of the reality they live in, Latin Americans showed me things the Bible has to say about servanthood and God's care for the poor that I could have found hard to learn elsewhere. African believers, not brainwashed by a desupernaturalized society as we Westerners are, often teach us vital realities of prayer and faith.

We have everything to learn from each other. As Paul says, every one of us should have a word of instruction to benefit the others; and the Body of Christ grows and builds itself up in love as *each* part shares its unique contribution (1 Cor 14:26, Eph 4:16). We each have insights to share; and insights that are true will not, ultimately, conflict with each other. So the themes highlighted in what follows are not presented as *the* priorities of the Bible books in question. There are many other ways to approach these books, other truths that God gives his people through them. As we each share what God gives, together we build towards the full, gloriously unattainable grasp of all he is saying; and meanwhile he will have yet more light to break forth from his holy Word!

The chapters that follow, therefore, are selective, are personal. I have divided them into sections that some people may find useful in daily readings, on the train for example. But why these particular passages? Because they happen to have been meaningful 'gateways' into God's presence for me; sections that have sent me out afterwards through the front door feeling fully fed and newly inspired. But there cannot be a part of the Bible that will not – through prayerful faith, commitment of our minds and the illumination of the Spirit – turn out likewise a 'gateway' to a new insight of God and of his will (cf. 2 Timothy 3:16). The wider we range, the broader and deeper will be our vision, our understanding, our discipleship. These are a few reports from just one traveller.

What follows, then, is an account of places that have been 'gateways to God' for me.[3] We're going to feed on four key new testament books: Ephesians, 2 Corinthians, Mark and 1 Peter, each of which has something enormously relevant for our twenty-first century situation. Then we're going to take a break and, on the basis of what we've explored, think a little more deeply about what can give us a truly life-giving spirituality for this challenging new era. Lastly, we'll 'pioneer' again, this time into some fascinating and fruitful regions of 1 John, Romans and Revelation.

My prayer is that what follows will encourage us each to pioneer. To trust the Spirit to teach us, whoever we are; to tunnel further into the depths of God's boundless revelation, and so to put down roots that will save us from shallowness; to grow in a spirituality that is shaped by his continual speaking; one that is marked by his priorities, his truths, his longings and will and desires...

'... *that we may have power, together with all the saints, to grasp how wide and long and high and deep is the love of Christ, and to know this love that passes knowledge... that we may be filled with all the fullness of God...*' (Ephesians 3:18-19).

Notes

[1] Phil 3:10.

[2] Luke 2:51.

[3] It seemed simplest to stick with the new testament; and I've avoided what a later chapter will describe as the 'core' passages, because the aim here is to focus on 'pioneering' a little off the beaten track.

I

The Vision of the Ultimate: Rereading Ephesians

Ephesians: A Rough Guide

Chapter 1	Paul's vision and Paul's prayers
Chapters 2, 3	The gospel that unifies Christ's Bride
Chapters 4:1-5:21	Living in tune with what God has done...
Chapters 5:22-6:9	...in marriage, family, work
Chapter 6:10-24	Spiritual warfare

Staring glory in the face (1:1-23)

Ephesians has been called the summit of the new testament. 'It must be manifest to the most casual reader that we are upon very high and holy ground here', said William Kelly a century ago as he launched out on his classic commentary.

From its very start, we sense that Paul's vision is possessed by the ultimate. A quick glance at the openings of other Epistles confirms that he is onto something special here. No other letter has an opening paragraph like this one, sweeping from before creation in v4 to the climax of time in v10. Paul begins almost in ecstasy – '*Blessed* be the God and Father of our Lord Jesus Christ, who has blessed us in the heavenly realms with every spiritual blessing in Christ!'

If we're feeling jaded, not moving spiritually, that joyous '*every*' sounds tantalizing – an uncompromising challenge that

God is doing more in us than we think. There is no explanation yet as to what so pregnant a promise will mean. But if we want to align with the spirituality of an apostle possessed by this sort of revelation, we probably need to join in with a conscious response: *Yes, Lord...*

No explanation yet, and maybe, in one sense, there's no explanation possible. Clearly there are spiritual steps forward that depend as much on divine, revelatory grace breaking in on us as they did at our initial conversion. That is what Paul prays for as the chapter proceeds: 'that God may give you the Spirit of revelation, so that you may know him better'(v17). Spiritual knowledge is inextricably supernatural in origin (compare 1 Corinthians 2:7-12). Without the Spirit speaking to us, there is nothing; it is not optional. (*Then Lord: please teach me!*)

As we read these first paragraphs, we sense Paul lifted up, overwhelmed, stretched for superlatives in his exuberant rejoicing over God's predestined plan for us. We're talking destiny here! Paul turns to one expression after another to convey something of God's goal for our existence. All of us who are 'in Christ', who have been 'included in Christ' by faith (1:13), have been chosen from the very creation to be 'holy' (v4). God's loving predestination brings us into the bizarre position of sons and daughters to the Almighty (v5). Our very existence is so that we might 'be for the praise of his glory' (vv6,12,14), and, ultimately, participate in 'the mystery of his will' when history is consummated – that inauguration of an unimaginable cosmic unity of 'all things in heaven and earth... under one head, even Christ'(vv9-10). He will do all this, promises Paul; we can collaborate or not, we can go the long way round or not, but as believers that is where we're going. That's the purpose; that is the vision for us. (*Lord: praise be indeed to the glory of your grace....!*)

He moves on. Now comes a chance for us to foster a habit crucial to a pioneering spirituality: to begin noticing those moments when *if I'd written this, I wouldn't have put it that way*... – and then ask ourselves, why not? Maybe that's how we catch ourselves reacting to Paul's habit of giving thanks for his sisters and brothers(v16). It is not a habit I would have developed if it wasn't for Paul (though it helps no end with delicate relationships!) Or, maybe, it's how we react to Paul's 'hit list' of three key prayer concerns that he 'keeps asking' (v17), the topics of vv18-23. Again, these are not three issues I'd have focused on if left to myself[1] – which suggests I've been missing the point somewhere. As a starting-point in developing our spirituality, we can pray about these three, specifically for ourselves, and then for someone we care about, as Paul does here.

Paul prays that the Spirit will 'enlighten the eyes of our heart' to know, first, the 'hope to which he has called you'. This is such a preoccupation in Ephesians that we'll need to reflect on it more deeply later; but let us just note here that 'hope' is vital to Paul's spirituality. In fact, in Thessalonians our 'hope of salvation' turns out to be nothing less than the 'helmet' that protects our thinking – just as for the writer of Hebrews it is an 'anchor for the soul', stretching beyond the veil that hides the unseen world (6:19) – firmly holding to the rock of the ocean floor so that we are not blown around by the waves on the surface.[2] *Lord, please help me understand this hope...*

The second enlightenment concerns 'the riches of his glorious inheritance in the saints'. This we are likely to reverse, thinking Paul is describing the riches of our inheritance in God. But if the NIV and NASB reading is correct – and the reference to us as 'God's possession' (v14) would confirm it – it's the other way round; Paul's concern is that we grasp how remarkably precious we are to God. To understand this properly we will need to grasp the passage about the Bride in chapter 5; but meanwhile it has all kinds of challenging implications for our self-image.

Ten years ago I went through a phase of feeling fairly discouraged, and during that time a Malaysian friend gave me

a simple plaque with Christ's words from John 15:9: 'As the
Father has loved me, so have I loved you.' For me, this took
some believing. That Christ loves us, in general terms, I
believed; that he could tolerate me personally, I understood
too. But that his love for each of us was equivalent to the vast,
infinite, oceanic love that the Father feels for his utterly perfect
Son – this took some faith. But so it is; that is how we are loved;
we are the inheritance he is waiting for. (Calvin compares God
to a husband saying, 'I seem to be only half a man when my wife
is not with me.'[3]) This is what Paul wants us to grasp here; it is
also a prime purpose of heaven, that God should show us the
'incomparable riches' of his love for us (2:7). (And the response
in developing our spirituality might at the least be, *Thankyou,
Lord...*)

The third enlightenment from the Spirit is that we might know
what is 'his incomparably great power for us who believe'(v19).
Immediately Paul goes on to compare it to the resurrection: power
that broke the grave, power that brought the dead to life – let
loose in each of us! Again, the horizons sweep back endlessly: if
that power is loose in *my* life, then there is nothing he cannot do;
no stronghold of darkness or resistance to truth that is
impregnable; no personality weakness, no emotional scar, no
past folly (compare 3:8) that is beyond the reach of his
transformation. We are not doomed to the prison of any habit
or addiction; what matters about us is not what we are, but what,
through this kind of power, we can become. Inside us or outside
us, as Paul puts it two chapters later, God can 'do immeasurably
more than all we ask or imagine'; it is a charter to dream about
the possible, based on the vision Paul is praying into us here.
We're surrounded by the media's silent insistence that God never
does anything. So our spirituality must build on this liberating
certainty of a God who is working way ahead of us, of power
that can (in his own time) do more than we are capable of
dreaming.

(All we can capture of this is just a drop in the bucket. But maybe now is a moment to move beyond studying the text, and to use it to worship the Lord. That is the heart of spirituality…)

The heavens now, and heaven to come (2:1-7, 1:9-14)

There's much more in Ephesians' first few paragraphs. What other themes do we find prominent? Not surprisingly, since Paul is expressing the vision of the ultimate, we find him talking about heaven. The surprise comes in what he says about it. It isn't the way we usually think.

Maybe the most surprising thing comes at the end of our section, in 2:6. For Paul, the 'heavenly realms' aren't just where we go when we die; they are where we believers are, *right now*. Already God has 'seated us in the heavenly realms' with Christ, he says; we are 'seated' with Jesus in the invisible realm, the real-est universe.[4] We don't sense it, of course: most of the time, anyway. Our five senses are firmly attuned to this world; and so – most of the time, apart from odd minutes, hints, glimpses in our lives' best moments that we sense and then they are gone – we don't actually experience the 'heavenly realms'. But vital things are happening there continually; and right now we share Christ's unseen authority there (2:6, 1:20-21), far above all the principalities and powers. That is why we can pray 'in Jesus' Name'. (It's a vital point in many two-thirds-world countries, where it's crucial that in Christ we're set far above the reach of all powers of darkness.) 'All the spiritual blessings' that, according to Paul, we already possess, have likewise to do with our position in these 'heavenly realms' (1:3) that we must perceive by faith.

(This is one reason why death will be the supreme, joyous adventure. Right now we're like people walking through the woods with a noisy Walkman. Outside the birds are singing, but there's too much noise pumping into our ears, and we can't hear them at all. Then suddenly the batteries go dead… and for the first time we hear what's really there! So when the heart stops, and we close our eyes for the last time to this world, and open them to the eternal universe... we shall suddenly see where we've been living, see the forces that matter: that overwhelming cosmos of angels and demons, God and Satan, powers of heaven and hell that we've been wandering blindly amongst all this time.   It will undoubtedly come as a shock; we'll see what misdirected priorities, concerns and fears we had! But it's going to be good; for above all we'll see Jesus...)

We are seated securely with Christ in the 'real-est world', then; remembering that let's return to 1:11-14, because it takes us a step further. God's Spirit who came to live in us when we were 'included in Christ'[5] is himself the 'deposit' or foretaste of heaven, in that sense in which we usually mean it (1:14). God has a glorious future 'inheritance' for us; but that radiant 'heaven' has a bridgehead inside us now, from which its transforming powers break into our decaying world; and one day – at death or the second coming – they will sweep through us completely.   But the foothold is there already.   Graham Kendrick has it right – 'Heaven is in my heart!'   When we were born again, we entered into heaven, and heaven entered into us. We are with God, he is with us; we are 'seated' with Christ now. *(Thankyou, Lord, for both placing your Spirit in me, and seating me now 'above... with Christ in God'; please help me get some idea of what this 'heaven' means for me, help me to 'set my mind' there* (Col 3:1-4).)

So we're involved with the eternal world, and 'heaven' is in us now; but 'heaven' is also where we're going.   Paul has a lot on his heart about the glory and loving oneness that will fill the heavenly cosmos of the future.   There's a profound revelation awaiting us here, with implications in a hundred directions.

First, the cosmos is to be reshaped by the reality of God. Christ 'fills everything in every way'(1:23), as the one who 'ascended higher than the heavens in order to fill the whole universe' (4:10).   One day the cosmos will reflect that. 1:10

sets it out: the Father's whole future purpose is to 'bring all things in heaven and earth together under one head, even Christ'. Paul presents us with a vision of relationships restored 'together' throughout a transfigured, reunified cosmos. That certainly isn't what we have now; universal alienation was the result of our snatching at our own autonomy[6] in the Fall. In Genesis 3, the man/God rupture caused by our attempt to run our own world developed quickly into broken relationships between man and woman (3:16), and between humans and nature (3:17-19). There followed the first murder (4:8), and Cain's alienation from his environment as a 'restless wanderer on the earth' (4:11-14), until eventually the whole earth became 'corrupt and full of violence' (6:11).

We have inherited the results. Generations of individuals have repeated the self-assertion and self-isolation of the Fall. We've inherited a divided world living by the survival of the fittest, broken by ethnic tension, class struggle, shattered relationships, gender misunderstanding, generational conflicts. But now heaven is coming. That alienated, individualism-driven world is being subverted, and will finally be swept away, by a resurrected, reunited universe: one brought back together under Christ, radiant with God. It will happen: Christ's love will flow into every wound and every corner, and 'the earth will be filled with the glory of God as the waters cover the sea'! All the brokenness gone, all relationships restored; it's a vision worth living for, and worth dying for. (*Father, I worship you...*)

Even now, therefore, God is reaching out (through us!), until ultimately in this unity 'everything has been put under him' (1 Cor 15:27). This fact has radical implications for our spirituality. (*Lord, please help me find my place...*) First, for the imperative of personal involvement with global mission to every geographical corner, ensuring a presence in God's triumphant final synthesis of 'every nation, tribe, people, and language' (Rev 7:9). Equally, for the glorifying of Christ in every corner of human endeavour: 'There is not an inch in the whole area of existence,' proclaimed Abraham Kuyper at the foundation of the Free University of Amsterdam, 'of which Christ the sovereign of all does not cry, "It is Mine"!' Equally, too, for our commitment to the love of God at work in every corner of our global society. The Lord demands, and will one day bring, justice and truth and wholeness in every inch of his creation.

There could be no greater vision! Inevitably this unity involves a total negation of all 'dividing walls of hostility' (2:14). 'There is neither Jew nor Greek, slave nor free, male nor female, for you are all one in Christ Jesus' (Gal 3:28). That's the theme of the second half of chapter 2, to which we'll soon turn. But first we must grasp another vital idea, introduced for us in the closing two verses of chapter 1. What unites us all, in God's glorious purposes, is something else for which we need the Spirit's revelation: the glory of Christ's Body, his loving Bride, the eternal Church.

The Bride and the Body　(1:22-23, 5:25-32, 4:4-16)

If we speed-read on through Ephesians (it's only five pages!), we will quickly notice the centrality of the Church to Paul's concerns. We'll see, too, that his vision of cosmic unity isn't something bureaucratic or impersonal. (Nor, we should remind ourselves, is it compulsory (4:18); there are those who 'reject God's purpose for themselves' (cf. Luke 7:30), remaining finally 'shut out from the presence of the Lord' (2 Thess 1:9), outside in the dark.) Rather, it is personalized to the highest degree.

Paul's 'vision of the ultimate' picks up here on one of the great themes of the Bible. Near the close of Revelation, John presents history's consummation in the Bible's final chapters; it is a panorama of the 'wedding supper' of the Church, the 'Bride, the wife of the Lamb'. We see her 'beautifully dressed for her husband'; she 'shone with the glory of God', and she will be Christ's companion forever (Rev 21:2-3,9-11). '*The*

Bride': human love, sex and marriage are a foreshadowing of this ultimate, rapturous union between the Lord and his people; it's the climax of history, and the theme of eternity! In Ephesians too, Paul's vision is of a universe irradiated (5:27) by the beauty of this glorious Bride of Christ. She is the Church that Christ will finally perfect; she is what Calvary (perhaps even our entire planet's existence?) was for (5:25-27, 31-32). Each of us who believes is part of her; and each of us will share in that triumphant consummation. (*Lord, I truly thank you that I can belong in all this...!*)

She will reflect, or rather be filled with, Christ's own nature. The Father is 'over all and through all and in all' (4:6); and, utterly one with him, Christ too 'ascended higher than the heavens in order to fill the whole universe' (4:10). So a 'reflective glory' of holy, loving oneness is also his purpose for his Bride (4:3-6). This was Christ's passionate longing as he prayed to his Father just before the cross: 'I pray for those who will believe, that all of them may be one, Father, *just as* you are in me and I am in you' (John 17:20-21). The Spirit's ministry is at work now for precisely this purpose, says Paul (just after his words about Christ 'filling the universe'), so that we may be built up 'until we all reach unity in the faith and in the knowledge of the Son' (Eph 4:12-13). This radiant unity of the Church will be at the heart of the heavenly universe. It is glorious, and it's already happening. Experience teaches that Christ spoke no less than the truth when he prayed to his Father, 'I have given them the glory that you gave me, that they may be one as we are one; I in them, and you in me' (John 17:22)![7]

We are Christ's Bride: what more could we ask or imagine? Yet there is more! In our reading of the book as a whole we'll find one profound image of the Church succeeding another as Paul struggles to express our destiny as God's people.[8] Or let's say our identity; our destiny is our identity. Grasp Ephesians and we grasp the glory of the Church – utterly vital if we are to have strength for working through the inadequacies of local churches that are the chrysalis of that glory. A further crucial image, then, is of the Church as Christ's *Body* (1:23, 2:15-16, 4:11-16), the extension of his personality on earth. Christ is this Body's head, and we are his *fullness* (1:23): his chosen expression, his supremely ordained 'genre' through which his personality and grace and love overflow into the world. We the Church are not what we appear! On earth there is, in the end, only one Church, one living Body: made up only of believers, but made up of all believers. The Church is not a human organization operating merely on a sociological level (many of its members are in the next life already); it is a supernatural, living organism, sharing the glory of Christ its head.

It is important for us to grasp that this Body is already a reality. The divisions that human beings carve into its skin are only externalities. Whatever our culture, century or denomination – Danish Lutherans, Welsh Calvinists, Nigerian charismatics, Dallas Baptists – we are being 'built together to become a dwelling-place in which God lives by his Spirit': the Body is One now, and we shall be so throughout eternity. (Still, as we read that 'built together' we see why 1 John, and the Lord's Prayer, make clear that closeness to God depends on good relations with our brothers and sisters.[9] Spirituality is incompatible with an unforgiving spirit; the peace of God is essential to life in the Body. *Lord, please help me see where that applies to me!*)

Two more things are crucial for us to grasp about the Body, particularly from chapter 4. First, its combination of unity and diversity. Paul is enthusiastic about the unity that God is creating ('making every effort' to maintain that oneness (4:3) is the climax of his argument in chapters 2 and 3, as we shall see); yet this does not blot out the individual. Instead – and this harmony is another reason why Ephesians is so life-giving – amidst the emphasis on unity, the individual becomes crucial. *Each* of us is a unique gift from God to his Church (4:7-8,11); 'to *each* one of us' God has given a part to play (v7); and the

Body will only grow 'joined and held together by *every* supporting ligament...as *each* part does its work'(v16). God's design involves innumerable sources of individual input building up his Body. There is, for example, a plurality of evangelists, a plurality of pastor-teachers (v11); the local church is to be 'built up in love' by many diverse insights and different approaches.

We are built to need those multiple insights on broader levels too, of course. Creating cross-fertilization between different traditions is one of the most valuable things the student Christian Unions, and also the national Evangelical Alliances, have contributed to the Church; increasing inter-cultural contacts in years to come will bring even greater mutual blessing, since other cultures – or indeed age groups – grasp quickly what we do not.[10]　I ask myself now: how much less would I have learnt about prayer and faith, if it were not for lessons learnt from African sisters and brothers? About awe at God's majesty, if not for Russians and Belarussians? We're built for the Body, and it is only 'with all the saints' that we can be filled to the fullness of God, as Paul says (3:18-19, cf. 4:13). Without a hunger to learn, from every other member of the Body, there will be needless limits to our growth.

This vision of the kaleidoscopic input we need has been tragically neglected in the history of the Church. Sadly, the Reformation failed to take a tough enough look at the idea of the 'minister', and carried into the new era the notion of a local church having just one 'priest': despite the insistence of, say, 1 Peter 2:9, that all God's people are priests. (It is astonishing – and impoverishing – to hear believers today describe just one church member as 'our priest'!) The result of this failure was that, for many Protestant churches, 'body-life' has amounted to little more than watching a single performer, just like in the middle ages. The vision of Ephesians is radically different. Everyone matters, every member has a job to do; and the body will only grow 'as *each* part does its work' (4:16, 1 Cor 12:20-22). No one is dispensable, in evangelism, worship, discipling or caring.

But there's more. The purpose of a gift is not simply to be exercised for passive reception by others. Rather, all the gifts and leaders are there to mobilize, encourage, equip and stretch others of God's people to get into the work (4:12).[11] The goal of everyone in the Body, then, is to work him/herself out of a job. As Roger Mitchell put it in the IFES magazine *In Touch*: 'It's like 2 Timothy 2: sharing the things you've been taught with other people who will pass them on to others again: training someone, making yourself redundant, and moving on' - so that those to whom the leader has ministered know everything (s)he does and can take over, and (s)he can go off and build something fresh elsewhere. (And when there is nowhere left to go, of course, the End will come: Matthew 24:14.) This is a vision that can transform our whole approach to ministry – and be a powerful stimulus to the Body's growth. *Lord, deliver me from holding on to my own place and power in an un-Christlike way; teach me how to work with you in this process; help me trust you enough to work myself out of a job...*

The other astounding thing is the goal of the Body's development. Doctrinal teaching and theology are not merely for the sake of abstract knowledge (when they become so they are clearly inauthentic), but so that we may 'grow up into Christ' (4:15). Paul phrases this in an astonishing way. In the end, he says, God has predestined us collectively to 'become mature, attaining to the *whole* measure of the fullness of Christ'(4:13), with all of his love, joy and power for goodness flowing out through us. ('That you may be filled with all the fullness of God', says 3:19; surely that will necessitate eternity!) This idea takes a certain amount of believing. Revelation 3:21's way of putting it is equally difficult: we will share his throne, says Jesus, 'just as I sat down with my Father on his throne'. (*Just as*? *Lord?*) But that is what ultimate unity and divine companionship finally mean; that is the Bride's destiny; that is heaven.

Meanwhile this world is the arena in which the Church goes through that maturing process. Here, says Paul, introducing a fourth picture, we the Church are God's '*workmanship*' (2:10), his 'artwork' or 'masterpiece'. (The Greek word is the one from which we derive the English word 'poem'.) The history of his Body is his drama, his symphony, where the free actions of numberless participants are orchestrated with boundless skill, to draw out his unfathomable glory. Paul feels a calling to 'make plain to everyone' the wonder of this reality, this 'mystery' (3:8-9). And, remarkably, not just to humanity. Paul adds that the matchless brilliance of this enterprise reveals 'through the church, the manifold wisdom of God... to the rulers and authorities in the heavenly realms' (3:10). God has purposes for the unseen worlds of which we know nothing: what is remarkable is that it is through us that his glory is revealed, so that he receives 'glory in the church' (3:21). In the cross God revealed his cosmic purpose in all its love, selflessness, wisdom and grace. As we then express it by his Spirit in the way we live, we participate in its revelation at levels we cannot imagine.[12] As Kelly suggested last century, even if the whole world rejected us, that itself would be an astonishing calling. (*Lord, may I live up to it...*)

One final image. The Church is Christ's 'fullness', Bride, Body, masterpiece; she is also his '*temple*' and '*dwelling*' (2:20-22). Built together on the Word, indwelt and irradiated by the Spirit; together we are the place where God has chosen to live, as truly as when he was a foetus in Mary's womb. 'God's temple is sacred, and you are that temple,' Paul wrote to Corinth (1 Cor 3:17). (*Lord, what does it mean to be indwelt by you?*) It is practical, of course: if I secretly look down on a fellow-believer, I am actually despising a temple of the Spirit. That goes for self-dislike too. Each of us as believers is an indispensable segment of God's holy dwelling-place: the temple that he chose, that with infinite competence he is beautifying, and that he loves, passionately.

Lord, thankyou for your love for us, and for the glory of your Church! Please give me a deeper vision of its grandeur; may it determine how I live and how I view your Church down here, so that I may be more use in it right now...

Learning about love   (2:1-3:21)

The practicalities flow out from all that. If our destiny is to be one glorified Body, totally one with each other, totally one with Christ... then if love is a feeling to be learned, we have a lot of learning to do on the way to glory. Christ's prayer for the Church was that she should be One (John 17:21), and she *is*, says Paul (Eph 2:14-16); but then we need to live (or love) that out.

Paul's starting-point in learning about love is really *seeing* the love of Christ; if God loved us this much, we also ought to love each other, as John too reminds us. So Ephesians has plenty to say about learning to 'know this love that surpasses knowledge' (3:19): 'the incomparable riches of God's grace' (2:7), God's enormous, utterly undeserved kindness to us that is his personality in its deepest expression. Indeed, learning the depths of that love is why he is bringing us to heaven (2:7)!

This love, this 'glorious grace', is a basic theme of chapter 2. But let's take note how Paul sets about helping us see its greatness. For him, the first essential is that we grasp how fearful our situation was before conversion: 'Remember!' (vv11-12).

There is a fundamental antithesis in Paul's thought here that can make our postmodern mindset uncomfortable. Clearly there are those who are 'in Christ', on the one hand, and those who are outside, on the other. We may not like this idea. But if we are serious about aligning our understanding with God, we have to follow his revelation here. Jesus talked much about there being 'sheep' and 'goats', and about a 'narrow gate' to life which only a few find.[13]

And it matters if we're outside the 'narrow gate'. Without Christ we were not just ignorant, not 'basically OK', says Paul: 'You were once *darkness!*' (5:8). In the most crucial sense we were totally 'dead' (2:1; 'separated from the life of God', 4:18); what had to be achieved was nothing less than our resurrection from the dead (2:5). When we 'followed the ways of this world' – when the surrounding world was setting our agenda – the norms we lived by were not neutral but were actually those of Satan (2:2).[14] What we were facing *(Lord, please help me grasp this)* was the unimaginable anger of God ('objects of wrath', v3); and it is this that Christ carried on Calvary. *(Thankyou, Lord...!)* We didn't find our own way home; without the divine initiative first, there would have been no salvation (v8). We had been 'separate from Christ, foreigners to the' (Jewish) 'covenants of promise' (v12). (We could pause to think how things might have been if God's 'covenants of promise' had indeed been for one race only: if, for example, you were permanently excluded from salvation unless you were black.) Ours was a life going nowhere, 'without hope and without God' (v12, very clear, very strong!): 'now you who once were far away have been brought near'– but at the cost of the blood, and the fathomless agony, of the Son. That is divine love.

Here is the indispensable 'bass note' of spirituality. If we have not grasped the depth of the darkness in us, we will not be raised up by a love astonished at the cross.[15] Genuine revival, Martyn Lloyd-Jones taught, stems from a 'sense of the awful majesty of God and the abject wickedness of sinful men and women in the presence of their holy Creator: in consequence a deep abhorrence of sin, and a grateful reception of the mercy and grace of God.'[16] This is one way in which 'the message of the cross is the power of God': love blazes up from a genuine grasp of Golgotha. *(Lord, help me to see, and to worship...)*

But then that Calvary love has radical implications for our relationships. Paul applies this in the second part of chapter 2 to the racial barriers between Jew and Gentile. (In fact the themes of our reconciliation to God and Jews' reconciliation to Gentiles are hard to disentangle here: they are (almost) the same problem, with the same solution.) What is the process by which God breaks our alienation? First and above all, by the cross: Christ 'abolished in his flesh' (vv14-15), at his cost, the root cause of the ethnic barrier. 'He is our peace' (v14); and what we receive when we receive him is a Spirit of 'peace' who transcends all such barriers,[17] finding them redundant and hateful. Next, Jesus creates in his Body a new organism, the Church, in which both parties are truly one, at a level deeper than they can grasp (v15) – and it is only as members of that Body that we are reconciled to God (v16). He then comes 'preaching peace' to both parties (v17); and finally, he himself 'builds us together' (vv20-22). *So thankyou, Lord, for the cross; thankyou for the Body! Help me to hear when you are 'preaching peace' to me...*

Then as we read into chapter 3, Paul moves a step further. Indeed, last time through Ephesians I found myself wondering: does the entire letter hinge around the verses 3:14-4:4? And is Paul's 'kneeling' in prayer in 3:14 the heart of his whole Epistle?

Look at the way he weaves the themes together here. 'For this reason' in 3:14 picks up the flow from the 'For this reason' he writes before getting joyously distracted at the start of chapter 3; it refers back to the verses preceding 3:1. 'For this reason', therefore – that at the cross, God has nullified all divisions in what Paul will now call the 'whole family', and that we now have this incredible privilege of being 'built together to become a dwelling in which God lives'(2:22) – 'for this reason', Paul prays (as in 1:17) for the 'Spirit of revelation' to help us grasp something that can only be perceived in partnership 'with all the saints' (so love is the qualification for revelation[18]): the vision of just how wide and deep is the love of Christ (3:16-18). We are reminded of his earlier prayer, that we will grasp how enormously God loves

us (1:18). (Which can be deeply healing for our relationships;
if we have truly perceived this love, we'll be set free from any
small-minded scrabbling after status or power or affirmation.)
What awaits us in the infinity of God's love is more than we
dare dream, says Paul, 'immeasurably more than all we ask or
imagine'.[19] *Lord, thankyou; to you be glory in the Church and
in Christ Jesus, for ever and ever* (3:21)!

Every time I reread these verses I think: this is colossal!
But the outflow of our grasping this vision, our beginning to
'know this love that surpasses knowledge' (3:18-19), must be
very practical: that we should be 'strengthened with power...
according to his power that is at work within us' (3:16,20;
compare, again, 1:19); and 'live a life worthy of the calling', in
which we 'make every effort to maintain the unity of the
Spirit' (4:1-4).[20] The message of chapter 2 was that all the
walls have been broken down. Now Paul longs and prays
that, through the power of God, the fullness of practical love
will flood in through the breach.

The vision hits the road (4:1-5:20)

Ephesians shows us how theory leads into practice. In fact,
these are not helpful categories to separate. 'Theory',
'doctrine', is the essential revelation that transforms practice;
it is the empowering for what we've got in hand to do. If the
vision, the 'doctrine', ever gets lost, the practical lifestyle soon
suffers too. That's why Paul's overwhelming prayer-concern
in both chapters 1 and 3 is that we grasp the vision.

So what we meet as we read the remaining chapters is not
some spaced-out dreaminess. Truly pietistic mysticism leads
straight into cutting-edge activity. It's very concrete: 'walking
worthy' of the calling and the vision (4:1) means 'making every
effort' (the Greek implies strenuous, deliberate urgency) to
maintain the oneness in our own situation (vv2-3). Holiness
does not come automatically just because we are members of

the Body; and Paul clearly feels that love's implications need working on very specifically in these chapters.

Love is not, for example, a sentimentalism that smiles benignly on doctrinal carelessness or on personal dishonesty. It's not a very postmodern thing to say, but the fact is that, biblically, love and truth go inseparably together. Our calling is always two-sided, 'speaking the *truth* in *love*' (4:15). We've been talking about seeing the process of 'salvation' in its broadest, most cosmic sense. Love means aligning with that process as it really functions, through faith alone (2:8-9) – and not turning a blind eye to false teachings as to what the gospel is, and how this salvation is to be attained.

That needs emphasis in our present situation. As the twentieth century has drawn to a close, our media-oriented, postmodern culture made it difficult to think with this kind of alert precision. But love demands that we must; we cannot afford woolly thinking when people's salvation is at stake. Sound doctrine is vital for the Body's life; the exercise of the gifts (4:11) is designed precisely to protect the Church from being 'blown here and there by every wind of teaching' (4:14). *(Lord, please give me your courage and your alertness...)* Not all traditions or doctrines or 'new waves' are acceptable, and the gifts of the Spirit are actually there to ward some of them off. Love, then, must always build on truth, otherwise it becomes gutless liberal sentimentalism (just as truth without love hardens quickly into legalism and doctrinaire sectarianism).[21] It is love likewise that necessitates our speaking 'truthfully' in general, the motivation being that 'we are all members of one Body' (4:25).

Again, love presupposes ethics, and holiness. The Spirit whose presence is the dynamic of the Body (2:22, 3:16-18) is a personal and *Holy* Spirit. Holiness is therefore so crucial that Paul will 'tell you this, and insist on it in the Lord' (4:17): 'Find out what pleases the Lord... Be very careful how you live' (5:10,15). To say that the Spirit is the dynamic of God's cosmic process is not a piece of safe, abstract philosophy. It means our relationship with him is so vital that we must take great care not to treat our local brothers and sisters in ways that would block it, that would put us out of touch with the mainline. Thus a key motivation for 'getting rid of all bitterness', and carefully restraining ourselves from 'slander', is the importance of not blocking that relationship, not 'grieving the Spirit' (4:30-31). *Holy Spirit, please help me see what to do to maintain my walk with you, and then to do it...*

Throughout this section we find vision transforming practice. It is being 'taught' the sheer glory of a new self 'created to be like God' that can motivate us to work at 'true righteousness and holiness' (4:22-24). It is as we've grasped the meaning of Christ's life-giving 'grace' flowing through his Body (4:7-12) that we also grasp our responsibility to live as its channels, to do what *'imparts grace* to those who hear', rather than the opposite (4:29 RSV). It is faith secure in Christ's enormous love (5:2) that liberates us from the greedy acquisitiveness which – 'of this you can be sure' (5:5-6) – could keep us out of the glory of heaven. [22] And it's being continuously, joyously 'filled with the Spirit' (5:18-20), beginning to enjoy heaven now, that – as the flow of 4:30-5:20 makes clear – is both cure and alternative to debauchery. (If we really desire that ongoing 'filling', we will want to discover what it is. The close parallel in Colossians makes clear that another way to describe the same process is a spirituality full of Scripture, where we 'let the word of Christ dwell in you richly' (Col 3:16-17).[23]) *Thankyou, Lord, for your glory and your love; help me in turn to 'be very careful' about 'finding out what pleases the Lord', day by day...*

Finding our way forward (5:21-6:9)

Above all, the vision sets the pattern for our relationships: 'Be imitators of God' (5:1). Paul makes the point repeatedly: Christ's utterly self-giving love at Calvary is the transforming model for us, for our forgiving each other ('just as in Christ

God forgave you', 4:32) and 'living a life of love' ('just as Christ loved us', 5:2). It is when we've seen how, in the 'oneness' God has created, service to difficult employers is service to the Lord (6:5) – as is right relating to parents (6:1) – that we will be armed to handle those relationships aright.

This is not at all easy. Mutual submissiveness (5:21) goes right against the grain. So it is precisely in the context of living out Christ's love in the family and workplace that Paul challenges us, 'Be strong in the Lord and in his mighty power', and spells out carefully how we can arm ourselves, aspect by aspect, against satanic attack (6:10-18). This is where spirituality is toughest; it is in our closest relationships that Satan most easily sabotages us and defiles our walk with the Spirit (cf. 4:30-32).

Space does not permit our exploring these sections in detail. But the supreme example of Christ as our pattern is in 5:21-33 – Paul on love, sex and marriage. As the sexual and the spiritual illuminate each other[24], this profound passage floods us with light in at least three directions.

First, it radically illuminates our marriages: we understand how we should love our partners by learning to take as our model the utterly self-giving, creative, patient care of Christ for his Bride. 'Husbands, love your wives, *just as* Christ loved the Church!' That seems a horrendous challenge… Yet if husbands can manage, through the Spirit's power changing us, to love our wives just a little more like Christ loves (Paul drives the point home three times (vv25,28,33)), we should not have many failed marriages!

So we understand the ever-deepening oneness of marriage and sexuality through the ever-deepening oneness of Christ and his Church. But at the same time, the passage illuminates the Church for us: we understand her through our understanding of marriage, as Christ's Bride, his partner-to-be that he loved so passionately he 'gave himself up for her… to present her to himself' (v25-27).[25]

And lastly it illuminates Christ for us too: our eternal Lover, the devoted Bridegroom, who endlessly, patiently, 'feeds and cares for' his Bride; washing her feet, 'cleansing her by the washing of water through the Word', until finally, one day, she will be 'without stain or wrinkle', all defilement gone; 'a radiant Church', ready to share his throne forever (vv26-29).[26]

It is a marvellous vision. In our next chapter we shall watch Paul working all this out amid great difficulties; in 2 Corinthians he faces, both in himself and in others, plenty of 'stains and wrinkles'. But it is in action, he insists here, in finding our way through the challenges of our closest relationships, that we come to understand and express more of the love of Christ himself. Vision will empower action; action illuminates vision.

So then get the vision, Paul challenges us; meditate thoroughly on it; it is the living Word that the Spirit will use to empower you for those everyday realities where the vision touches the ground...

Father, thankyou for the vision. Thankyou for the Calvary love of Christ. Please help me treat my sisters and brothers in such truthfulness and love. Help me treat my employer and employees in a way marked by the vision of Christ. Help me treat my wife in the devoted way you treat us in your Church...

Our indispensable armour   (6:10-22)

'Finally, be strong in the Lord.' Having presented the vision, Paul now says: you'll need to do something about it. It will take you beyond your comfort zones. It will expose you to merciless assault. Expect that, says Paul, and prepare for it – now!

Why? Because we have enemies. There are intelligences in this world that are not human, that apparently predate humanity and are marked by unceasing hatred towards the purposes of God and to humans who identify with them. And they have a great deal of power; Paul even terms them 'the rulers, the authorities, the powers of this dark world'. It is essential that we see where our real enemy is. 'Our struggle is not against flesh and blood,' says Paul (although he faced plenty of human opposition at Ephesus; see Acts 19), 'but... against the spiritual forces of evil in the heavenly realms.' There is a war on, and we will face trouble if we let that reality slip out of our consciousness: 'Therefore put on the full armour of God.'

What for? Surely, both for attack and for defence. In our evangelism we aren't merely engaged in mental wrestling-matches, our brains against unbelievers': 'Our struggle is against the spiritual forces of evil.' 2 Corinthians will make this very clear: Satan has 'blinded the minds of unbelievers, so that they cannot see the light of the gospel of the glory of Christ' (4:4). Those we seek to reach are currently, if unknowingly, 'following the ways of this world and of the ruler of the kingdom of the air' (Satan, Eph 2:2). We have to recognize where the real problem is, and the kind of response that will be needed. We are wasting our time if we think the captives of darkness can be liberated by a few wise words, without our consciously making use of the armament Paul is about to describe. This is a vital chapter.

But the defensive aspect seems prominent in Paul's mind right here. 'Put on the full armour of God, so that when the day of evil comes, you may be able to stand your ground, and after you have done everything, to stand.' 'Days of evil' do happen; times of unrelenting assault – suffering, problems, depressions, doubts, persecution – when there is no real question of our seeking to advance: our task, indeed all we can do, is to 'stand'. (Job is a good example.) So this, says Paul, is how to prepare for them. It will be too late when the whirlwind is upon us; what we must do is ensure we have God's 'full armour' already 'in place'(v14) beforehand.

As we read on, we find this is made up of seven pieces: five primarily for defence, perhaps, and two for attack.

First, the *'belt of truth'*. The day-by-day, week-by-week absorption of God's truth equips us with what we need to be effective in liberating Satan's captives; it is the truth that sets people free from Satan (cf. John 8:44,32). But it is also vital defensively, to keep us from being swept away when the 'evil day' comes. If in some small measure we face a situation resembling Job's, it can make all the difference if we have read and absorbed the truth in Job 1: that whatever Satan does is limited by the loving sovereignty of God; that there is a limit beyond which Satan cannot go.[27] The 'truth' about heaven is another vital part of our armour, as we'll see in a moment. So a 'pioneering spirituality', clothing us with deeper and deeper reserves of 'truth', is indispensable for spiritual warfare. But there is another way of looking at this 'belt of truth'; it may also refer to integrity, truthfulness. If our lives are not marked by such sincerity, our evangelism will be hollow – and defensively, there will be all kinds of inconsistencies that will offer ways in for destructive powers when the assault begins in earnest. We don't need to choose between these interpretations, because surely they go together. A life of integrity is built on the full expression, in our lives, of what we learn from God's Word; but the truths we learn there are meaningless unless they lead to consistent truth-full-ness of lifestyle. *(Lord, please lead me deeper in both these aspects…)*

But the Word's living truth goes with the liberating power of the Spirit. And we cannot battle in partnership with the Spirit if we do things that 'grieve the Spirit' (Eph 4:30). Therefore, the *'breastplate of righteousness'* is vital for our witness; otherwise the Spirit's power will be lacking and we will be ineffective. Yet still more is this essential for defensive spiritual warfare. Unless we maintain the 'full armour' of holiness, there will be gaps (from dishonesty, refusal to forgive, pride) that satanic power will exploit when the assault begins. Therefore, said Paul two chapters earlier in the context of maintaining good relationships, 'Do not give the devil a

foothold'(4:27). *(Lord, please grant me alertness as to where my
carelessness about sin is leaving an opening for the devil himself...)*

Our third step is to have our *'feet fitted with the readiness
that comes from the gospel of peace'* – or, as the Good News
Bible helpfully puts it, the 'readiness to announce the good
news of peace'. Again, here is a mindset vital for the war of
spiritual liberation: one that is continually, prayerfully
expectant, watching alertly for those windows of opportunity
to share the truth that sets people free. *Lord, please help me
cultivate this expectancy...* But defensively this is important too.
Times of intense difficulty can be rendered meaningful if we
are asking: But how could this provide an opening for the
good news? 1 Peter makes this clear: in a chapter directed at
believers facing intense difficulties, he encourages them,
'Always be prepared to give the reason for the hope you have.'
The reality of something in us that sustains us, even through
the toughest times, can be as powerful a piece of lived-out
'good news' as our neighbours will ever see.

The fourth item comes with quite a warranty! – 'the *shield
of faith*, with which you can extinguish *all* the flaming arrows
of the evil one'. What stops us being swept away, in any and
all satanic assault, is the firmness of our grasp of God's
faithfulness, our conviction of his love, wisdom and power.
'The just *live by* faith' – which was a key truth that God gave
to Habakkuk to arm him for an evil day (Hab 2:1-4). 'It is by
faith you stand firm', says Paul in 2 Corinthians 1; and in that
passage we see the steps God takes to develop this essential
ability to trust him. (In fact that seems to be why the 'evil
days' are sometimes permitted, as we'll see in a few pages'
time.) Again, therefore, we need to grow in this mindset now,
so that it is in place when a real conflict comes: learning to
live in a way where it matters whether God is real or not.
Father, please help me to grow in my trust in you...

'Take the *helmet of salvation*' – or, as Paul expands it in
1 Thessalonians 5:8, 'the *hope* of salvation as a helmet'. What
protects our heads, our minds, is the hope that Paul was

praying for in chapter 1. If we have truly grasped the glory of what God has in store for us, we will be secure against the many kinds of satanic attack that depend on taking this world too seriously. Covetousness (materialism) is one; bitterness is another; concern for status is another. Maybe Hebrews 10 gives us the clearest 'worked example' of this: 'Remember those earlier days after you had received the light, when you stood your ground' (as in Ephesians 6) 'in a great contest in the face of suffering... You sympathised with those in prison and joyfully accepted the confiscation of your property, *because you knew* that you yourselves had better and lasting possessions' (vv32,34). (Our deep conviction of heaven and hell's reality also give weight to our evangelistic attacks on Satan's kingdom, of course.) *Father, please help me to 'take' – to fill my mind with – this certainty...*

And finally come the two more aggressive weapons. Paul presents no esoteric, complex secrets here about addressing demons or the use of candles or liturgy; what enables us to defeat the 'spiritual forces of evil' is two simple things, the Word of God and prayer. First, *'the sword of the Spirit, which is the word of God'*. We see this in practice in evangelism (and in pastoral care): 'My opinion is...', or, 'Historically, Christians have thought...', has far less ability to lodge in the mind than 'See, this is what God says...' – or better still, 'Do you know, just yesterday I was reading what God says about this...' (Which is why the freshness of our own times with God's Word correlates directly with our fruitfulness in evangelism.) Yet defensively, too, the Spirit's sword equips us for combat in the realm of our thoughts. We watch this in the classic temptation in Matthew 4. Satan approaches Jesus with a temptation to materialism: Jesus parries, taking up a relevant truth from Deuteronomy, that it's rather by 'every word from God' that we live. Satan tries a different temptation; Jesus wards him off again – again using Deuteronomy. Satan tempts again; Jesus parries again – yet again using Deuteronomy! (We learn here the value of

a 'pioneering spirituality' that, day by day, grows equipped
by God's 'every' Word![28]) *(Thankyou, Lord; please help me!)*
Satan cannot take too much of this, and the battle ends.

Alongside that comes *'praying in the Spirit'*. (Note the
repeated role of the Spirit here; the Word, too, is the *Spirit's*
sword, because the Word and the Spirit go together. These
weapons have no effect without us seeking continually to
be full of the Spirit (5:18) who empowers them.)   Prayer
must have a regular, all-encompassing character, so that we
are advancing (and protected) on every front: 'On all
occasions with all kinds of prayers... always keep on praying
for all the saints!' (That helps us grasp how much 'growing'
we have to do in prayer, and how many things deserve and
demand our intercession.)   Specific prayer opens the
windows in people's hearts; it is a central expression of
our 'readiness to announce the good news of peace'. But
specific prayer is also essential for our defence. Sometimes
we sense problems converging in a way that has no human
explanation but almost feels like some purposefully
malignant mind on the attack. That impression may well
match reality; we need to act on what we're sensing, because
if there is a spiritual dimension to it, then our enemy can
only be dealt with by prayer. 'Be alert' says Paul (repeating
the advice Jesus gave his disciples in the 'evil day' (Matthew
26:41)), 'and always keep on praying.' *Lord, I have so much
learning to do in all these areas; please help me to grow in
using this essential armament for spiritual warfare...*

The summit (6:23-24)

But in the end, we're not just created for warfare. Ephesians'
vision is of a cosmos that, one day, will be gloriously freed
from all evil, unified totally with the goodness, love and joy
of Christ (1:9-10). This is what God has made us for! So in
the book's final verse Paul comes exultantly back to the 'heart
of the whole matter': love for CHRIST!

Of course. He must; we must. If we miss this, we miss the whole point. And we all have, haven't we – when God's good but smaller things rise up and dominate our thinking: abstractions of theology or doctrine, activism for social righteousness, getting the mechanics of outreach right, repairing the damage the enemy causes, oiling the wheels of the church... And suddenly the thought comes, as it did to me while running a conference recently, *Christ, that's someone I used to care about....*

A book about the vision of the ultimate cannot be devoted to anything but the 'unsearchable riches' of Christ (3:8). Heaven, for us, means being in Christ (2:6). The Church is for Christ (5:31-32). And if you want to compile a doctrine of Christ, Ephesians isn't a bad place to go looking. (Using a concordance to find all the 'in him' and 'in Christ' verses is a good way to start.)

In the end, everything is in, from, through Christ. That is made clear when Paul begins Ephesians with his cry of joyous praise because of Christ: 'Praise be to the Father', because 'every spiritual blessing' is now ours – '*in Christ*' (1:3). Christ, God, is infinite, and ultimately everything of value must be bound up with him. *Thankyou, Lord...!* (Learning to make the effort to worship is a discipline crucial to grasping these things!) With him we received everything we could need, when we were 'included in Christ, when you heard the word of truth' (1:13).

Again, it's only 'in him' that we are redeemed (1:7). This is not a colourless 'legal fiction', as liberals sometimes say, but a profound cosmic mystery: it is because we are brought into Christ that we find ourselves benefiting from the price paid for our sin 'in his flesh' (2:15), and find ourselves also 'made alive with him' (2:5), 'raised up with Christ' and 'seated with him in the heavenly realms' (2:6).

Yet again, God's grace is 'freely given us' – 'in the one he loves' (1:6). It's 'in him' we were chosen (1:4,11), 'through him' we were predestined to be God's sons and daughters

(1:5), and 'in him' we were 'marked with the Holy Spirit' (1:13). *Hallelujah!* Only 'in him and through faith in him' can we 'approach God with freedom and confidence' (3:12). 'In Christ' we are 'created to do good works' (2:10), and it's 'in him' we are 'built together to become a dwelling in which God lives by his Spirit' (2:21,22). It's as 'members of the one body' of which Christ is the head that we are 'sharers together in the promise' – again, 'in Christ Jesus' (3:6, 1:22-23). The whole cosmic plan is 'purposed in Christ' and 'accomplished in Christ' (1:9,3:11); Christ is its climax, Christ its head and consummation (1:10). 'To him be glory in the church – and in Christ!'(3:21) And so Paul brings his Epistle to its logically inevitable conclusion, with another cry of prayer and adoration: 'Grace to all who *love* our Lord Jesus Christ with *love undying!*' (6:24)

It is Christ who is, in every sense, the ultimate. *Lord, I can't hold it all; but insofar as I can, I love, and I worship...*

Notes

[1] John White has an excellent exposition of the lessons for intercession contained in this prayer, in *People in Prayer* (1977), pp.125-40. White's whole book is a classic example of a pioneering spirituality.

[2] Paul returns to this theme at the end of Ephesians, in 6:17.

[3] Quoted in John Stott's *Bible Speaks Today* commentary, *The Message of Ephesians* (1979), p.63.

[4] These unseen 'realms' include more than we conventionally mean by 'heaven'; they contain warfare too, 6:12. (Cf. 1 Cor 8:5 or Gal 1:8.) But Paul rejoices that we are 'seated in the heavenly realms in Christ'; there may be conflict there, but we have a secure place in the unseen, real-est universe.

[5] Jesus describes this moment as when we are 'born of the Spirit' (John 3:7-8).

[6] The fundamental temptation to which the first human beings succumb is to 'be like God'; to attempt to decide ourselves what is right and wrong, good and evil, in autonomous isolation from the revealed will of the Father; to run our own universe (Gen 3:5).

(The fact that there was a tempter implies that that rebellion mirrored an earlier, satanic 'snatching at autonomy' in the 'heavenly realms'.) 'Repentance' – recognizing we're wrong, returning to God, bowing to the Lordship of Christ – reverses precisely that folly of self-isolation and independence.

[7] 'Why wasn't Jesus' prayer answered when he prayed that we might be one?' a Welsh student asked me. Surely it was: what's in view here is not the unification of anything so temporary as denominational structures, but an infinitely more profound unity of all who are in Christ, something that is a tangible reality across cultural and denominational divides. The usual snag with the bureaucratic processes we think of when we talk of unity is how far (or how little) they represent 'unity in the faith'. One wonders anyway how much they are a mid-twentieth-century issue; perhaps, as the twenty-first century unfolds, denominational divisions are not so much being dismantled by complex agreements as simply becoming irrelevant. And most believers who spend time in a distant culture will confirm the powerful sense of far deeper unity with fellow-believers there than exists with not-yet-believing fellow-citizens back home. Where there is real 'unity in the faith'(4:13) we experience also 'unity in the Spirit'(4:3).

[8] Anyone who has heard Roger Forster expound Ephesians will recognize some ways of thinking underlying this section.

[9] It is difficult to avoid the feeling, from the flow of Paul's argument in 1 Cor 11:17-34, that the central Christian experience of communion is designed, among other things, to refocus our awareness of the Body, as we partake together of that bread that also 'is my Body'. We remember Christ's Body broken for us in the past (v24), but Paul would have us also take care to remember the Body all too easily broken now by actions such as vv20-22. (Note the 'So then…' in v33, which seems to define (at least in part) what he means by 'without recognising the Body of the Lord' in v29.)

[10] These two principles are very evident in 1 Corinthians 14, where vv29-31 encourage a plurality of input and insights to build up the local church (something too few congregations succeed in developing); then v36 underlines the crucial importance of cross-fertilization with the wider Church.

[11] Is it legitimate to see the allusion in Matthew 25:27 to 'bankers' as referring to this kind of leader, who can develop others' gifts and set them to work?

[12] In the last few decades, the strength of scientific humanism has been such that evangelicals have become nervous of saying much to do with the other world. The starvation of spirituality in the wider culture is a partial result. But the task of the Church in the presence of the unseen world is a theme that appears several times in Paul: for example, 1 Cor 4:9, 1 Cor 11:10, 1 Tim 5:21 and possibly 2 Thess 1:10. We might think also of Job 1.

[13] Matthew 25:31-46, Matthew 7:13-14. Numerous other passages could be cited, of course.

[14] Cf. 1 John 5:19: 'We know that we are children of God, and that the whole world is under the control of the evil one.' Or indeed Eph 5:16: 'The days are evil.'

[15] This is why the most prominent lesson from many of the earlier parts of the Bible seems to be the absolute importance of holiness (in much of the Pentateuch, for example), and our utter inability to get it right on our own (e.g. in Numbers or Judges or the books of Kings, taken as a whole). After those lessons, we are ready to learn about the Messiah and the cross. At least that is the way in which, historically, God has chosen to reveal himself, though obviously the themes of his enormous love and his rescue shine out also from Genesis 3 onwards.

[16] *Martyn Lloyd-Jones: Chosen by God*, ed. Christopher Catherwood (1986), p.172. As Lloyd-Jones observes in his commentary on Romans 1, the wrath of God is the starting-point of Paul's gospel (see Rom 1:18). 'The fear of the Lord is the beginning of wisdom'; we are only ready for repentance that lasts when we have grasped our deep need to be forgiven.

[17] It is the Spirit who is the life at the heart of this process; 'peace' is a 'fruit' of the Spirit. It is through our joint sharing in the Spirit that we both have access to the Father (2:18, cf. 1 Cor 12:12-13); through the Spirit we receive the revelation of divine love (3:16-19); in the Spirit our unity is grounded (2:22). Implying, incidentally, that if our view of the Spirit rebuilds barriers between lovers of Christ that the Spirit himself is destroying, something may be wrong with it.

[18] Jesus seems to make a similar connection in Mark 11:22-26 between the release of God's power to do the unimaginable (cf. Eph 3:20) and the quality of relationships within the Body.

[19] Is there a contrast here with 4:18-19, where those who are 'separated from the life of God' are described as having 'lost all sensitivity' and therefore 'given themselves over to sensuality'? What we have in 3:18 is the Spirit stretching our sensitivities to the limit (as does great art) – so that we might grasp the depth of God.

[20] 3:14 seems to be Paul's second attempt towards expressing his interrupted thought of 3:1. But the repetition of 'as a prisoner of the Lord' suggests that what he aimed to say in 3:1 is only finally expressed at 4:1-2.

[21] If truth without love is like a dry skeleton, isn't love without truth like a boneless jellyfish?

[22] And that liberates us also to use wealth for its true purpose: 4:28.

[23] Being (truly) filled with the Word and (truly) filled with the Spirit have exactly the same effects, in worship and thanksgiving; compare Col 3:16-17 with Eph 5:19-20.

[24] It is worth noting that the authentic biblical response to the debauched sexuality of Ephesus is not the normal ascetic reaction of human religion, understandable though that would be (cf. Col 2:23). God's response is not so much external restraint as internal transformation. If we truly see how totally devoted sex, totally mutual and permanent self-giving in security and generosity, reflects and expresses in-Christness, then promiscuity becomes senseless, a bone-headed abandonment of what sex is fundamentally about. The vision glorifies sex, rather than excluding it in the manner of celibate monasticism. (Jack Clemo has a wonderful passage on this topic in *The Invading Gospel* (1972), pp.75-82.) We might add that changing our behaviour by applying the biblical vision in this way is itself an instance of the beautifying of the Church/Bride by 'washing with water through the Word' (5:26): that is, 'sanctifying by the truth, your Word' (John 17:17).

[25] The implications of this for our attitude to our own local congregation are spelled out by Paul in 2 Corinthians 11:2-3. It becomes a serious thing to despise the only tangible manifestation of the Bride that Christ loves so much...

[26] Of course the experience of singleness also 'conforms us to Christ', and helps us to know him better: he has waited an enormous length of time for *his* Bride.

[27] See also 1 Cor 10:13.

[28] It is also why carelessness about the Bible's authority and trustworthiness become crippling in any church or spiritual movement, in terms of spiritual warfare. 'Did God really say?' is where temptation starts (Gen 3:1).

2

Broken Pot Spirituality: Rereading 2 Corinthians

2 Corinthians: A Rough Guide

Chapters 1-3	How Paul copes with pressure
Chapters 4:1-5:8	Stress and glory
Chapters 5:9-7:1	New life in practice
Chapters 7:2-9:1	Paul's big project in the multi-ethnic church
Chapters 10:1-13:14	Paul faces disorder

I suppose anyone exploring Ephesians ends up with the sense the poet Day-Lewis expressed when he said a poem is 'never finished, just abandoned'. It is impossible to seize more than a hint of the depth and the glory; we are children catching the tiniest fragment in our buckets as the waterfall cascades down. There is enough in Ephesians for a total spirituality, for a century's reflection.

'But God has more light to break forth from his holy Word': sixty-five books of it, to be precise. And that's good. There are times when we feel a thousand miles away from Paul's triumphant starting-point in Ephesians; and a spirituality deep enough to last will need to feed us in those times too. Times when we feel something like this: 'I was under great pressure... far beyond my ability to endure... I despaired even of my life...'

Stress and what we can get out of it

That is how 2 Corinthians begins. And if we read, say, its first seven chapters (five pages) through at a sitting, we realize what an enormously human letter it is. Paul writes on the very edge of depression: hence, perhaps, the repeated 'Therefore we do not lose heart'(4:1,16,5:6,8). Once we've noticed that, one of the questions with which we approach this letter must be: So why does he not lose heart?

Paul is having a really rough time. Both throughout the early chapters, and in the passionate final section, we see him feeling criticized, and needing to defend himself (1:8 and 1:12-2:4, especially vv14,17,23; 11:7-12:19). What makes things worse is that he keeps on realizing he had not wanted to get pushed into that posture of self-defence (3:1-2, 5:11-12, 10:18, 12:11,19, 13:7). The same sense of guarding himself against accusations from people he loves recurs in 6:3-4, 6:8, 7:2, 10:15, 11:7 and 12:16-18. Over and over again he needs to state that he has operated in 'holiness and sincerity': 'not peddling the Word of God for profit... we speak before God with sincerity', 'not using deception' (1:12, 2:17, 4:2, 8:21).

And that's not all. His lack of training as a speaker is being used against him (11:6), and we sense the emotion with which he responds (see, perhaps, 2:17 and the reference to plain speech in 4:2). He himself had planted this church in Corinth, but now they are 'demanding proof that Christ is speaking through me'(13:3): 'His letters are weighty and forceful', they were saying, 'but in person he is unimpressive, and his speaking amounts to nothing'(10:10). It must have been desperately painful for Paul to write, more than once, 'Make room for us in your hearts'(7:2, 6:13, 12:15). He is stressed 'daily' by these concerns (11:28) (anxious in Troas (2:13), still troubled in Macedonia (7:5)), and very deeply saddened by the failure of others (2:4, 11:29). Indeed, he has real fears that he may have failed himself (12:2 and maybe 7:8, 13:7). He is certainly coming face to face with the local church's 'stains and wrinkles' from Ephesians 5.

Most of us know how criticism preys on the mind. (I received an unhelpful letter just before leaving on a three-week preaching trip while writing this section, and it took most of that time for the shadow to lift.) How do we cope with such things? What kind of roots can we put down so that we do not get blown aside by the criticisms and pressures?

Armed with that question[1], we can map out the flow of the first few chapters, looking out for Paul's main responses. (It doesn't matter if we get it wrong – in itself the exercise ensures we know the book better.) We will find that the first three chapters give us at least four answers.

How Paul copes (1:1-24)

First, and above all, Paul's anchor is his *faith*.

This is the point of Paul's first full paragraph. Paul has absolute confidence that if there is suffering in his life, then there will also, somewhere, be 'comfort' (1:5, cf. 1:7); and, indeed, that if there is suffering there must also be benefit released somewhere in the Body (1:6, cf. 4:11-12,15). Suffering comes in part, he says, so that we will be equipped to comfort others (1:4), by passing on God's comfort in a credible way that shows we have been there too; it equips us to be genuine encouragers. On reflection, we know this is realistic. When we are in trouble, we turn to people who have been through hard times themselves. And the suffering we have passed through with God (broken family? doubt? bereavement?) can likewise be what enables us to get alongside others; it is what makes us pastorally fruitful, a crucial 'gateway for grace' in our own 'history with God'.

Paul copes, then, because (usually, anyway) he is 'living by faith' (cf. 5:7) in the reality of this process; faith that, ultimately, God knows what he is doing, and, ultimately, it will be for good. It's a mark of new testament spirituality that the 'just' '*live by faith*' and faith alone (Rom 1:17, Gal 3:11, Heb 10:38). We are not only born again by faith, we *live* thereafter 'by faith in the Son of God' (Gal 2:20). And that applies specifically to the times of pressure, when the criticism starts to fly: it is faith in God's goodness and loving sovereignty that anchors Paul, and us, and keeps us from trying to manipulate people and play politics (cf. 1:12). 'By faith you stand firm' (1:24).

So we are not surprised when Paul goes on to say that this faith's development is, in itself, a goal of all the pressures: 'This happened that we might not rely on ourselves but on God, who raises the dead'(1:9). God permitted Paul's heart-feelings of helplessness and impending death (feelings which proved mistaken, v9) to bring him to a deeper grasp of how resurrection power breaks into hopeless situations.

It happens to us, doesn't it? Sometimes, like Jacob in Genesis 32, we have to be brought to a point where our strength is gone, and we can only hang on in dependence and trust that God will bless us. If we are watching for the way he acts in our lives we will recognize this process. On my first trip to Africa I had serious visa problems. Day followed day without a solution, until my schedule was three weeks behind. Finally, on the last possible day that the trip could be salvaged, I travelled in on the underground knowing my embassy 'contact' was away that day, and said to the Lord, 'Only you can salvage this now.' And then he did. At such times we can only pray, 'Lord, I didn't want to get into this situation, and there's nothing now I can do about it; yet I believe this is your will, and I trust you to see it through.' And he does.

As something of a pessimist by temperament, I find this faith a hard lesson to learn. But it seems God's will for us is to learn a childlike expectation of deliverance ('On him we have set our hope that he will continue to deliver us', 1:10), rather than bracing ourselves for disaster. (We will be looking at this again when we come to Mark's Gospel.)

So we find a sense in this chapter of Paul making the deliberate mental choice to trust: 'We have *set* our hope'(1:10).

Faith isn't just a matter of getting what we want. (The man of faith never misses the bus! His car never breaks down! His baby never cries inconsolably at 3 am!) Rather, for Paul, faith is that loving relationship in which we choose to keep trusting the Father, even though things don't turn out as we wish. (See, for example, the marks of a 'servant of God' in 6:4-5: 'great endurance, troubles, hardships and distresses; beatings, imprisonments and riots; hard work, sleepless nights and hunger'.) Nor does faith lead to passivity; it creates a very practical need to stir up prayer, because deliverance will come in response to collective prayer (1:11). Such faith becomes an anchor for us. *Lord, I know it will not be easy; but please help me learn to live more by faith!*

Beyond the measurable goals (2:1-17)

In the last part of chapter 2 we find a second anchor. Faith involves a life-choice to trust in what God's loving sovereignty is bringing about, and particularly in our witness.

Paul has real fears that he has been a failure. Other people in Corinth are doing plenty to help him feel that way; and in chapter 2 in particular he is involved in a pastoral situation of that delicate kind where one can never feel over-confident. Yet in 2:14 comes this cry of confidence: 'Thanks be to God, who *always* leads us in triumphal procession in Christ, and through him spreads *everywhere* the fragrance of the knowledge of him.' *In Christ*, as he had told Corinth earlier (1 Cor 15:58), our labour really is not in vain in the long run; we can trust there will be something to show for our pains.

However, that 'something' isn't always growth and the spread of new life: it may even be 'death' (2:16). This can be hard if we have not yet learnt to live by trust rather than by sight. The application of management-thinking to ministry has taught us all to look for visible, measurably positive results. Not long ago we met with a funding group who wanted a statistical projection of just how the numbers of believers in

our work would grow if they backed us. It sounded daft –
but my own heart craves the same. I see in myself a longing
to know that the Christian groups I work among are growing:
something visibly positive, something I can *see*, to prove I'm
not wasting my time. The trouble is that God doesn't always
work this way. 'Here am I, send me', Isaiah prayed in one of
the Bible's great missionary passages (Isaiah 6:8-13), and found
God giving him a most unattractive message to proclaim (v9).
'Then I said' (not surprisingly) '"For how long, O Lord?"'
Well, actually, said the Lord, until the cities lie ruined and
without inhabitant, until the houses are left deserted and the
land is utterly forsaken (vv11-12). Measurable results, in the
ministry of the old testament's greatest prophet...

*Father, have mercy on my weakness, I doubt I could cope with
something like that. But please help me to be faithful.* Only
faith can grasp the kind of results God promises. What God
guarantees, Paul says here, is that, as we 'spread the fragrance
of the knowledge of him' (a strange, thought-provoking
phrase), the gospel will bring its true fruit, one way or the
other. If we do what we have been given to do, then those
crucial encounters will indeed result that determine eternal
destiny: both 'among those who are being saved and those
who are perishing. To the one we are the smell of death; to
the other, the fragrance of life' (v15-16).

If human freedom is genuine, we cannot demand that the
response to our work should always be positive. If the gospel
is fully presented, many will reject it; that happened with Jesus'
preaching too (John 6:60-66, cf. Matthew 10:12-15). Either
way, the messenger is doing all they can. And we will be
liberated from the tyranny of visible results as we believe in a
God who 'always leads us in triumphal procession'. Such a
confidence – that 'always' – will anchor us and enable us to
carry on. *Lord, please help me to do my part, and to trust you
for what follows...*

Ministering the Spirit (3:1-6)

In chapter 3 we find Paul's third anchor of 'confidence' (v4) amid the stresses. It's one that can transform our attitude to evangelism.

Paul may be criticized, people may say scornfully that he is 'unimpressive'. But, deep down, Paul trusts God, trusts that he is doing something supernatural. He is enabling Paul truly to *minister the Spirit* (3:3,6,8).

An odd phrase, we notice? Well, let's think about it. For Paul, it seems that helping to 'make disciples' isn't only about passing on fresh ideas; it is bringing the activity of the Spirit into the lives of others. The Corinthians are Paul's 'letter' 'read by everybody', and the 'ink' with which he 'wrote' that letter is the Spirit: the Spirit flowed out from Paul like ink from a pen, he says(v3).

Well, we feel, that's what we would expect; Paul, unlike us, was an apostle. Not so. Jesus promised us that he will flow in the same natural way from every believer: '"*Whoever* believes on me, as the Scripture has said, streams of living water will flow from within him." By this he meant the Spirit' (John 7:38-39).

Now that is a remarkable promise. Each of us who believes, 'impressive' or not, says Christ, is a walking channel of the Spirit, and through us his life flows into the desert of our culture. That assumes, of course, that we aren't blocking the channel ('grieving the Spirit'[2]) by sin. Or, rather, that as sin happens day by day, so we get the channel unblocked by daily repentance – he is the *Holy* Spirit, and expects holiness from us – and on that basis ask, daily and confidently, for his renewed filling.[3] (*Lord, help me actually to make a habit of doing these things.*) But if the channel is clear, then Christ's promise is equally clear: as we're drawing on his nature through his Word and prayer, something of the Spirit's life, his love, joy, peace and power, will be flowing out to others through us. (If a believer works in a particular office, there will normally be a certain presence of peace and gentleness that was not there before. And it happens, doesn't it?)[4]

As we think of all the pain and darkness around us, this becomes a crucial promise. Each of us is at the cutting edge, fountains of the Spirit's life into the world. Whoever we are, whatever we're doing, we bring him too; 'impressive' or not, we are containers, walking 'temples', of this personal Spirit (1 Cor 6:19). Trobisch writes how the Spirit works in believers until sharing his new life, sharing our faith, becomes 'natural': 'Not as a duty that they must add to their many other Christian duties. Not as a programme they have to adopt, a special technique they must learn. Not as a *must* at all...' The Spirit's way, he says, is that our faith 'flows out of Christians without their even realizing it. It arms them with contagious health. It becomes... *natural.* To use a biblical term, it becomes *automatic* – something which goes on even though the communicator – the sower – "knows not how" (Mark 4:27).' The Spirit will flow, promises Christ, from '*whoever* believes on me'; that is the conviction Paul builds on here.

Such a faith affects our whole approach to evangelism. Many churches have so little impact on our surroundings. And often it is because we think only of activities and our involvement in them, rather than building conscious friendships with outsiders through which this 'ministry of the Spirit' can happen. If we've grasped Paul's confidence here, we'll want to ensure that we all have relationships where not-yet-Christians can be touched by the Spirit, reaching out to them from within us.[5] Like Corinth, we are called to be a 'letter from Christ... known and read by everybody'!

This 'confidence' surely doesn't mean we pretend to be perfect. Far from it. The church is a hospital where broken people get mended; and sometimes we are very broken indeed! But we're called to believe God's Word here, to trust that, even while we don't have perfection, we do each have reality. (We see that reality most easily in the lives of others, of our friends who are serious about Jesus.) 'Such confidence as this is ours through Christ... Not that we are competent in ourselves... but our competence comes from God. He has made us ministers... of the Spirit' (3:4-6). It's his work, and Jesus clearly expects us to trust him to do it; that every believer who really wants it, and pursues it in prayer and holiness, will find the Spirit himself opening ways for his truth and love – 'random acts of senseless beauty' – to be expressed through them.

Lord, thankyou; I believe you! Please help me to seek your Spirit's fullness, day after day, and to notice your possibilities for its expression...

Right to the heart of God (3:7-18)

Paul's third anchor, then, is this certainty that he is 'ministering the Spirit'. Is there a fourth 'anchor' here that helps him survive? Surely yes: his sense of the incredible privilege of working with God.

In these next verses he aims, as a leader, to strengthen others (cf.1:4) by enthusing them with joy at the ministry of evangelism. (Christian leaders might ask ourselves how central that is to our ministry; or whether we get fired up only by organizational projects?) The flow of Paul's thought here seems to climax in 4:1: 'Since through God's mercy we have *this* ministry', the glory of which is the theme of chapter 3, 'we do not lose heart!'

Lord, please help me sense this glory about the gospel you've given us to share. It is an astonishing privilege to have God's own nature incarnated through us in this 'ministry of the Spirit'; and, amid all his pressures, Paul is hugely enthusiastic about it (3:6-11). He helps us to grasp its glory better by taking us back through the Bible to Moses, and the story of Exodus. The 'tablets of stone' Moses brought down from Sinai were accompanied by dazzling glory, Paul reminds us (vv7,3). And rightly so; they came from God himself, and contained instructions we urgently needed. And yet, says Paul, what

God is doing now, as we 'minister the Spirit', is something still more glorious. Why?

The difference is, first, that Moses' message could only 'bring death' and 'condemn men' (vv 6,7,9). What it announced was a law no human being could keep or be saved by – so that we would see our need of a Saviour (cf. Gal 3:24). That law wasn't the 'good news'; something greater was still to come. And now it has! Underlying Paul's whole message here is God's liberating announcement of Jeremiah 31:31-34: Israel has totally failed to keep the external law, but now God promises he will 'write it on their hearts' (internally, therefore effectively!), and 'I will be their God and they will be my people...I will remember their sins no more.' (This 'new covenant' that transcends the law (v33) must surely be the one Paul 'ministers' in 2 Corinthians 3:6.)

It's astonishing how people fail to grasp this. Not long back, two Jehovah's Witnesses knocked at our door. Then, sitting on our sofa, they explained how, if we kept God's laws, we could go to paradise. Surely the most depressing message in the world! God's law: Love the Lord with *all* your heart, soul, mind and strength; keep that and you'll go to paradise? We can't keep it, we told them; we try, but we fall far short, and so do you. And love your neighbour *as yourself?* We don't keep that either; we're on the way, we hope, but we fail, all the time. We'll never get to paradise if we have to keep the law. (Well, they admitted, that's true, but we trust God to be merciful. Interesting, we said: here you are going round this estate preaching about keeping the law, yet your hope for your own souls is a faith that God will be merciful!)

Paul's (and our!) message is far more joyous. Set against the bondage offered by the cults that ignore the gospel; set, even, against that essential sense of utter unrighteousness that comes from grasping the law as God's 'opening lesson'[6]; the gospel we can carry shines out as life-giving (v6), glorious (v8) and liberating (v17). *(Thankyou, Lord!)* Too often even conservative Christians can fail to embody the enormous contrast Paul points to here. Our spirituality can slip back into a legalism marked by negativity, death and condemnation, rather than glory; as Watchman Nee says, 'ministering death rather than life'. The joyous difference, says Paul, is that the gospel of faith in Christ does what the law could never do; it gives us free access now, to 'look steadily' into the glory of God (vv7,18)! At Sinai, the people could not face Moses when he returned shining with God's radiance, so he had to wear a veil (vv7,13). But in the 'gospel of the glory of Christ' that veil has gone, and now we see God freely through 'the light of the knowledge of the glory of God in the face of Christ' (cf. 4:3,4,6). That freedom is God's astounding gift to all who believe; and this, exults Paul, is what our ministry brings!

It is hugely important. 'We are very bold... We with *unveiled* face reflect the Lord's glory', drawing near to our God directly, says Paul (3:12,18). It is the same life-giving insight we find at the heart of Hebrews, where we're challenged that, unlike old testament Israel, we can have complete 'confidence' to enter the very 'holiest of all' (Heb 10:19-20). In the old testament time, sin had not yet been dealt with; so in the temple, God's presence had to be shut off in that holy place behind the veil, and only the high priest could go there, just once a year (9:7-9). When Christ died, however, all the barriers were swept away, and that temple veil was ripped open dramatically from top to bottom (Lk 23:45) *(Hallelujah!)*. We have been given a way into the very heart of God, 'through the veil', by faith (Heb 10:20,22).[7]

But how this good news gets diluted! It's amazing to see how many parts of Christendom have 'recreated the veil' – re-establishing in the churches a 'holy place' separated off by an old testament-style barrier (the Orthodox *iconostasis*, for example), behind which only special 'priests' can go. What does that say to our spirituality? Surely, all too clearly, that the ordinary believer doesn't belong in the deepest heart of God. Something in our natural 'religious' mindset gets uneasy at the thought of direct encounter with God for everybody.[8]

Then, as our confidence of access to Christ is weakened, we feel a need for someone holier to do our praying for us; or else, perhaps, we have confidence only to pray to someone lesser than God – to saints, to Mary, to angels. What a loss – for ourselves and, we dare say, for the Father who longs for our company! Or, we are left with a fear of a barrier remaining, of sins still unatoned, of God still needing to be pacified – I have so much guilt, I dare not enter his holy presence.[9] It is a 'spirituality of sorrow', rather than of the joy God intends for us.

Paul's spirituality is radically different, in ways we must never lose sight of. It rejoices over the sense of direct intimacy with God. Paul is thrilled because all the barriers have been broken, once and for all; Christ has died for our sins, and by faith we may all come 'with unveiled face' into God's very heart! Indeed, God actually comes to live inside us as we are 'born again of the Spirit' (John 3:3,8); the Spirit now flowing from each of us who believe *is* the presence of God. To 'minister the Spirit', then, is to help others encounter God's very presence! *(Again, thankyou, Lord!)*

Channelling glory (3:12 (again!)– 4:1)

Amid all our pressures and stresses, therefore, we'll be strengthened if we grasp the incredible privilege of 'ministering the Spirit'. But now Paul suddenly starts to talk about Bible reading (3:14). Whatever for?

Well, as Anfin Skaaheim puts it, the words of Jesus are not just symbolic expressions about the presence of God, they *are* the presence of God. 'The words I have spoken to you are Spirit,' Jesus said, 'and they are life' (John 6:63). As always, our encounter with the Word (3:15-16) and the ministry of the Spirit (3:17-18) go together. As we read his Word, with his Spirit opening it to us, we are in the presence of the Lord; to minister the Word is to minister the Spirit.

But Paul has a serious, even controversial, point for us here; like Jesus,[10] Paul was not afraid to be controversial if enough was at stake. 'Even to this day', says Paul, that 'same veil remains' when those who have not submitted to Christ read the old testament. The barrier 'has not been removed, because only in Christ is it taken away'(vv14-16). That's a vital issue for Christians today, in the training of our future leaders. If Scripture is made plain above all through the Spirit's presence, it follows that, for scholars who do not 'follow Christ' according to the biblical gospel, the 'veil' will remain, and false understanding will be inevitable. A grim example is Dibelius, one of the fathers of 'form criticism', who dared write that a 'monstrous illusion' (that the End was about to come) 'lies at the basis of the whole mission of Jesus'.[11] So wrong a foundation inevitably leads to warped interpretations; without close contact with the Spirit, the point of whole passages will be missed. And people shaped by such approaches will learn a warped agenda too. Yet that is often how we train our future leaders... Obviously all this is a key area of spiritual warfare (cf. 4:3-4). If God has really spoken in his Word, then a major concern of the Enemy will be to ask continually, 'Did God really say...?'(Gen 3:1) – to confuse or render distant and obscure the meaning of the Word. It is not difficult to see that happening in the history of biblical scholarship.

Such issues are vital, because our encounter with the Word is central to the marvel the Spirit is accomplishing in us. Paul's remarks about Bible reading (vv14-16) now lead into a dramatic promise: as 'with unveiled faces' we contemplate God's glory in his Word, the result will be our own 'transformation', or transfiguration, into glory (v18)! Paul's choice of word here is thought-provoking: it's the term used for Christ's transfiguration in Mark 9:2.[12] So as we read the Gospels, for example, 'beholding as in a mirror'[13] the 'glory of God in the face of Christ' (cf. 4:6), it may seem a mundane thing to do; but in fact something remarkable is occurring, and we are invisibly being 'transformed into his likeness with ever-increasing glory'. (*Lord, please help me understand, and believe, what this means!*)

The idea of such a transformation is astounding, a wondrous finale to our salvation; as Paul says elsewhere, it will culminate in nothing less than our being 'conformed to the likeness of his Son' (Rom 8:29). In later chapters he will set out its implications for relationships, money, and ethnic divisions; here, however, he's showing us how it works, through our gazing at Christ's glory, and specifically in Scripture. It's what we saw in Ephesians 5: Christ preparing for himself a 'radiant church', transfigured through the 'washing of water with the Word'.

At the heart of our spirituality, then, must be time spent gazing, meditating on, contemplating and ultimately reflecting the 'unveiled' revelation of Christ; absorbing the Bible personally, grappling with it collectively in a Bible study group, absorbing it through exposition in church. To see Jesus is to grow like him. M'Cheyne's sane advice is relevant here[14]: take ten looks at Christ for every one you take at yourself. The key to our transformation is not self-examination – that is, using the mirror to scrutinize ourselves. Gazing into the abyss of our self can be endlessly fascinating, especially in times of stress; but what we see reflected back may only be something introspective, damaged and inadequate – a broken pot, as Paul will say in chapter 4. There is a role for that 'one deep look' inside; but its main role is to help us grasp our inadequacy for change; the power has to come from elsewhere. (We'll see this process again when we look at the shift from failure on our own in Romans 7 to God's empowerment in Romans 8.) Real transformation comes from gazing at the Lord. 1 John speaks in similar terms: 'Dear friends... what we will be has not yet been made known. But we know that when he appears, we shall be like him, *for*' – why? – '*we shall see him as he is*' (3:2). And it is in the Word that we see him right now.

Therefore, concludes Paul, in a cry of confident faith that lifts him beyond all the pressures and accusations: 'Therefore, since through God's mercy we have *this* ministry' – this quite astonishing ministry of glory, channelling God's Word and Spirit to others – 'we *do not lose heart!*' (4:1).

The weapons of our warfare (4:1-6)

Paul does not lose heart, nor give way to deceptiveness[15](4:2), because he knows the Word is genuinely working (4:1; 3:4). The Spirit is actually being ministered through us (3:6) and we and many others are being transformed (3:16-18). But we face a recurring problem, taking many forms: the veil, the barrier.

Wyn was a Welsh nationalist. One day we talked at length about the historical evidence that Jesus really was raised from the dead.[16] It is true, and in that room, at that moment, I think he knew it. Logically, then, he went on to worship the risen Christ? Not at all. A daft remark followed, and he switched the conversation. We're called to give a 'reason for the hope we have' (1 Peter 3:15), but in the end we can't simply argue people into the kingdom; there is a problem that goes far deeper than that.

The real problem in evangelism is supernatural. There is a demonic blinding of the ego that prevents those who are not yet believers from 'seeing the glory of Christ', says Paul in 4:4. Against such a supernatural blockage, only supernatural weapons will do. As Paul will say later: 'The weapons we fight with are not the weapons of the world. On the contrary, they have divine power to demolish strongholds. We demolish arguments and every pretension that sets itself up against the knowledge of God'(10:3-5).

What are those weapons? Our minds turn back to Paul's classic account of our spiritual armour in Ephesians 6, with its twin weapons for attack: the 'sword of the Spirit which is the Word of God', and prayer. Evangelism is never just an intellectual wrestling-match. Unless the supernatural blindness is broken by persistent prayer, and until God indeed 'makes his light to shine in our hearts', nothing can be achieved.

We see this many times in student evangelism. Over and over, the crucial work for university missions is done in prayer meetings beforehand. 'I never cease to be amazed how these prayers are answered,' wrote Roger Mitchell in *In Touch*; 'the people we've listed for specific prayer make up many of those who become Christians.' It's no accident that African countries with huge evangelical student groups – sometimes a thousand believers in a single university – are also marked by weekly nights of prayer attended by hundreds. It underlines the truth of Hallesby's memorable exhortation: 'Pray every day for your non-Christian friends. Surround them with your prayer.' (*Help me do it, Lord!*) 'Each time you pray you plunge a holy explosive into their soul, and one day it will scatter the ice from around their hearts!'

And the other weapon by which our 'ministry of the Spirit' 'scatters the ice' is our gospel: the 'sword of the Spirit which is the Word of God'. As we saw in the previous section, the simple, unvarnished Word that we share is no less than the channel for the 'glory of Christ'; it is our remarkable privilege that, through our faltering words, the Spirit is ministered. (We'll see this again when we come to look later at 1 Peter 1:25.)

This gospel, says Paul, is not merely about abstract ideas. We are called to share the 'knowledge of the glory of God in the face of Christ' (2 Cor 4:6). (*Lord, may what I say give others a sense of that glory...*) Relevant apologetics, and careful explanation of the gospel, are indispensable. But equally important is that we learn to share something of what we're perceiving, day by day, of the glory of God in the face of Christ; since he is, as Hebrews 1 says, the clearest of revelations, the ultimate 'radiance of God's glory and the exact representation of his being'. That is why the freshness of our own times with God, absorbing 'the Lord's glory' (3:18), links directly to our effectiveness in witness: they give us something living to say. That is also why, all over the world, so many people meet Christ through group studies based on his self-revelation in the Gospels. The goal of all our evangelism is to promote an informed, worshipping answer to the question, Who is Jesus, and how should I respond to him? The Gospels, *par excellence*, are the place to tackle that question: channels through which he 'shines in our hearts to give us the light of the knowledge of the glory'.

Specific prayer and the Word, then, are the means by which the 'ministry of the Spirit' bursts through the 'veil' over human hearts. (*Thankyou, Lord! Please help me use them both*...) But, Paul now tells us, there are situations through which God's power is specially released: our pressures, and our sufferings.

Confessions of a cardboard box (4:7-11)

'More love, more power', goes a well-loved chorus, 'more of you in my life'. And there is power within us for astonishing ministry, says Paul: power to minister the Spirit and the Word that conforms us to Christ; power to break through the deepest blindness that the Enemy has inflicted on humanity. But now he relates this to the pressures he and so many of his fellow-believers have suffered. We have this power in 'jars of clay', he says – cheap, disposable containers, indeed containers that are falling apart. And God creates this distinction between the contents and the packaging, so that it will be clear that 'this all-surpassing power is from God and not from us' (4:7).

It's not always easy to be a clay pot – or, let's say, a cardboard box. Feeling – discovering – as many of us do, that one is such second-rate, inadequate, failing and broken material for God; hoping, often, that not too many other people will notice. Why does it have to be this way? Could not God's Spirit be carried around in 'containers' a little less prone to falling apart? What can we learn from chapter 4 as Paul explores this further?

First, it is *normal*. The issue plagued Paul – and many others before him. One wonders if, as he wrote this, Paul was thinking of Gideon – someone else whose story concerns light hidden in clay jars (Judges 7:16-21). Gideon, too, came to see God's strength revealed in absurd human weakness.[17] He recruited an army of thirty thousand to liberate Israel from the invader. Then, first, God told him to send home any who were frightened; so much for all his efforts in recruitment and motivation. That cost him two-thirds of his army. Next, God separated the rest into two groups, one nine thousand seven hundred strong, the other a mere three hundred. And just when (one imagines) Gideon was feeling relief that this time he would lose just three per cent more, God told him to send the nine thousand home; so that Israel's faith would be in God, not their own strength (Judg. 7:2, cf. 2 Cor 1:9).

Finally came God's battle plan. He told Gideon to give each man a light in a jar, and encircle the enemy's camp. In the middle of the night, the invaders woke to hear trumpet blasts and the smashing of clay jars, and to see lights flaming out in every direction around them. In the panic that ensued, the enemy was put to flight completely. But if this lesson was in Paul's mind, he will have remembered the cost: the clay pots had to be broken (the cardboard carton has to be ripped open) for what was inside to shine out.

At any rate that is what is happening to him. 'We are hard-pressed on every side, but not crushed... struck down, but not destroyed,' he writes. 'We always carry around in our body the death of Jesus, *so that* the life of Jesus may also be revealed in our body' (4:8-10). It's a central spiritual principle: the divine power of the resurrection goes with the brokenness of the cross. The principle was most clearly set out by the divine 'wounded healer', Jesus himself, in John 12:24: 'Unless' – *unless* – 'a grain of wheat falls to the ground and dies, it remains a single seed. But if it dies, it produces many seeds.' *(Thankyou, Lord, that you have been this way.)* That was the way of the cross, and, said Jesus, there is no alternative route to glory: 'Whoever serves me must follow me' (John 12:26,23).

Paul knows it is happening to him: in the pressures, the criticisms, the pitiless disclosures of his own human weakness. They connect to this 'carrying around in our body the death of Jesus'. In fact, they are part of the process of being made like Jesus, 'transformed into his likeness', that shone over Paul's horizon in 3:18. Growing into Christ cannot exclude the cross that was so central to his incarnation here. But to recognize this is to find meaning inherent in our stresses, our inadequacy, even our failures (cf. 12:10). Somehow, they make us useable; they are inseparable from the release, somewhere and somehow, of God's power, of 'the life of Jesus' (vv10-11). (It may even be, as a Japanese colleague counselled me late one night about an issue I felt was genuinely harming my own work, that our difficulty is our strength.) It's okay to feel bad; but 'therefore we do not lose heart'; even when (to quote Eric Clapton) we're down to 'running on faith'.

In all the pressure, then, Paul lives, survives, by faith. *(Thankyou, Lord. Please help me trust too.)* Faith that in all the problems – even as the 'cardboard box' or 'clay jar' that he has become is 'wasting away'(v16) – so the gospel is furthered, God is glorified, and others benefit (v12,15). '*In* all these things,' as he says in a similar context in Romans 8:35-37, 'we are more than conquerors.'[18]

Living for glory (4:12-5:8)

In the new testament, suffering and glory seem to go together like the two sides of a coin. (See Romans 8:17-18 or 1 Peter 5:1.) So a letter with plenty to say about pressure should also have plenty to say about glory. If we do a quick survey of chapters 4 and 5, we'll note at least three striking aspects to this.

First, the 'clay pot process' that makes Paul's weakness so obvious also ensures God's glory, in a very straightforward way. It means that when people think about Paul, they may also be thinking, 'But in person he's unimpressive' (10:10). It's an error of judgment; but meanwhile the process ensures that, for whatever reason, the glory goes where Paul would want it, and where it belongs: to God (4:15, cf. 1 Cor 1:28-29).

This is a serious matter. Adulation of the 'big names' was a problem in Corinth (1 Cor 3:18,20-22), and Paul had to rebuke his own 'supporters' about it (1 Cor 1:12-13). A glance round the evangelical scene today shows how easily the demonstration of spiritual power – a powerful preacher, an effective evangelist, a healing ministry – attracts admiration to the human being at its centre. And God's glory is stolen. (The dramatic story in Acts 12:20-23 helps us grasp how serious this is.) Paul doesn't want that. His passion, for which he is willing to pay the price, is that glory and thanksgiving go to God. The goal of what's happening in 1:11 is that '*many will give thanks* on our behalf for the gracious favour given us'; in 4:15 it's 'so that the grace which is reaching more and more people may *cause thanksgiving to overflow* to the glory of God'; the aim in 9:11-13 is that 'your generosity will *result in thanksgiving* to God. This service... is overflowing in many expressions of thanks to God.' The glorifying of God is (as the Westminster catechism says) the chief purpose of our existence; and we sense Paul wanting to live so as to stimulate praise and thanksgiving. (*Lord, I take this moment to worship you. Give me a heart like Paul's; please help me encourage others to give you glory!*)

But that's not all. Secondly, the glorifying of God is bound up with our own growth into glory. We will not be clay pots forever. 'Therefore we do not lose heart', repeats Paul, because we hold to faith that 'our light and momentary troubles' are actually '*achieving for us an eternal glory*, that far outweighs them all' (4:16-17). Being a clay pot isn't easy. But the body we have now is the chrysalis of new life, that will one day soar into the heavens. Chrysalises aren't much more attractive than clay pots, of course, and the butterfly finally soars only when the chrysalis finally breaks; but that's not the end for what really matters. Again we remember Hebrews 6:19: our hope is our anchor; suffering is borne through our sense of glory to come. (Psychiatrist Larry Crabb applies this helpfully to the times when we're badly hurt by others. The vital issue, he says, is how far our legitimate disappointment turns into a bitterness that eats us away. But bitterness occurs only when we forget that, ultimately, all that matters is safe in glory, beyond the reach of others' malice or carelessness.[19] Our hope is our anchor.)

For Paul, then, inward renewal amid the pressures depends on 'fixing our eyes' on heaven, and a deep grasp of what the Word tells us of glory (4:18). (*Lord, I believe: help my lack of faith – before it gets me into trouble!*) But what is this 'grasp'?

As a teenager, I learnt a lot from a missionary to India. One day she shared with me what meditation meant for her. Over the years, she told me, more and more Scripture gets written into our memories; and that makes possible a fruitful form of meditation where our thoughts roam out from our daily reading to related passages, and then we turn them up with a concordance.[20] Here we catch Paul's vision better as we respond also to Jesus' words: 'Store up for yourselves treasure in heaven... for where your treasure is, there your heart will be also' (Matt 6:20-21). Or to Colossians 3:1-4, again talking about where our 'hearts' are set: 'Since, then, you have been raised with Christ, set your hearts on things above, where Christ is.'

This deliberate grasp, this 'fixing our eyes on what is unseen'(4:18) and 'longing for our heavenly dwelling'(5:2), is highly un-contemporary. But for Paul, it comes close to the core of Christian life. In Romans 5:2, to be 'justified by faith' means to begin to 'rejoice in hope of the glory of God' (*Yes, Lord!*); in 1 Thess 1:10, Paul presents the longing for the change of worlds at Christ's appearing as a fundamental aspect of discipleship.[21] Staying hungry for 'things above' is at the heart of 'living by faith': we notice that when Paul uses that key phrase here, it's clearly tied to his passion for heaven (2 Cor 5:6-8).

So a spirituality that has learned from Paul keeps a deliberate place for longing, dreaming, giving thanks about the glory to come. (*Please help me build it in, Lord; walking across the park, or on the bus...*) 'No ear has heard, no mind has conceived what God has prepared for those who love him', Paul challenges our imaginations (1 Cor 2:9). It will be 'more than we can ask or think'! But this we can be sure of: to be totally in the presence of God, face to face, must logically mean experiencing the fullness of his infinite love and joy, his peace and gentleness. Heaven exists because the Lord loves us and wants our company; his longing is that we should be with him, to see all his glory (John 17:24, Eph 2:7). What we have now isn't the fullness of what 'life' means. We've only ever caught brief and limited glimpses, here on earth, of what undiluted joy or love are like. There, we're going to taste them fully.

Cartoonists imagine heaven as somehow vaguer, paler, duller than here. Paul's grasp ('Now we *know*', 5:1) is of a world far more vital than this one, far more exuberantly alive – one might even say far more physical; a world where our mortality is 'swallowed up by life' (5:4). (*Please help me grasp that idea, Father...*)   God cares about our bodies. Our destiny isn't to be 'unclothed', stripped of physicality (5:3-4), as Eastern thought teaches, but rather to be 'further clothed;'[22] our 'lowly bodies' will be 'transformed' (that word again) to 'be like Christ's glorious body' (Phil 3:21). This bizarre fact can preserve us from ideas of heaven as dull, insubstantial and passionless. Jesus came to bring us 'life to the full' (John 10:10). We shan't be drifting round as colourless ghosts. Rather, we shall experience the life we were made for, for the very first time.

1 Corinthians 15 explains it at length: our bodies may be as unimaginably different from what we have now as the full-grown wheat is from the shrivelled seed. Yet, like the wheat's

relation to the seed, what wakes up may be profoundly better, but it will still be *us*. Perhaps the first moments in heaven will be like that first day of feeling strong and restored after a long illness – that strange sense of flexing our limbs more easily, remembering what it feels like to be healthy. So, probably, after death: we shall stretch out in surprise and know, for the first time, what it means to be fully human, fully whole. Dream about it, long for it; *this* is what we were made for, says Paul (2 Cor 5:5). (*Thankyou, Lord!*)

But – thirdly – there's more. We're not just called to desire: the realities of heaven start now. God has made us for heaven, says Paul, '*and* has given us the Spirit as a deposit, guaranteeing what is to come'(5:5). ('Hope does not disappoint us,' he adds over in Romans 5:5, 'because God *has* poured out his love into our hearts by the Holy Spirit.') The clay pot is falling apart; but even now, inside us, there is the 'treasure' of the Spirit, a pointer to the future, a foretaste or deposit of glory.

Often we don't grasp what a crucial, life-giving idea this is for Paul. But we saw it in Ephesians 1:14 and 4:30, we'll meet it again in Romans 8:23, and this is the second time in 2 Corinthians. In Galatians 3:14 he goes so far as to say that the whole purpose of redemption was that we might receive this 'promise of the Spirit'.[23] And it is the Spirit who is the revelatory channel of glory in 2 Corinthians 3:18, in Ephesians 1:17-18 or 1 Corinthians 2:9-10. Any spirituality for the coming century must take seriously Paul's vision of the Spirit's centrality as the gateway of heaven. (Non-charismatics doubtful about other parts of charismatic theology still need to think hard how to take this on board!)

So the God who sealed us with his Spirit as the guarantee of glory beyond our imaginations is the one who ensures that, ultimately, we 'stand firm' (cf. 2 Cor 1:21-22). '*Therefore*', repeats Paul the walking clay pot - when everything's falling apart, even as the pot itself crumbles and this time what's cracking is us – '*therefore we are always confident*' (5:6)...

Salvation spreads (5:9-21)

What follows from all this?

As usual with Paul, mysticism and action come together as his letter continues. Or, we might equally say, faith comes together with works. The next chapters are incredibly practical, impacting one 'private' area of our lives after another.

It starts with a heart-orientation. Paul's grasp of eternal reality includes deep awareness that 'we must all appear before the judgment seat of Christ'(5:10). Faith in heaven is far from being an opiate. The sense of the reality of the other world, the awe-inspiring thought of explaining to the Father how we used the lives and abilities he gave us ('Each of us will give an account of himself to God', Rom 14:12), gives profound urgency to evangelism. (*Lord, help me grasp that this is not a fable; please renew in me this sense of urgency!*) 'Since, then, we know what it is to fear the Lord, we try to persuade men' (5:11).

I had a few hours recently in a dull airport, waiting for a flight to Lithuania; and (as this section was in the mix) it seemed an opportunity to skim through chapters 6-13. Speed-reading like that is always good for getting the flow, seeing how or why one section or idea leads into the next; and this time I found myself wondering why there was this big emphasis on the gospel, here and in 5:18-6:2. Was it that the criticisms were still weighing on Paul, and the one on his mind here was that he'd been far too passionate about evangelism? Does this underlie his keenness to explain why evangelism is such a glorious task, in chapter 3? It does seem as if he needs to explain (5:11-15) why he's such a man of passion: 'If we are out of our mind, it is for the sake of God... for Christ's love compels us'(vv13-14).

It may be. But then the next question comes: what fuels such a glorious passion?

Surely it is a sense of the hugeness of the gospel. Let's follow the flow. A theme (or a vision) running through

5:14-17 is the implications of the cross: 'the gospel' in its broadest, most far-reaching sense. 'Christ's love compels us'; if Christ has died for all, says Paul, all of us have died, with him, to ourselves and our world (vv14-15). Everything has changed; since our new birth we are finished with our old existence; nothing is to be viewed from the world's perspective any more (v16). Radical holiness, in short, which will be the theme of 6:14 onwards. Paul has glimpsed something colossal here: 'If anyone is in Christ, he is a new creation; the old has gone, the new has come!'(v17). God's heavenly 'new creation' has broken into our world, taking shape in our actions now, leading us triumphantly towards the 'everything new' of Revelation 21:5. Our gospel of the cross, then, that colossal act of love, death and resurrection, is about complete transformation, such as we saw thrilling Paul in 3:18. This, by definition, will have sweeping consequences, as salvation spreads from the 'deposit' of the Spirit now within us, outwards across the components of our personality. The cross has implications without limit for us – 'He died for all that those who live should no longer live for themselves but for him who died for them...'

It's quite a gospel. What we're proclaiming is complete 're-creation', into a God-oriented rather than self-oriented life; becoming the way we were built to be! But what does my having 'died'(v14) and risen into newness with Christ mean for my own life, right now? This 'gospel' challenges my entire being and existence. All my emotions, my imagination: to reorientate from being 'self-centred' to being 'Christ-centred', finding their place in the 'new creation'. Each of my values, my dreams, my ambitions: ditto. My use of time and gifts and money, my lifestyle, my marriage and career plans: likewise. Quite an agenda to seek to recognize and assess. (*Lord, thankyou for the cross and the 'new creation'; please help me work consciously on finding the next steps, by your Spirit...*)

Here is true 'transformation'. To be born again was to die with Christ and to begin an entire new life with him.[24]

Through the cross, everything is becoming new; holiness is indispensable. My heart-commitment to this 're-creation process' is basic to the gospel. It's what 'repentance' means...

A sixfold passion (1) (5:16-7:1)

'If anyone is in Christ, he is a new creation!'

'Making disciples', or 'following-up new believers', means helping others grasp this dramatic vision, the concrete implications of this spreading transformation – just as we seek to help ourselves. We see Paul embodying it in at least six areas in the next chapters. They are basic to our spirituality. Let's look at them briefly.

The first, as we have seen, is a *passion for evangelism*. Paul no longer views anyone as he used to, but rather as someone facing God's judgment and needing to be 'implored'(5:20) to do something about it. Being transformed into Christ's likeness includes having his love (v14) compel us to *'implore'* people to hear the gospel: 'on Christ's behalf... as though God were making his appeal through us'(v20). Paul's transformed mentality, his sense of eternal reality, motivates him to passion about the only gospel that saves. (*Lord, I don't feel I've 'implored' anybody 'in Christ's stead' for some time now...*)

A second is a *passion for spiritual seriousness*. In fact these two go together; in 5:20-6:2 (as in 12:20-13:5) it is hard to say if Paul's challenge to Corinth is evangelistic – are they truly 'in the faith', have they indeed repented and believed? – or confirming whether they live in a way that shows their repentance was real. No holiness means no genuineness; as 1 John 3:6,9 puts it, noone born of God can happily continue to sin. The question is whose life it is. An attempt to run our own lives, to delay obedience, asserts precisely that rebellious independence ('It's my life') which could not coexist with true repentance. Saying 'Not yet' is saying 'No' to God: 'It's my life and I will hand it over when I choose.' (Which, as Paul reminds them, is foolish. 'Now is the time of God's favour'(6:2); it would be absurdly arrogant to demand that God's offer of his presence and redirection recur just when we decide we want it.)

But then why does Paul write 6:3-10 at this particular point in the argument? Is he reminding them what's involved in real seriousness – in following Jesus even if the way of the cross leads out beyond our 'comfort zones'?[25] 'In great endurance; in troubles, hardships and distresses; in beatings, imprisonments, and riots; in hard work, sleepless nights and hunger... glory and dishonour, bad report and good report'(vv4-8). It is scarcely 'prosperity Christianity'! ('Poor, yet making many rich; having nothing, and yet possessing everything'(v10).) Godly seriousness is even 'sorrowful'(v10), as Paul grows like Jesus the 'Man of sorrows'; we think of Paul 'imploring' those who are headed astray, and our minds return to Acts – 'For three years I never stopped warning each of you night and day with tears' (20:31, cf. 20:19). Yet we sense a glory revealed – automatically – in character that perseveres through such suffering by God's grace; it fits into Paul's vision of being 'transformed into Christ's likeness'. It is an astounding privilege to be 'God's fellow-workers'(6:1), through whom Christ's glory flows into the world. But if suffering and glory go together, then it's not surprising if 'knowing Christ and the power of his resurrection' also involves us in this 'fellowship of sharing in his sufferings'(Phil 3:10).

Spiritual reality: are you in it with us?, Paul asks the Corinthians. 'One died for all... that those who live should no longer live for themselves.' Thirdly, then, Paul moves on to what we can call a *passion for holiness*: 'Do not be yoked together with unbelievers... Let us purify ourselves from everything that contaminates body and spirit, perfecting holiness out of reverence for God.' We often apply this to love and marriage; because here above all is a 'yoke' where you're committed to doing things together, and so it's crucial to have, at the deepest level, the same desires. Anyone married for more than a few years can testify how much conflict is spared if both of you are committed to the same fundamental priorities and life-goals. Inevitably there will be trouble if, at the deepest level, one of you is a 'temple of God' – ultimately dedicated to God's worship – and the other a 'temple of idols' – ultimately committed to other life-priorities (v16). Long-term, getting this wrong cripples our Godward relationship. The force of Paul's language is striking: 'What fellowship can light have with darkness?... What does a believer have in common with an unbeliever?' 'Nearly everything', we may answer when we're in love. It may only be after several years of marriage that we grasp that, here too, Paul's words were inspired by God.[26]

But love and marriage are not the only issues here; rather, 'let us purify ourselves from *everything* that contaminates body and spirit'. Again, this is scarcely a contemporary way to talk; to be called 'pure' today is more an insult than a compliment![27] I find it hard to cultivate the instinct that notices, 'Hey, this that I'm reading makes me feel defiled, it leaves me a little away from God.' In our present environment, that sense is easily blunted; we have to develop the habit of hearing it, and acting on it, rather than overriding it. The issue here is seriousness about cultivating the white heat of passion for holiness: how much we want to stay sensitive to Christ and his voice. Articles in the Sunday paper, web-pages or videos we pump into the imagination, are a gospel issue, a transformation issue.

Inevitably there is something about this passion for holiness that feels 'narrower yet deeper'; just as for a woman to marry a man is to shut herself off from all other potential partners. Yet above all holiness is positive and relational, not negative and life-denying. We will be motivated to it if we grasp God's astonishing words here: 'I will live with them and walk among them... *I will be a Father to you*, and you will be my sons and daughters' (6:16,18). (Or, as in 4:10, 'so that the *life of Jesus* may be revealed in our body'.) 'Since we have *these* promises, dear friends' (or 'dearly beloved' (AV)), 'let us purify ourselves' (7:1). *(Thankyou, Father, for your astounding gift of your presence; please help me cultivate a separateness for you!*)

A sixfold passion (2) (7:1-9:15)

Fourthly, we are confronted, in the next three chapters, by Paul's *passion for other brothers and sisters*. 'You have such a place in our hearts that we would live or die with you!' (7:3).

This motivates the tremendous urgency (and relief) with which we sense him repairing endangered relationships throughout chapter 7. There is Christ-like depth ('Christ's love compels us'?) about a mind that could feel no peace, until Titus confirmed that Paul's relations with his brothers were back in shape (7:5-7, cf. 2:13). The same passion marks the following chapters too. Here, as in other Epistles, we sense Paul's deep concern for his financial aid project for Jerusalem, that would bind the churches together across the historic ethnic divide. (And it did. That the Macedonians 'urgently pleaded with us' for the chance to be involved in the giving (8:4) is particularly remarkable; the Greeks viewed the Jews as barbarians.)

Such love is a mark of spiritual reality. We have seen it in the evangelical student groups worldwide. In the white-supremacist era in Zimbabwe, the university Christian Union was the only effectively multiracial group on campus, with a presidency sometimes black, sometimes white. At one tense phase during the ethnic turmoil in Sri Lanka, the student movement's national camp was described as 'the first time since the upheavals that people from both sides had met and studied (let alone lived!) together anywhere in the country'. In Burundi, believers were severely beaten or even murdered during the tragic Hutu/Tutsi genocide, because they cared for fellow-Christians who belonged to the 'others'.

Of course the record isn't always so positive. Critics may remind us of roles played by some (but certainly not all)

'Christians' in Ulster or South Africa.[28]   But such incidents say nothing about true faith; they merely show how tribal hatred can clothe itself in twisted religious ideology. Similar links between virulent nationalism and nominal religion have been evident throughout eastern Europe. (The flag can creep surprisingly close to the pulpit in the West too.) Religions identified with the bulk of a community, and that blur the line between nominal and true believers, are particularly vulnerable. It's been tragic, in former Yugoslavia for example, to watch how little was done by church hierarchies (from the Pope downwards) to restrain ethnic hate by clear church discipline. It's hard to see how someone can claim to be a true Catholic, or Protestant, or Orthodox, if they don't implement such central commands of Christ as 'Love your enemy'. A pastor once took me through a militantly Unionist part of Belfast, with pavements painted red, white and blue, and described it as '100% "Protestant", utterly pagan. Everybody here's "Protestant", nobody goes to church.' Such tribalism has nothing to do with spiritual reality.

Thankyou, Lord, that you died because you cared enormously for 'all people everywhere'. Please help me grasp what that means for me. Jesus-, or Paul-style passion for fellow-believers of all ethnicities must have practical consequences. A contemporary parallel would have implications for our politics: for choices to vote for parties who see that a small percent of our economic growth matters less than the policies draining huge sums from destitute lands, causing malnutrition or crippling illness for children of our brothers and sisters.[29]   Likewise, it implies huge questions about our ability to work for companies profiting by aggressive arms marketing, massively worsening the injuries to our brothers caught in African ethnic strife. (Isn't this living out the 'vision of the Body' that we saw in Ephesians?) And it implies perceptive, deliberate holiness when we catch ethnic scorn surfacing[30] back home in our own thoughts: 'purifying ourselves from everything that contaminates body and spirit; perfecting holiness out of reverence for God'(7:1). Paul too knew how venomous ethnic feelings could be (eg. Acts 18:2,19:34,21:28-30,22:21-22). His dream for this collection from the Gentile churches, with its tangible proof of love across the divide, is set out in 9:13-14. 'People' (the Jewish recipients) 'will praise God for the *obedience that accompanies your confession* of the gospel of Christ; and for your generosity in sharing with them and with everyone else. And' – the Body is bound together, ethnic hostility is shattered – 'in their prayers for you their hearts will go out to you!'

It is logical, then, that in this section we see both Paul's passion for others, and his *passion for giving*. In chapter 6 we saw the transformation of sexuality; we've seen how the cross transforms ethnic loyalties; now we watch it touching another of our deepest drives. If the pocket has truly been liberated, the heart is surely liberated too! 'Out of the most severe trial, their overflowing joy and their extreme poverty welled up in generosity,' writes Paul of the Macedonians (8:2). Our culture expects riches to lead to joy; once we've learnt that joy comes from elsewhere, we can put riches to their proper use. Like prayer, giving is a channel by which God's blessing can be passed on into one area after another. The challenge, as in 4:18, is to 'fix our eyes not on what is seen, but what is unseen'. And the question is how to do that: how to learn the joy of generous giving by breaking the addiction to material things. These are big issues for parents bringing up children, and couples embarking on or reviewing their marriage. *Lord, please help me hear your voice about your next steps for me in this...*

Here too, transformation comes as nothing less than a direct gift from God (8:1). Again, this is the 'day of salvation', and Paul urges[31] the Corinthians to be consistently obedient to the impulse from heaven (8:7), to see it through when the initial excitement has subsided (8:11). Faith is meaningless (cf. Jam 2:20) unless it bears real fruit in action, hence Paul's emphasis on proving the reality of their faith (7:12,8:8,24,9:13). In this gospel of transformation, giving is not one or more isolated charitable acts, after which we have 'done our bit'. Rather, it flows from a far deeper 'giving ourselves first to the Lord' (8:5). Probably this 'giving ourselves' is something each of us should pray, explicitly, once or more each day. If we truly grasp the insight that 'we are not our own' (1 Cor 6:19), then the issue is no longer how much we give 'away', but how much of God's money we allocate to ourselves. Again the cross is the heart of the matter: 'For you know the grace of our Lord Jesus Christ, that though he was rich' – we can consider in what sense Christ was 'rich', if we want to understand true wealth – 'yet for your sakes he became poor, so that you through his poverty might be rich' (8:9). (*Lord, I worship*...) Liberation and transformation come as we grasp the cross, and grow like Jesus.

And at the section's close we glimpse a sixth passion: Paul's *passion for stimulating praise*. His concern for giving acts out one of the 'great commandments', loving our neighbour; it's not surprising that we find the other here too – loving the Lord with all our heart, the centre of Christian life. 'Your generosity will result in thanksgiving to God. This service that you perform is not only supplying the needs of God's people but is *also* overflowing in many expressions of thanks to God. Because of the service by which you have proved yourselves, men will praise God!' (9:11-13). It seems that Paul plans, preaches, contrives to set people praising God, all round the Mediterranean!– to be a 'helper of your joy', in short (1:24 AV). And a key aspect of praise here is one believer glorifying God for the particular 'grace' he has revealed in other believers (9:14).[32] A central part of Paul's own prayer life was praising God for other sisters and brothers, as we've seen (1 Cor 1:4-5, Eph 1:15-16, Phil 1:3-5, 1 Thess 1:2-3, 3:9, 2 Thess 1:3-4). (*Lord, I don't do very much of this, I need to plan to.*) It's a fruitful part of worship.

Again we recall the chief purpose of life, according to the Westminster catechism: to *glorify* God, and *enjoy* him forever.

Paul's passion here shows us his heart; he would want these to be far more than empty words for us!

Weakness in the world where the cross happened (10:1-13:14)

At 10:1 the tone changes dramatically. Bruce[33] suggests that even as Paul was writing, reports had come in of new follies at Corinth. And here, perhaps, comes the heart of the whole letter.

Space does not permit our covering this section in depth; but it fits closely with what has gone before. Chapter 10 makes clear that Paul's method for dealing with a difficult church situation is still the 'broken pot spirituality' of chapter 4: trust in God, in the midst of his own weakness. 'We do not wage war as the world does.[34] The weapons we fight with are not the weapons of the world.' (*Lord, what methods am I tempted by that are really the 'weapons of the world'?*)

We can apply this to the traps we sometimes fall into in today's Christian community: internal politics, manipulation and building of 'parties', minor deceptiveness, slander, power-plays and self-aggrandizement. These can even be what's advocated ('as the world does') in secular assertiveness-training; and we can relish feeling 'tough' and 'uncompromising', whether that is a 'Sermon on the Mount' approach to our situation or not. The modern management ethos is shot through with such attitudes, and church leaderships (and 'management teams' of Christian groups) have no automatic shield from infection. Roger Mitchell, expounding Luke 4, sees the power-temptation as so ubiquitous in spiritual warfare that it should be a regular prayer concern to see where we're succumbing. 'We have conducted ourselves in our relations with you,' says Paul in 2 Cor 1:12, 'in the holiness and sincerity that are from God... not according to worldly wisdom, but according to God's grace.' Grace, because, if we renounce the political and self-aggrandizing methods of the world, we may be left with our own weakness and (10:10) 'unimpressiveness'; and only faith can assure us that the 'way of the cross' will produce whatever results God actually wants. But in contrast, to work by 'human wisdom', 'as the world does', may be to do without God's power. (*Lord, help me in my life to discern these issues; to trust you; and to live accordingly...*)

And so it is in a very practical context of conflict, criticism and his own possible failure (13:7), that we find Paul setting out the principle that has run through 2 Corinthians. He tells now of a major problem that 'tormented' him. Three times, he says, he 'pleaded' with the Lord for deliverance. 'But he said to me, "My grace is sufficient for you, for my power is made perfect in weakness." Therefore I will boast all the more gladly about my weaknesses, so that Christ's power may rest on me. That is why, for Christ's sake, I delight in weaknesses, in insults, in hardships, in persecutions, in difficulties. For when I am weak, then I am strong' (12:8-10). Paul knows that this is the Way, because it means conformity to the ultimate pattern of the cross: 'Christ... was crucified in weakness, yet he lives by God's power. Likewise, we are weak in him, yet by God's power we will live with him to serve you' (13:4). The cross makes it clear: weakness is strength; suffering is glory.

Here is the faith by which, as we saw at the beginning, Paul lives and survives. Faith strengthened by the vision we noted in Ephesians 1, of God's 'incomparably great power for us who believe'; faith, therefore, that in difficult situations can say to God, 'Lord, I don't enjoy what you're doing, and I don't understand it, but go on.' Faith that then sets out somehow to 'give glory to God', like Abraham in a similar situation: 'Without weakening in his faith,[35] he faced the fact that his body was as good as dead... He was strengthened in his faith and gave glory to God' (Rom 4:19-21). Presumably that deliberate, difficult thanksgiving, that 'giving glory', matches the 'most gladly... delight' here in 12:9-10.

Such faith falls back on Paul's conviction that God's weakness is stronger than human strength, and that therefore God has chosen the weak and foolish things of the world to be his partners (1 Cor 1:25,27). Having our own resources can be perilous; numerical strength, financial strength, resources of technique or manpower, gifts of intellect or experience can all dilute our sense of the need to live by faith alone.[36] The way of the cross, says Paul, is often the way of weakness, so that it is clear that the 'all-surpassing power' is from God and not from us (2 Cor 4:7). 'I came to you in weakness and fear, and with much trembling... so that your faith might not rest on men's wisdom, but on God's power,' he wrote earlier (1 Cor 2:3,5).

This definition of 'Christ's power resting upon us'(12:9) is Paul's gift to us in 2 Corinthians. Ultimately, it is liberating, peace-bringing. We are weak, imperfect people: cardboard containers for God, tin cans, broken clay pots. But we 'do not lose heart', because we trust that God is shining his light and ministering his Spirit through us. We pray – we are weak, but the Spirit who answers prayer is strong. We share our Christian life – we are imperfect, but the Spirit's living water that flows through us is real. We share what we're discovering as we 'pioneer' in the Bible – we don't understand it all, but the Spirit makes it his 'sword' that pierces darkness, revealing 'the glory of God in the face of Christ'. Broken pots: we suffer, our weakness is revealed – and even here, such is his creativity, as the 'clay pots' show signs of cracking, so the glory, somehow and somewhere, is released. In that situation we may not be able to 'delight' quite as Paul does, but at least we can set out in that direction: holding to faith that 'when I am weak, then I am strong'.

Broken pot spirituality is central to Christian life because it is cross spirituality. And following Jesus is about the cross. In 1 Corinthians, Paul summarizes Christianity in two words: '*Christ, crucified*'(1:23, 2:2). 'The cross alone,' said Luther, 'is our theology'; the cross embodies the very heart of our faith and life. It is the centre of history, the place where all roads meet; throughout eternity earth will be remembered as the place where the cross happened. We will never 'outgrow' a deepening grasp of the cross, because the cross, above all, revealed God, what he is like and how he acts.[37] If we want to know how God's glory is revealed, it is by the cross; when Jesus said 'The hour has come for the Son of Man to be glorified', it was the cross he meant (John 12:23).[38] "Tis in thy cross, Lord, that we learn/ What thou in all thy fullness art.'[39] It is in the cross that we understand the meaning of what happens in our own lives; and how, as Jesus-followers, to respond.

Notes

[1] There are many other ways we could approach 2 Corinthians. This is just one!

[2] Eph 4:30.

[3] Eph 5:18. Seeing the importance of this 'ministry of the Spirit' helps us grasp why the Spirit's power is so basic to the Church's evangelistic task in Acts 1:8.

[4] Rugby international Jason Robinson, for instance, told the *Independent on Sunday* (31 December 2000) how watching the life of his Samoan teammate Va'aiga Tuigamala made him 'put my faith in Jesus': 'I saw a peace in him that I wanted. He was the only believer in the team and I wanted to find out what it was about this man who never got carried away.'

[5] One of the best books on this topic is Rebecca Manley Pippert, *Out of the Saltshaker* (new edition, 1999). (The Trobisch quotation is from his preface to the 1979 American edition.)

[6] To quote David Gooding's illustration, the law is like a thermometer, an essential tool for recognizing our sickness. But a thermometer is not the same as the medicine that heals us; for that we need to look further, to the gospel.

[7] The Greek word for Moses' veil is not the same as for the temple veil, but the point is surely the same: an exclusion from the heart of God which the gospel removes.

[8] What has gone wrong with our spirituality in this case? Often, we've lost our grasp of the forgiveness and enormous change

brought us in God's gift of free, once-for-all new birth by faith; and we've drifted into thinking of spiritual life as something that comes (or goes) insofar as we keep up a repeated participation in the sacraments. (Or, in the Protestant version, church services.) In practice, the difference is huge; it means our spirituality becomes marked by a sense of uncertainty and distance from God. The 'holy place' of his heart is no longer where we naturally belong, as our home ('seated with Christ in the heavenly realms', as we saw last chapter); instead, it becomes somewhere we might possibly reach one day, if we do everything right. Paul's gospel offers us far, far more than that (cf. too John's confidence in 1 John 5:13-14): new birth through faith leading to a joyous assurance of absolute closeness to God.

[9] This sense of a guilty conscience is precisely the issue again in Hebrews 10: 'Since we have confidence to enter the most holy place by the blood of Jesus... let us draw near to God... in full assurance of faith, *having our hearts sprinkled to cleanse us from a guilty conscience*' (vv19-22).

[10] Cf. John Stott's excellent *Christ the Controversialist* (1970).

[11] M.Dibelius, *Jesus* (1949), p.70.

[12] And for our being 'transformed by the renewing of your mind' in Romans 12:2.

[13] F.F.Bruce's preferred translation: cf. *New Century Bible Commentary: I and II Corinthians* (1971), p.193.

[14] Quoted in George Verwer's brilliant little book on discipleship, *Hunger for Reality* (1972), p.75.

[15] There is an issue here for our apologetics. If we are confident that the Word really is *true*, and does its own work, then we are free from any pressure to 'twist the evidence'. Deceptiveness reflects a need to do God's work by our own strength, rather than trusting him to do it himself. We can afford to say we don't know; we can recognize that some issues (the problem of suffering, for instance) remain, as Stott says, in our 'pending tray'. Truth can stand on its own; because we are not putting our faith in our own persuasive abilities, we can relax and trust God's power.

[16] An impressive and academically credible summary is Sir Norman Anderson, *Jesus Christ – the Witness of History* (1985).

[17] If Gideon's story is indeed in Paul's mind in 2 Cor 4, it's interesting that it starts with Gideon being able to look face to face

on 'the angel of the Lord' – indeed, in some sense, on 'the Lord' himself (v14) – without being killed (Jud 6:22-23). This is fascinating, because that same issue – how we can contemplate the Lord's glory with unveiled faces – is precisely the one at the end of 2 Corinthians 3.

[18] Thus the Chinese writer Watchman Nee, in his classic *What Shall This Man Do?*(1971 edition): 'Life, Paul tells us, is that with which he serves the Church, and in doing so he defines the thing upon which all true ministry in the Church is founded. Death, working in the servant of God, produces life; and because he has life, others too have life. The Church receives, because some are willing to bear the Cross... By allowing God to work through their trials and testing, praising Him and submitting to His will, His children make it possible for Him to bring life to others. But only those who pay the price receive this costly ministry. For life is released through death, but only so... Thus we see two ministries by which the Body is built up – gifts and life; and we may ask ourselves: In which do we discern God's highest purpose? I reply: not in gifts, but in the life from Christ which comes through death'(p.117).

[19] Larry Crabb, *The Marriage Builder* (1982), chapter 7. Crabb's immediate context is marriage, but his point can be enormously healing for other types of hurts as well.

[20] She was assuming a moderately good memory. Another route is to keep a file (on computer or paper) in which we note our discoveries, including related passages, about particular Bible books – from our quiet times, from sermons we hear and books we read. Little by little this will come to play a similar part. It does for me.

[21] Cf. also Rom 8:23 and Phil 3:20.

[22] Bruce's translation of 5:4.

[23] Cf. also Gal 4:4-6 or John 16:7.

[24] Paul explores all this more fully in the first part of Romans 6. We'll be turning to that passage later in this book, but it's worth glancing at as a helpful cross-reference here.

[25] One assumes he isn't talking just about himself; it is hard to believe that 'servants of God'(v4) was already a technical phrase for 'full-time Christian workers', describing Paul but not his hearers. After a similar list in 2 Tim 3:10-12 he adds that these will mark 'everyone who wants to live a godly life in Christ'.

²⁶ 'So from now on we regard no one from a worldly point of view... We fix our eyes not on what is seen, but on what is unseen'(5:16, 4:18).

²⁷ But for Jesus, 'purity' was vital; see Matthew 5:8.

²⁸ But in many ways believers paved the way for the astonishingly peaceful transition from white minority rule in South Africa. And has it not been believers who most powerfully voiced the call for forgiveness in Ulster; for example, after the Enniskillen killings?

²⁹ The Christian-inspired Jubilee Campaign has made a major impact with its call for cancellation of the poorest countries' debts. These debts mean that, every year, those nations send to the West millions of pounds that should be spent on health and education. (Some ten million children die each year from preventable diseases or famine, for example.) The campaign's inspiration has been the 'jubilee year' of Leviticus 25, a key passage where God puts a careful timelimit on the worst that can happen if someone falls into poverty. Paul Handley, writing in the *Independent*, observes, 'We feel that we've been duped... While we were congratulating ourselves on how much we raised for charity, somebody somewhere was siphoning back nine times as much, in our names... We find ourselves in need of forgiveness; and as our Lord taught us, our own forgiveness is linked (chained) to our readiness to forgive our debtors.' Tearfund are also active in this area; their website is www.tearfund.org.

³⁰ 'Perceptive', because these issues arise when we might not expect them. The racist attitude most acceptable to many right-on believers is anti-Americanism!

³¹ Paul is quite deliberate about 'spurring one another on to love and good deeds' in this regard (8:7-12, 9:2, cf. Heb 10:24). But in view of the godless excess to which fundraising can go, it is worth raising a question here: If we survey all the Epistles, isn't it true that Paul fundraises more fervently the further the recipients are from himself? Is this a case of 'Carry each other's burdens, and in this way you will fulfil the law of Christ'(Gal 6:2)?

³² It is worth noting Jack Clemo's idea that this process (of praising God for the particular gift of his 'grace' we see in others) lies close to the heart of Christian sexuality too. When a Christian man falls in love with a woman, he says, 'something distinct about her faith... arrests him and fills him with a great longing to fuse

himself with the facet of Christ which she reflects'. (*The Invading Gospel* (edition of 1972), p.78.)

[33] Bruce, p.169.

[34] This passage supplies lessons for general spiritual warfare; but the context here for his discussion of spiritual power is the personal conflicts within the church – as it is in 13:1-4,10 and 1 Cor 4:18-21. Indeed, these are a key area of 'spiritual warfare'. A Russian friend recently expressed to me deep frustration about being part of a church that prided itself on its 'spiritual warfare', yet was riven by conflict and power struggles.

[35] He almost did weaken. In the Genesis 15 original of this story, Abraham is struggling with deep doubt and depression. It is striking that this classic example of someone whose 'faith was credited to him as righteousness' isn't an untroubled giant of faith, but rather another 'broken pot', someone who can only just maintain his trust. Another example is Habakkuk, the original of 'the just shall live by faith'.

[36] The lukewarm church of Laodicea would be a good example. 'You say, "I am rich; I have acquired wealth and do not need a thing." But you do not realize that you are wretched, pitiful, poor, blind, and naked'(Rev 3:17). As Jesus said, it can be hard for those who are rich to truly enter into the reign of heaven (Matt 19:23). And sometimes, as we noted above with Jacob and with Gideon, God has to weaken us: to reveal our weakness, leave us stripped of contingency plans and thrown back on his grace – so as to make room for his power. I remember Hans Burki challenging an IFES leaders' event that leaders often want to appear strong and omnicompetent; but that is an unhelpful model for those they lead. So, if we aim for that as our image, there will be times when God has to shatter it.

[37] Cf. Phil 2:5-8.

[38] Cf. John 12:31-33 also: to be lifted up in glory was to be lifted up on the cross.

[39] From a hymn by Edward Denny.

3

Believe Some Good News!
Rereading Mark

One of the most faith-destroying, soul-destroying things is the way bad things happen to good people. Another is the way they happen to us.

'God, I thought you answered prayer. God, I thought you wanted your work to go forward. God, I thought you cared.' Not all of us have these thoughts, maybe, but many of us do. And if the just are supposed to live by faith, well, acting like the just isn't always easy.

And yet the Bible warned us it could be this way. There is the slow enormity of the pile-up of disasters that clatter down on the hapless Job. First, much of what he owned is wiped out in a surprise assault by Sabaeans. Then, much of the rest gets destroyed by what seems, of all things, the 'fire of God'. Then the knockout: a building collapses and bereaves him, at one horrifying stroke, of all his children.

There is Habakkuk: watching the triumph of violence and injustice, and the swallowing up of the righteous by the wicked; appealing to God, and receiving a chilling answer that runs, approximately, 'If you think this is bad, you ain't seen nothing yet, and by the way, the just shall live by their faith in God.'

These things we know, with our heads. With our heads we recall Christ's warning that in the world we shall have tribulation. This world is not yet heaven. It is fallen; it is a war zone; and it is *'in* all these things', as Paul (no stranger to pain) puts it in Romans 8, that we are more than conquerors.

With our heads we know these things. It is in our hearts that the problem comes: claiming an apparent promise from God that consistently fails to materialize; watching a project disintegrate that seemed be so valuable; seeing a church fellowship torn apart by dissension; finding a key Christian worker taken off the frontline by some totally avoidable sin or folly. Or it may just be the extended experience of singleness or unemployment; and the deep sense these can generate of unfulfilled potential, creating a spirit somehow calloused, a secret cynicism that doesn't really expect God to 'come through'.

With our heads we understand: the Bible warned us to expect these things. But inside, we feel the 'Yes-God-is-good-in-general-but-not-to-me' syndrome. Inside, something is dying.

Kingdom, come (1:1-6:44)

Rereading Mark recently, it struck me how helpfully it speaks to these questions.

So we're going to look at Mark in this brief section. As we said at the very beginning, this volume concentrates on 'pioneering' into passages we may not know so well, hence it's largely omitting the Gospels. But this one section aims to 'pioneer' within Mark, taking an angle that, for me at any rate, was a little new. We'll be taking Mark at speed, in large chunks (four to eight pages at a time – not too much, when you compare it with how we read other books), because we're just looking at one issue. But moving through a Gospel at that speed gives us perspectives we miss when we focus more closely. It's something we all need to do from time to time.

So, I was rereading Mark. I'd been through it several times before, as most of us have. But this time, right at the start, a question arose that was fresh to me. (Which is what we trust the Spirit to do, if we're alert: to highlight new issues, to turn even the 'old' passages into pioneering fields for us.)

It had to do with Mark 1:14. Mark's Gospel begins with Jesus advancing dramatically into Galilee, 'proclaiming the good news of God'. But what is this good news, this 'gospel'? 'The kingdom of God is near. Repent, and believe the good news!'(v15).

Of course it is good to see that what Jesus focuses on are the same issues we have learned to make central; that we didn't 'lose the plot', that the authentic gospel here concerns that same combination – repentance and faith – as Paul proclaims in Acts 20:21. (If we're talking about what leads people to heaven or hell, it matters that we get it right!) But as I reread those verses I found myself asking: Yes, but 'believe' *what* 'good news' in particular?

If someone asked the same question of us today, the answers would be obvious. Good news of salvation through the cross: forgiveness, peace with God; new birth; the gift of the Holy Spirit; ongoing new life with Jesus; and so much more. But this is before Calvary. So what exactly is the 'good news' in which Jesus summons his hearers to trust, and that he demonstrates in the events that follow?

Let's read on. Surely the answer becomes plain: that the kingdom is right at hand (1:15). That God has visited his people (as implied in 1:2-3). That he is here. That the Son of Man is actually doing things now *on earth* (2:10). That God's reign *has* come, that he *will* work in triumphant loving power for goodness and healing and forgiveness and hope – right now, right here.

If we speed-read the next few sections and write down their themes, we'll start to grasp the nature of this reign, this kingdom.[1] 1:21-45 chronicles that first astonishing advance, where Jesus reveals his power to put things right in the face of ignorance, sickness and demons. A key point in the healing of the paralytic is precisely that Christ demonstrates his power for goodness this side of death, that the kingdom is come *here* (2:10). The next section expresses the joyous positiveness of this power (2:19,22,23-28,3:4-6), the way its love has strength to draw in the excluded (2:16-17) (a contrast to the fears we might have, that the coming of God's kingdom could mean final exclusion for us[2]). Again, it is power for good, here, now.

Then, after the kingdom's rejection (ch.3) and Jesus' comments on that (ch.4), there comes a further section revealing its power in action, triumphant over destructive nature, demonic evil, even death itself (4:35-5:43). Jesus' challenge to Jairus – infuriatedly impatient, we may imagine, when Jesus pauses to care for the woman with the flow of blood when he should be coming to heal Jairus' daughter, and then in agonized despair when the daughter dies in the meantime – is 'Don't be afraid: just believe' (5:36); God is in control, he cares, now, and his power knows no limits, even death. *(I praise you, Lord!)*

The feeding of the five thousand (6:35-44) is a further sign of that loving care from God. And it isn't something that functions only in life-threatening situations. Let's think about this incident: the crowds surely weren't facing actual starvation – it's unlikely that so many would have put themselves in serious danger, and it was clearly possible for them to 'go to the surrounding villages to buy themselves something to eat' (v36). Indeed, the disciples themselves had set off for this place with no food at all (even the five loaves and two fishes were borrowed, John 6:9). So starvation wasn't a danger. What this central sign (it's selected for record by all four Gospels) shows us isn't that we have some minimal supernatural safety net, where God will step in, but only when life itself is at risk. Rather, what it reveals is the enormous love of our King, his generous affection and his delight in providing, day by day, for his children.

Thankyou for your kindness, Lord! These chapters also present Christ giving purpose to individuals (1:16-20,2:13-17), astonishing the villagers with huge new vistas of truth (1:27,38), and bringing joyous liberation ('new wine') from the constrictions of false religion ('old wineskins', 2:21-28). The 'good news' is firstly about forgiveness of sins (2:5), because dealing with that blockage is the gateway to everything else; but through this gateway a whole glorious new order floods in. Where Christ comes, the kingdom comes, and the kingdom reveals the heart of God: bringing truth where there was falsehood, love where there was hate, wholeness where there was brokenness. Above all, what Jesus brings is *good*.[3] 'The Spirit of the Lord is upon me,' he said elsewhere around the same time, '...to preach *good* news to the poor... to proclaim freedom for the prisoners and recovery of sight to the blind, to release the oppressed, to proclaim the year of the Lord's favour!' (Luke 4:18-19).[4] This is what our God is like! *I worship you for all your goodness, Father!*

But we also notice something else. This revelation of the 'powers of the age to come' is not given just for us to watch as spectators. We are summoned to *'believe'* the good news. From 1:17 onwards, those who see are called to follow: to step out into a life of faith in the good provision of the kingdom; by that faith to (1:20) leave boats[5] and (2:4-5) knock holes in ceilings. In 6:5-6 we learn that lack of such faith in Christ's hometown created a situation where he 'could not do any miracles'. Two verses later he sends his disciples out with instructions designed precisely to demonstrate the effectiveness of living by faith in God's caring power: 'Take nothing for the journey – no bread, no bag, no money' (6:8, cf. 10:21).

If our minds turn to Matthew's account of the same period, we will recall that the challenge to a lifestyle of consistent faith was central there too. Jesus both announces (Matt 4:17) and demonstrates (4:23-24) that God's kingdom has come near; that a different order bringing his goodness and wholeness has broken into our world of tragedy. He heals the sick, extinguishes pain, liberates the demon-possessed, restores the paralysed. And the crowds love it (4:25). Whereupon he sits them down and explains unmistakably that if we want to be part of the new kingdom, it will involve total, trusting commitment to the

kingdom's radically alternative lifestyle. 'Blessed are the poor
in spirit... those who mourn... the meek... the pure' – all the
things the old system would never say. Go for radical purity,
demands Jesus; shun divorce; don't resist an evil person; give
to the one who demands from you; love your enemies; forgive
those who wrong you; don't store up treasure on earth; don't
worry about tomorrow, but in faith seek first the kingdom
and trust the Father to see to the consequences (6:32-33).
You've seen the kingdom, says Jesus; it's right here to hand;
but now you must, in the deepest sense, *believe*.

Mark doesn't set out all these details, but in Mark too we
notice how often Jesus begins to raise a hard question about
their faith: Don't you trust me to care for you? 4:35-41 is
crucial: the disciples are in the boat in a furious storm, Jesus is
asleep; the boat is nearly swamped, they wake him up:
'Teacher, don't you care if we drown?' His response is: 'Why
are you so afraid? Do you still have no faith?'

(Lord, do I?)

Jesus poses the tough question (6:45-8:30)

Let's read on in Mark. We'll see that this same, fundamental
challenge to faith gets re-emphasized as the Gospel progresses.
We need to understand it.

Mark 6:47-52 is a good example. Once again, the disciples
are having a hard night voyage. They've just helped in Christ's
feeding of the five thousand, but now they're tired. Suddenly,
to their horror, they see something approaching on the water;
in their exhaustion they fear it's a hostile spirit. It turns out,
of course, to be the Lord. 'Take courage! It is I. Don't be
afraid', he says, and as he climbs into the boat the wind dies
down. 'They were completely amazed,' says Mark, 'for' –
and here is the unexpected phrasing, the one to look out for
in 'pioneering' – 'they had not understood about the *loaves*.'
(Loaves aren't usually what matters when you're facing a
headwind or a ghost; but those loaves that had fed five

thousand should have assured them they were competently cared for.) '...Their hearts were hardened.'

We find the theme again in 8:17-21. They get anxious about having forgotten to bring bread. (Here, they're overlooking not only the recent miracle, but also Jesus' challenge not to worry what they should eat, drink or wear.) So again he reminds them of the spectacular revelations of God's kingdom provision that they had witnessed: in the feeding of the five thousand (v19, 6:30-44) and the four thousand (v20, 8:1-9). And then he asks, 'Do you still not understand?'

'Why are you so afraid? Do you still have no faith?' Sometimes they didn't. And maybe we need the same question. Agreed, it seems God has more than one way of working, and there is a special clarity about how he revealed the kingdom around Jesus. The coming of the old testament law, we recall, was surrounded by an unusual flood of miracles; that 'flood' wasn't permanent, lessening considerably (though not totally) by the time of David.[6] Just so (Hebrews 2:3-4 implies), God released a special outburst of 'signs' to validate the new testament revelation, and this too wasn't permanent. Indeed, even within the Gospel period, the kingdom's powers are manifested differently in different phases. Toward its end, Jesus reminds his disciples how he had taught them faith by sending them out without purse or provision; God had answered prayer, all their needs had been met. And then he asks them, "'When I sent you without purse, bag or sandals, did you lack anything?" "Nothing", they answered. He said to them, "But now, if you have a purse, take it, and also a bag: and if you don't have a sword, sell your cloak and buy one"'(Lk 22:35-36). They were in a different phase now, where the kingdom would operate differently.[7] There's something equally 'special' about the Acts period; we don't expect healing by a Christian leader's shadow (Acts 5:15) or his handkerchiefs (19:12) to be normal for ever after, because these were, as 19:11 says clearly, 'extraordinary miracles' for a particular moment of revelation. So the kingdom works in different ways at

different times. (Still, Mark does hint (2:5, 6:5-6, 11:22-23) that
that difference can be linked to the collective faith there is on
our side, as well as to God's developing plan.)

But on the other hand, Mark cannot be irrelevant for us.
These chapters are given to us for a purpose; and at their very
heart lies Jesus' 'good news' of Mark 1:14. His challenge is,
believe that the powerful reign of God has come; that he cares,
that things are being put right supernaturally – on earth, right
here. We know that that caring reign may vary in style, and
will remain 'incomplete' till the second coming[8]; and we can't
be sure what precisely it will mean for us (how and when it
will operate through the release of God's miraculous power,
or how and when it may be the way of 'living by faith' under
pressure like Habakkuk). But we cannot be facing a total loss
of what Jesus announced and demonstrated.

That becomes clear if we turn back to Acts. The kingdom
is the theme signalled both at its start and its end. It is the
kingdom that Christ is teaching about in Acts 1:3; and it is
when the disciples ask when that kingdom will be restored
(v6) that he responds, 'You will receive power' (God's reign
is obviously, among other things, about power for good) 'when
the Holy Spirit comes on you, and you will be my witnesses'
(1:8). We the Church, then, are the presence of this kingdom
of goodness spreading into the world.[9]   Again, Acts' final
summary of Paul's message, in the book's closing verse, is
'Boldly and without hindrance he *preached the kingdom* of
God and taught about the Lord Jesus Christ' (28:31).[10]
Implying, surely, not that the kingdom is in some way
suspended, but that, as Acts closes, it is what the Church is
still announcing and living by.

So Mark's 'good news of the kingdom' is for us! The exact
nature of the continuity between our era and Jesus' may not
be clear; but continuity there must be. Mark does not belong
on another planet; whatever the kingdom means at the close
of Acts, it must be related to what Christ demonstrated. The
kingdom isn't locked away from us in the past, on the wrong

side of the closing of the canon. Christ challenges *us* to trust that his reign is come, acting lovingly and powerfully for good, in our situation, right now. *(Lord, I do believe in your goodness, and in your power. Please help my unbelief!)*

Learning faith (8:31-11:25)

So far so good. But now we must return to the questions and disappointments with which we began. The life of faith does not always work out the way we hope. What does Mark have to say to this?

There are 'Habakkuk-times' when God doesn't seem to act in power when we want, at least as far as we can see; situations when we are called to be the 'just' who go on living by faith, that is, 'believing' (cf. Mark 5:36). Mark tells us of various such times. In chapter 5, Jesus puts an unknown woman's need first, and Jairus' sick daughter, who he was coming to heal, dies in the meantime (vv23-25,35). Mark 6 has another example: Jesus sees the disciples 'straining at the oars, because the wind was against them', but it isn't until 3 am that he comes to help them (6:48).

We recognize the truth of this. As Hebrews 11 says, there have been giants of faith who conquered kingdoms, gained what was promised, shut the mouths of lions and received their dead back to life again (vv33-35); which is marvellous. But, the same chapter reminds us, there were other giants who didn't: who were tortured and didn't get released in this life at all; who were stoned, sawn in two, put to death by the sword: the 'way of the cross' (vv35-38). Jesus' summons to discipleship in Mark 8:35 evidently includes a calling to follow in this way as necessary. Faith may link to power for suffering, as well as to power for glory. It happened in the first century, it happens in this one; and in some terrible way this, too, is the reign, the strength, of God.

I find this hard to think about. Clearly there are two ways that the kingdom works. Yet treating these two categories of events as if they were equal may bring us towards a paralysis of faith and prayer.

The real danger is that we start to feel as if it's a toss of a coin whether an uninterested God will hear our prayers. We catch ourselves saying, 'Well, I guess we'll just have to trust the Lord', as if we were depending on an unreliable plumber. Worse, we can start to feel as if God's inactivity, on this side of death, is the norm. ('Heaven remained rigidly on the other side of death,' says Graham Greene of the depressing world of his novel *The Heart of the Matter*, 'and on this side flourished the injustices, the cruelties, the meanness...') So it is striking to see, as we now reach Mark 11:22-24, the uninhibited, positive way that Jesus challenges us to 'Have faith in God... If anyone says to this mountain, "Go, throw yourself into the sea," and does not doubt in his heart but believes that what he says will happen, it will be done for him. Therefore I tell you, whatever you ask for in prayer, believe that you have received it, and *it will be yours.*' Does that sound 'unbalanced'? Possibly, but it isn't the only time he does it. Consider his further remarks in John 14:14, 15:16: 'You may ask me for anything in my name, and *I will do it...* The Father will give you whatever you ask in my name!'

Yes, Scripture shows us that there are exceptions to these promises (unless we think none of Hebrews' tortured heroes ever prayed for release). Mark itself makes that clear. Three chapters later it shows Jesus praying a desperate, unanswered prayer for deliverance. We read in 14:36 of the agony where he himself lived out the obedience of faith: 'Abba, Father, everything is possible for you. Take this cup from me.' That request was not granted (and therefore we are saved; *Thankyou, Lord...*). Exceptions surely do happen; and the Father knows why. But what Jesus emphasizes in Mark 11 (and John 14) is that prayers get answered. And he doesn't feel it necessary to add that good prayers from good people can get answered with 'No'.

In other words: such times are not the norm. The norm, Jesus implies, is that we get serious about prayer[11] and our prayers bear fruit. The norm is that things *happen*; that the caring power of the kingdom *is* released, 'on earth', by prayer; that 'mountains' are swept away and God's will is actualized on earth as it is in heaven, in response to a praying Church opening the floodgates God gave her. True, God is sovereign and reserves the right to do things differently, when long-term that is the most loving thing he can do. But doesn't it seem that these times are the exceptions, since Christ did not feel it necessary to refer to them as he taught us?

The Bible shows us, too, how grasping the 'norm' will help us through the 'exceptions'. God has plans to develop our faith through the 'exceptions', through those times when we have to 'walk by faith, not by sight'. (See 2 Corinthians 1:9.) Our faith, our trust, matters to him; and the times when we don't 'see' what he is doing are times when that trust can be expressed.

So the Gospels show us how to grow in this also. Two months ago I was sitting in a Bible study in St. Petersburg, where my colleague Jenny Brown reminded us that Mark's triumphant kingdom-narrative starts with a situation where the kingdom apparently didn't work at all: '*After John was put in prison*, Jesus went into Galilee proclaiming the good news of God' (1:14). It is striking to see how Christ handles this 'exception'. For John in prison, the kingdom's apparent failure was so depressing that he began to doubt Jesus altogether; having actually seen heaven opened and the Spirit descending on Christ, he now questions whether Jesus is the Messiah at all.[12] Christ's response is instructive. He doesn't spirit John out of prison (as he would Peter in Acts 12); the kingdom, for John, was to be manifested in his faithfulness to the end. Rather, he focuses John's attention on what have been called the 'paradigm events', the ones that display reality most clearly: 'Jesus replied, "Go back and report to John what you hear and see: the blind receive sight, the lame walk... the deaf hear, the dead are raised, and the good news is preached to the poor" (Matthew 11:4-5).

These, Jesus suggests, are God's norm; fill your mind with them. And we too must fill our minds, from the Word, with what these writers 'heard and saw'.[13] ('The tempter would lead us to judge of God by the dark shadings of many a passage of our history here,' the nineteenth-century writer J.G.Bellett says. 'But the Spirit of God would have us acquaint ourselves with Him in the beauteous light of the Gospels.'[14]) They will give us strength to trust, to live by faith, as the 'exceptions' come.

Indeed, Mark implies, this strength will be an issue even in the 'normal' times. Why does his Gospel have such an emphasis on the need − even for Jesus − for recurrent withdrawal to recuperate (6:30-32, 46; cf. 1:35 at the close of the opening section expounding the kingdom)? Is it because, no matter how much of God's goodness we are seeing, tiredness can drain away the sheer energy to exercise faith? Is it not exhaustion that sometimes makes it hardest to trust God's care? It is tempting to speculate on the reasons for the disciples' failure to trust in 6:52, despite all the miracles they had seen and performed. It is odd that people who had just driven out 'many demons' (6:13) suddenly panicked at a ghost. Were they 'burnt out' through being unable to take the break Jesus had arranged in 6:30-34? Is there a relation between exhaustion and faith-weakness? Seriousness about Sabbath rest links to the strength to believe, the strength to pray. And absorbing the Gospels in bulk at such times of rest is often a key to recovery.

And so Christ's kingdom-challenge comes to us, as it did when he came to earth: choose to believe the good news − and pray in partnership with it! Believe that God reigns and he really will see that things happen; that his Church is built, his gospel preached and his kingdom forwarded. Pray in hope, in adventurous expectation; pray to get as much of heaven on earth as possible, as a church-planting friend of mine puts it.

It is clear that God works in different ways for different situations; but how he wants to work in our situation we shall only know if we press forward and pray. More: believe that he cares about us as individuals and our intimate needs: cares enormously. Believe that he is our 'Abba', our 'papa'; and that if an earthly father wouldn't answer his child's plea for bread with a stone, then – unless he truly sees a deeper benefit – so much more will our heavenly Father give good things to those who ask him. (*Thankyou, Abba, that you are worthy of my trust...*) Believe (on the authority of God's Word) that what Christ feels towards us as individuals is a love as vast as the infinite, oceanic love that the Father has for his perfect Son (John 15:9), and that that love is backed up for us by infinite wisdom and power.

Of course, Mark reminds us, that love has implications. Jesus says, 'Whatever you ask in prayer, believe that you have received it, and it will be yours' (11:24), and then adds immediately, 'And when you stand praying, if you hold anything against anyone, forgive him' (11:25). (*Lord, help me see where that applies for me...*) Presumably this links to the concern John expresses for us to know a radical 'confidence' in prayer: 'We have confidence before God and receive from him anything we ask, because we obey his commands' (1 John 3:21-22, cf. 5:14). Trusting and obeying go together; to see the power of the kingdom, we must live by the principles of the kingdom. 'Your kingdom come, your will be done' – 'getting as much of heaven on earth as possible' – starts in our own hearts. Christ's loving reign must be real in us if his lordship, his kingdom, is to flow out through us into the world.

Believe, therefore, Christ challenges us, that in the longterm, things will go right; that the colossal, creative power of loving grace that originally called heaven and earth out of nothingness is affectionately active for us in our situation. Believe that he will be at work, here and now, as we – seriously – pray. Live in a way that matches that kingdom. Cultivate the mental reflex that thankfully expects God to act for good around us, rather than the reflex that expects him to have some good reason for not doing so. Draw strength from the way God works in Scripture, and from reflecting gratefully on his kindness in good things we can identify in our own past. If indeed the just are those who '*live* by faith', then this faith is vital for us to grow in. *Father, I do not understand all these things, but please help me to walk with you...*

Have *faith*: that is one of Jesus' key challenges in this Gospel of Mark. Reach out for grace for that choice, for making the mental effort for faith. Use it to fuel your prayers. 'Lift up your heads.' The God of goodness has not left us. He is here.

Notes

[1] Of course there is far more in Mark's (and God's) definition of the kingdom than we can pick up in what follows. For example: the opening chapter seems to imply (like Acts 1:3-8) that what we will see happen has much to do with the Holy Spirit (vv8,10,12). But then in Christ's fundamental (4:13) illustration of the kingdom, it has above all to do with sowing the seed of the Word (4:1-11,14), and most of chapter 4 is designed to give us deeper understanding of how that operates; once again, then, Word and Spirit stand together at the heart of the spread of the kingdom. A classic study of the biblical meaning of the 'kingdom' is G.E.Ladd, *The Presence of the Future* (1974). Ladd defines it as 'the dynamic reign or kingly rule of God, and derivatively, the sphere in which the rule is experienced... The Kingdom is God's reign and the realm in which the blessings of his reign are experienced'(pp.262, 277).

[2] We should not forget that, but for the cross, those misapprehensions and fears would have been all too realistic; we the self-excluded would have stayed excluded from God's presence. The old testament's closing verse warned Israel that either they mend their ways or the coming of the Lord would be very bad news indeed –'or else I will come and strike the land with a curse,' in the old testament's final words. Apart from the cross the coming of 'God with us' in the Bible's next chapter (Matt 1:23) would have meant judgment, not enormous joy. But then we cannot imagine God 'apart from the cross': the rescue in the cross, and the joy of the King's coming, display his deepest nature.

³ Reading how the new creation bursts into our world in these chapters, are we not reminded of the repeated refrain describing God's handiwork in Genesis 1: 'And God saw that it was *good*'? The 'first sign' Jesus does in John's Gospel, the rescuing of the wedding in Cana, is also primarily a manifestation of God's *goodness* in answer to prayer (John 2:1-11).

⁴ Jesus' original in Isaiah 61 adds, attractively, 'He has sent me to bind up the brokenhearted... to bestow on them a crown of beauty instead of ashes, the oil of gladness instead of mourning, and a garment of praise instead of the spirit of despair... They will rebuild the ancient ruins and restore the places long devastated; they will renew the ruined cities that have been devastated for generations.' Christ's reign reaches out with power to transform every area of need, whether communal – e.g. the regeneration of devastated cities such as those still recovering from communism (or our own); or personal – e.g. our own liberation from depression and despair.

⁵ It is not by accident that Jesus' call of Peter, Andrew, James and John to leave their boats and follow him comes right here. 'Come, follow me'(Mark 1:17) is a splendid 'gospel summary', a fine expression of what is involved in the gospel of faith.

⁶ See also Psalm 44. But the old testament makes clear that God retains the sovereign right to return to a much more 'miraculous' mode whenever he chooses. The era of Solomon does not contain much of the 'supernatural'. But when Israel gives in to paganism in the period of Elijah and Elisha, the supernatural returns with full force.

⁷ We see these 'different phases' in Mark's Gospel if we take it as a whole. Doesn't Mark break into two halves around the confession of Christ, and the climax of kingdom-revelation (9:1) at the transfiguration (8:27-9:8)? (Luke certainly seems to; see David Gooding, *According to Luke* (1987), pp.179ff.) The idea makes a lot of sense; in that case Mark begins both halves by speaking of the gospel (1:14-15, 8:35), God's confirmatory 'You are my Son' (1:11, 9:7), and the challenge to respond to the gospel by following and leaving all (1:17-20, 8:34-36). But whereas the first half begins by proclaiming the kingdom come (1:14-15), the second half begins by announcing the cross (8:31-32); and it emphasizes throughout how committing to the way of the kingdom involves suffering, the way of the cross, where things may not always go as we wish. The repeated announcements of the cross and resurrection (8:31-32, 9:9,12,31, 10:33-34,45) make clear that this,

rather than (other expressions of) God's caring power, is now the primary theme. Chapters 9 and 10 have a lot to say about how we enter the kingdom, and here the 'following' that expresses kingdom-faith is more about the way of the cross (8:34) moving through suffering to glory (10:28-30). Nonetheless, even in the second half the emphasis is still on the kingdom's ethos as a simplicity of faith (10:14-15), faith so trustful of and committed to God's fatherly care that it has no need to hold onto security through possessions (10:21-25,28-30,50, 12:44, 14:3).

[8] 1 Cor 15:24 describes the final, full coming of the kingdom as the completion of an extended process and as belonging to the future: 'Then the end will come, when he hands over the kingdom to God the Father after he has destroyed all dominion, authority and power. For he must reign until he has put all his enemies under his feet. The last enemy to be destroyed is death.' 'At present we do not see everything subject to him' (Hebrews 2:8). Cf. the song at the climax in Rev 11:17: 'We give thanks to you, Lord God Almighty... because you have *taken* your great power and begun to reign.' In Ladd's famous formulation, there are aspects of the kingdom, the 'reign', that are with us 'already', and others that are 'not yet'.

[9] And the 'kingdom' marks our gospel till the End. It is when this 'good news of the kingdom' has finally been spread to involve all nations that the end will come (Matt 24:14).

[10] Paul's final warning to the Jews (Acts 28:26-27) repeats almost exactly Jesus' warning about the kingdom in Mark 4:11-12. There are other continuities with Mark. The question in Acts' opening section is, will God restore the kingdom *at this time?*; compare Mark 1:15's 'the time has come' – in a section having much to do with the Spirit, like Acts 1.

[11] Blackaby and King make the helpful observation that life with God depends on aligning ourselves with God's activity, with the loving initiatives he is taking; so knowing this kind of fruitfulness in prayer depends on being sufficiently in his presence to sense what he is doing and how he would have us pray. (Henry Blackaby and Claude King, *Experiencing God* (Nashville, 1994), p.162.) Cf. John 15:7: 'If you remain in me and my words remain in you, ask whatever you wish, and it will be given you.'

[12] Matthew 11:3. Does a proneness to depression tend to accompany the prophetic temperament? Elijah had it too (1 Kings 19:4).

[13] This is also the value of exposing ourselves to contemporary situations, or accounts of them, where God's kingdom power is revealed especially clearly ('revival situations'). When I was a younger believer, Brother Andrew's *God's Smuggler* and David Wilkerson's *The Cross and the Switchblade* were very important in this respect. (So, I should add, were accounts of the kingdom's other aspect, God's power strengthening believers to stand through unrelieved persecution: like Wurmbrand's *In God's Underground*.) When I got to university in Wales, it was obvious how vital memories of God's power in the various Welsh revivals were as 'paradigm events' for the strength of many people's spirituality. Missions involvement, and exposure to the realities of what God is doing in the two-thirds world, can be enormously strengthening for the same reason.

[14] *Footprints for Pilgrims* (1976 edition), p.65.

4

Life in Exile:
Rereading 1 Peter

There are two sides to the Christian life. We've seen them both in the two preceding chapters.

The norm – and this cannot be said too strongly, because Jesus said it strongly – is that God answers prayer. The 'kingdom' has *already* arrived through Jesus, and we are called to pray in the light of that; God's reign and God's power have arrived on earth, putting things right.

But in our lives we face a *'not yet'* about the kingdom too. We still live in a fallen world; the reign of God's grace will not be fully completed until the second coming, what Peter calls 'the time for God to restore everything' (Acts 3:21). And so there are times when God's power is not putting everything right. They are the exceptions, not the norm; but all of us encounter them periodically; and sometimes they are 'serious'. 'In this world,' Jesus warned us, 'you will have trouble' (John 16:33).

But here comes a complication – and a vital one for us to understand. The new testament uses the term 'kingdom' in an almost technical sense, as it speaks of God's reign coming in a far clearer, more active way than before, with Jesus' arrival and the subsequent spread of his Church, his Word and his Spirit, repairing the tragic consequences of the Fall. But that cannot mean God was absent before. Even before this kingdom came at the start of the Gospels, God, obviously, was in control. His 'reign' was expressed more in terms of the outworkings of his law: that sin creates a sphere of alienation, futility and death, where humankind lives away from God amid a natural order rendered tragic by rebellion; condemned to existence largely outside the sphere of his blessing. That is not the way his reign would be expressed with the coming of the new testament 'kingdom' grounded in his forgiveness through the cross, and displaying more fully his presence, his love and his transforming power, 'on earth as it is in heaven'. But those earlier outworkings of God's law were still the marks of his control; still his rule had been the fundamental, underlying reality. Who gave humanity bread to eat? Who sustained the physical laws that kept their planet in place?

This is true even in the darkest moment of the old testament. Insofar as the 'kingdom', the 'manifested', restoratory reign of God, was revealed before Christ's coming, it focused especially on God's house[1] in Jerusalem. (See particularly 1 Kings 8, with its emphasis on things being put right as people pray 'towards this temple'.[2]) But there came a tragic moment when that temple was ransacked and razed. And God did nothing. The miracle-narratives of Israel's past had told how people had been struck dead merely for touching the temple's contents (e.g. Uzzah in 2 Samuel 6). But now nothing happened: the soldiers of Babylon carried off the temple's treasures with impunity and put them in the temple of their own god. If ever a book opened on a note of the absence of the power of God, it is Daniel (1:2). But if we read through Daniel and write down a key lesson or two from each chapter, one theme will recur again and again: the Lord is in control, 'heaven rules... the Most High is sovereign over the kingdoms of men' (4:25-26,32). When Jerusalem falls, God is still almighty; what has occurred is the outworking of his laws by which he reigns.[3]

Even in the darkest moments, then, the Lord is ruling: but he manifests his rule in a different mode. And here is the issue for us. As Christians, our bodies are the point where heaven's kingdom intersects earth. Our bodies, now, are the dwelling place of God, the temple of the Holy Spirit (1 Cor 6:19). Already we are (not 'will be') seated in heavenly places in Christ (Eph 2:6); the kingdom is in our hearts. And as we saw in the last chapter, the gospel we preach is the 'good news of the kingdom': through the cross God invites humanity into a sphere where his reign begins to be revealed in a new way, 'on earth as it is in heaven'. So through the Word, through the Spirit and his fruit and gifts, through prayer, things begin to be put right on earth; the 'kingdom of heaven' pours into the world through us as his channels.

The 'norm', then, is one where heaven extends a step ahead of us, flows out in transformation through us. But it isn't always so. In us, heaven enters a world shaped by the results of human rebellion. And so at times our own hearts are, we may say, the frontier of the power of heaven; it doesn't extend beyond them, not yet. Around us is the world of tragedy; things go 'wrong'; and God's reign is manifested in the way his strength enables us to go on living, by faith, amid the desperate anarchy of events the healing 'kingdom' has not yet touched. At worst there are the 'Gethsemane' moments; the moments when we are caught up, as Jesus was, in the horror of a fallen world alienated from God: massive hunger and savagery; miscarriage or cancer; assault or rape. And here, ultimately, the only way to survive is by faith: somehow finding the strength to believe still that 'the Most High reigns', to 'let God be God in the way that he chooses'. (Like Job, amid all his anguished questionings: 'Though he slay me, yet will I hope in him.'[4]) It can be almost unbearably hard; it is only by taking in, becoming armed with, the grace, the strength, of God that we can live. 'Only by grace': in the 'exception', then, as much as in the 'norm', everything depends on the varied expressions of the strength, the reign, of God.

Peter himself experienced this 'change of mode' in Luke 22, as we have noted. Jesus asks the disciples in v35, 'When I sent you without purse, bag or sandals,[5] did you lack anything?' 'Nothing', they reply; as they had gone forth, the 'powers of the kingdom' had seen to everything. But now something different is happening, says Jesus. There is going to be a time when God's loving action will seem absent: 'But now if you have a purse, take it, and also a bag; and if you don't have a sword, sell your cloak and buy one' (v36).[6] Now would be a time of far more intense conflict, indeed of the apparent withdrawal of God's power as his own Christ is arrested and killed. We have shifted mode; as Jesus tells his assailants just seventeen verses later, 'This is your hour - when darkness reigns' (v53). Such times are permitted, within the overall loving sovereignty of God. Job knew them; Daniel knew them; so did Peter. Normally prayer is answered and what we need is given us as God's power is released; but there are times when it is not.

We do not know which of these 'modes' God has in store for us at particular phases of the drama. 'If we are thrown into the blazing furnace, the God we serve is able to save us from it... *But even if he does not* —', Daniel's friends tell Nebuchadnezzar (Daniel 3:17). 'Lord, *if* you are willing, you can make me clean', prays the leper in Matthew 8:2; and that is enough for Jesus. Faith isn't about the ability to look over God's shoulder and know for certain what he will do. What we are sure of is what he *can* do - his power, and his love, and his wisdom. Biblical faith prays on the basis of passionate certainty about these things.

Perhaps we may say, then, that the Christian lives on a spectrum of experience between two poles: 'kingdom' and (to use the Daniel picture) 'exile'. The norm is for us to live in his presence; sometimes, however, we learn to live by faith through his apparent absence.[7] On the one hand, the kingdom of heaven is *already* in us, and spreads out through and around us. Ephesians has this perspective; or if we seek an old testament parallel we might look to Joshua, the story of Israel's growth and victory in the Promised Land, the land where the promises came true. But on the other hand, the kingdom is *not yet* fully come; we are not yet 'at home', and meanwhile we face experiences of the wilderness – because God has chosen to put us there for the time, and/or because of the sin, stupidity or lack of faith of ourselves or others.

From the old testament, many people would read Numbers this way.[8] The new testament book that helps us with 'living in exile', 'living away from home' as 'aliens and strangers in the world', is 1 Peter (1:17, 2:11). *Father, please help me understand this...*

So let's look at it more closely. We'll find it a very personal letter. Doesn't Peter's own experience lie at the heart of what he writes? Don't we sense memories of his own moments of despair, as we watch him seeking to guard his readers (4:1) from failures like his own denial of Christ in Luke 22, and to strengthen them for experiences of suffering – such, indeed, as he knew lay ahead in his own future (John 21:19)? Don't we sense echoes of his last (and probably life-shaping) encounter with Jesus in John 21:15ff, as we read his concern that God's 'shepherds' care for God's sheep through tough times (5:1-2)?[9] *Father, please help me to be strengthened, and to learn to strengthen others, as I feed on this book...*

What is God's word for exiles? (1:1-12)

As we read Peter's letter, we indeed sense its recipients working through the experiences of 'exile'. They are facing pressure from the authorities, marriages that are in poor shape, working relationships that are entirely unjust. Plenty of problems; and the context Peter writes into doesn't seem marked by miraculous solutions as does, say, Acts. It's not a well-known

Epistle, in my experience. But it is striking to set alongside 2 Corinthians. In it we see how Paul's questions about living under pressure are handled by someone with a different temperament and insights.

What, then, do we notice in Peter's opening?

Just like Paul, Peter matches his greeting to his overall theme: he writes to those who are 'strangers in the world, scattered' (1:1). Then immediately he focuses on their source of security: they – we – are 'God's elect', 'chosen according to the foreknowledge of God the Father'. A further striking point is that the whole Trinity is involved with us in our exile (v2). (*Father: thankyou!*) We may also spot something surprising: the focus of what we are 'sanctified for' here is not forgiveness, but obedience.[10] As we go on reading, we may well decide that when Peter speaks of 'salvation', what matters to him is the entire journey of obedience through the world, rather than just the initial moment of new birth, crucial though that is.[11] Or, we may conclude that he uses 'obedience to Christ' in v2 as a technical term for new birth, because he sees new birth as a moment of profoundly 'obeying the truth' (1:22-23), a repentance that commits to deep, lifelong obedience by the grace of God. It is from an 'empty *way of life*' (1:18) that we were redeemed, and into a meaningful way of life that we have been brought: even in exile.

Then what are the main ideas, as he moves into the first part of his message? It is worth reading through the next few verses and then listing them.

First – again as with Paul – we find an outburst of praise. Why? Psychologically, because the deliberate choice to praise is vital for staying alive in the wilderness. But praise for what in particular? The issue especially meaningful for Peter is our 'new birth into a living *hope*'.[12] As he writes to the 'exiles', his mind moves immediately to the goal of the salvation-process, an 'inheritance that can never perish, spoil or fade, kept in heaven for you... In this you greatly rejoice!' A grasp of this reality – not just an intellectual assent, but a heart-grasp expressed in joy and praise – is our basis for survival.

Right at the start, then, Peter confronts us with what we saw in Ephesians and 2 Corinthians: the sheer centrality of our hope of heaven as our 'helmet', our 'anchor'. It is astonishing that we evangelicals can be so ashamed of heaven. We tend to see it as part of an embarrassing nineteenth-century spirituality. The fact is, of course, that we have lost our nerve. We've grown over-defensive after liberal accusations that our faith is only about 'pie in the sky when you die'. And in our concern to reaffirm God's kingdom this side of death, we've grown embarrassed by the afterlife. But deep faith in heaven does not contradict deep commitment to world evangelism, or passionate evangelical concern about the arms trade or the quality of education in our inner cities. (In fact, if we look closely at the inner-city churches we'll probably find that deep faith in heaven is what keeps many of their members alive.) One suspects there is another factor too. Particularly in the mainline denominations and the seminaries that serve them, evangelicals have had to spend so much energy defending the very core of supernaturalism – the virgin birth, the resurrection, the ascension – that a weariness arises at having to take responsibility for aspects of biblical supernaturalism which don't seem so vital. And so these get down-played, almost out of fatigue.

In the end, of course, it won't do. The human being is built for the supernatural and for heaven; and if we don't find it where God intended, then our hearts make us look elsewhere. The churches adapted their image to avoid scandalizing the late-nineteenth-century mechanistic worldview that has dominated liberal protestantism ever since; but as a result we are ill-equipped to handle the challenge of the postmodern era, and 'New Age' with its sometimes nonsensical responses to our hearts' genuine longings. The flourishing of alternative spiritualities should have reminded us that we are built to be 'hungry for heaven'; and as Nigel

Lee put it in the IFES magazine *In Touch*, if that hunger isn't
satisfied in the contemporary biblical vacuum, then we'll turn
to poisoned bread. Heaven is necessary for our whole
psychological dynamic. It is already obvious that, worldwide,
the fastest-growing churches tend to be those which view the
supernatural absolutely realistically; and failure at this level
certainly won't wash for the twenty-first century. Peter isn't
weak in this regard. What do the exiles need to hear first of
all? *'Praise God for a new birth that will take us to the glories of
heaven!'*

The next major concern we notice is the 'trials' we
encounter, and the response of faith (vv7-8). Peter's priorities
here and in v11 underline the reality we saw in 2 Corinthians
and Ephesians: the 'suffering' of exile and the 'glory' of heaven
go together like the two sides of a coin. (Look how they're
linked further in 4:13-14, 5:1 or 5:10.) Lindsay Brown has
pointed to the lack of a working theology of suffering as a
major weakness in many charismatic churches; this linkage
of suffering and glory is a key component for such a theology.

God values enormously the true faith that can pass through
suffering. It belongs to 'glory', says Peter; the 'all kinds of
trials' come 'so that your faith – of greater worth than gold –
may be proved genuine, and may result in praise, glory and
honour when Jesus Christ is revealed' (1:7). It is faith that
'stands firm to the end' that truly belongs with this final
'salvation' (cf. Matt 24:13), because such faith has been 'proved
genuine', proved to be truly 'not of perishable seed, but of
imperishable' (v23).[13] What God has already done in us
'imperishably' guarantees what he will continue to do in us
(cf. Phil 1:6).[14] But what connects with that power on our
side is our faith: we 'through faith are shielded by God's power'
(v5). Again we see the centrality of 'living by faith' (or 'by
grace through faith'). Faith alone connects us with the grace
that will keep us alive – which is why God values it so highly
and wants it tested, proved and developed. *(Father, please help
me to 'live by faith'...)*

Faith, then, for Peter, is the anchor. And now he moves on: at the heart of this faith is a deep longing for our 'inheritance', for what is hidden but will soon be 'revealed' (Peter uses the word repeatedly, in v5, v7 and v13). Heaven, and something greater still: union at last with the Christ we love but 'do not see' (v8).[15] There is an unashamedly emotional feel to Peter's writing here: 'Though you have not seen him, you love him.... You are filled with an inexpressible and glorious joy!' Isn't this the core of Christianity – not even the way of salvation, or discipleship, or Christian lifestyle, or mission, central though all these are, but passionate love for Christ? Some of us have to take a conscious step in permitting ourselves to express these feelings (*Lord, right now I want to make myself say it: I love you and I worship you!*); but how impoverished we are if we do not!

Heaven, and seeing Jesus at last – as Peter says in 5:12: '*This* is the grace of God!'

The power of desire (1:13-14)

1 Peter 1 is an extremely rich chapter; it gives us a whole succession of seminal ideas. But as we read it, looking for its thought-flow, doesn't v13 seem the 'hinge-verse', linking what is gone before with what is to follow? Here Peter re-emphasizes the longing for heaven; but he also moves on to explain what that longing means now. (Think heavenly; act locally!)

The giants of prophecy[16], indeed the majestic angels themselves who inhabit the fiery glory of heaven[17], have been utterly fascinated by the 'grace that was to come to us', says Peter (vv10,12).[18] As his fellow-apostle had put it, we the Church are those 'on whom the fulfilment of the ages has come' (1 Cor 10:11). '*Therefore,*' he now urges the exiles, 'prepare *your* minds for action'(v13).

This 'preparation for action' has two aspects. First, there is the deliberate mental choice of '*setting your hope fully*' on the reality of that glory to come – his letter's opening theme. Then, there is being *'self-controlled'* in holiness now – the dominant concern of the rest of the chapter, down to 2:3. For Peter these two are evidently linked. Fostering the longing for heaven, developing this conscious mental stance, supplies a vital 'arming vision' (to adapt an idea from 4:1); we will be 'armed' against the temptations we face in exile by the way we 'set our hope'. Again, it is tragic that so much of contemporary Christendom is so terrified of sounding 'pietistic' that we miss out on this central, life-giving new testament idea. Hebrews insists repeatedly that 'looking ahead to the reward' is what will keep us going through the pressures we experience as 'aliens and strangers' (see 10:34, 11:13-16,25-26, 35); it also calls us to 'fix our eyes' on 'Jesus, who *for the joy set before him* endured the cross' (12:2-3). Peter himself will restate the idea in 4:7: 'The end of all things is near. *Therefore*, be clear-minded and self-controlled.'

For there is an alternative motivation available to our hearts: the power of wrong desires. 'Set your hope fully' on heaven, says Peter in vv13-14, rather than 'conforming to the evil desires' we had as unbelievers. This 'clash of desires' is a very deep concern for Peter.[19] 'Abstain from sinful *desires*, which war against the soul', he will tell us in 2:11; the same challenge to liberation from 'evil human *desires*' reappears in 4:2-3. Indeed, in Peter's second Epistle this issue of the choice of desires becomes central to his entire argument. What's wrong with false prophets is that they 'follow the corrupt *desire* of the sinful nature' (2 Peter 2:10) and foster the same 'lustful *desires*' in others (2:18). 2 Peter 2 presents a stark vision where only the grace-spark of revelation delivers us from the garbage heap of the universe, from a pit where we wallow like animals, driven by brute desire ('like brute beasts, creatures of instinct, born only to be caught and destroyed... Of them the proverbs are true: "A dog returns to its vomit"'(2:12,22)). What snatches us out to another realm, enabling us (in a remarkable phrase) to 'participate in the divine nature and escape the corruption in the world caused by evil *desires*', is a firm grasp of God's 'very great and precious promises' (1:4).[20]

Promises, longings: we are shaped by one set of desires or the other. The people 'following their evil desires' are also those who deny the promised second coming (2 Peter 3:3-4); whereas holiness comes 'as you look forward' (again the note of longing) 'to the day of God... we are looking forward to a new heaven and a new earth, the home of righteousness' (3:12-13). Peter had listened to Jesus himself emphasizing the importance of setting our desires – our 'eye' – on treasure in heaven rather than on earth (Matt 6:19-24). One set of desires will in time drive out the other: either longing for the promised heaven will eclipse wrong desire – or else the opposite will occur.[21]

Peter's emphasis on the fundamental role of desire sounds very much like C.S.Lewis[22] – or, indeed, very postmodern. Desire is central to our nature: the question is, what are we longing for? It is our desires that shape our actions, and motivate where we invest our efforts. (*Lord, what are the longings that drop into place in free moments in my own mind? Status? Achievement? Security? Money, sex and power?*) So-called 'prosperity Christianity' can be tragically destructive at this point, because what it can do is foster precisely the wrong desires. ('Think about it – God wants you to be rich!') But even the concern to keep our ministry going, or our social action, can drown out our longing for heaven. We have vital tasks on earth, yet desire for heaven is indispensable. For Peter, that deliberate mental stance seems close to the heart of the 'faith'. (*Thankyou, Lord, for heaven. Please rekindle in me – I deliberately ask – the fire of a passionate longing!*)

Three roots of transformation (1:15-2:3)

So this deliberate 'setting our hope', our desires, 'fully' on the glory to come provides an 'arming vision'; it gives an essential emotional base for holiness that stays on its feet amid the buffetings of exile. What else will arm us for such a lifestyle? As we list the next verses' themes, we find Peter focusing on three more vital motivations.

The *first* is a vision of the reality of God himself: 'Be holy, because I am holy' (vv15-16). (*Lord, I pause here to glorify you for your holiness – minimal though my grasp is of what that holiness means...*) We have the astonishing privilege of growing in God-likeness, participating in that fiery glory of the divine nature. But a profound seriousness follows from that privilege. This God is also the one who will 'judge each man's work impartially'; therefore, says Peter, 'live your lives... in reverent fear' (v17). (We saw this same awareness in Paul also, in 2 Corinthians 5: 'Since we know what it is to fear the Lord...' *Lord, please help me grasp what this means.*)

Again, if as 'pioneers' we're listening out for the unexpected, we catch a note here that has been alien to much twentieth-century spirituality – and that we must now rediscover. It matches the 'be self-controlled' (NASB has 'keep sober') in v13. I was deeply struck by this while working with Dutch Christians: their commitment to 'reverent fear' in lifestyle, to the enormous importance of carrying through whatever is the will of God, no matter how un-contemporary it may be. Loss of this deep determination soon leads us into religious triviality, into spirituality without the guts and robustness for real counter-cultural radicalism. *Lord, please give me that gift of utter seriousness about your will...*

Holiness is serious for Peter. At the same time, it isn't negative. It points joyously to glory – and it is all about love. For where do we find Peter's specific application of holiness? Surely in v22 (and 2:1): 'Love one another deeply, from the heart.' Indeed, as we speed-read further in search of the book's flow, we'll see this theme runs on from 2:11 to 3:18: holiness is about learning the transformation of the broken relationships we face in exile, on the foundation of Calvary. 'Be holy, because I am holy' is the command of an eternally *loving* God.

It's not surprising, then, that in chapter 1 the *second* thing inspiring Peter for holiness is the outrageously costly love of the cross. 'Live your lives in reverent fear, *for*' ... because you, we, I, have been redeemed with the blood of God himself (vv17-19). On the one hand, that unimaginable commitment on God's side gives us profound security.[23] But the sheer costliness of what he has done gives holiness enormous importance. If we have even begun to understand the cross, holiness cannot be a hobby pursued merely when we feel like it. *(Lord, please help me grasp this...)* It involves change of lifestyle, commitment to a conscious break with the 'way of life' normal to our culture (cf. 4:3) and our tradition. The way of the Father takes precedence over the norms of our fathers (1:18); or our business colleagues, or our peers.

That, indeed, is what is involved in the *third* motivation Peter now presents: the radical nature of repentance and new birth (1:22-2:2). Our first response may be puzzlement. Peter could so easily have moved from exhorting us to love in 1:22 straight on to 2:1. What is he doing instead?

He presents two linked ideas. First, there is the absolute necessity that genuine new birth results in truly transformed relationships; but second, the enormity of what new birth means in itself. And somehow, the second empowers the first. 'Love one another deeply, *for* you have been born again, not of perishable seed'(v23); 'This'– the 'imperishable' Word of v23 – 'is the Word that was preached to you. *Therefore*, rid yourselves of all malice'(1:25-2:1). What is he saying here?

Let's chew on that 'perishable/imperishable' first, because it fits a repeated theme we've probably noticed. Here in the 'wilderness', there are things that stand out as valuable, 'precious': things worth suffering for[24], things truly worthy of our desire. What marks them out is that they are 'imperishable'. The inheritance held out before us in heaven is one that 'can never perish, spoil or fade' (1:4). On earth too there are things 'of greater worth than gold which perishes', namely our faith (v7), which in turn is grounded in the 'precious blood of Christ', of so much greater worth than 'perishable things such as silver or gold' (vv18-19). (*Father, please help me grasp this sense of value.*)'You have been born again, not of perishable seed, but of imperishable, through the living and abiding Word of God'(v23).

So what makes these things precious? Peter goes on to explain: they partake of a different universe, one beyond decay, 'where moth and rust do not destroy' as Jesus said. What vv23-25 present is the same crucial idea we saw underpinning Ephesians and 2 Corinthians: heaven gets a bridgehead in us now, through our faith and through the Word.

The Word reaches beyond – or from beyond – the Fall. Peter spells it out, quoting Isaiah: '*All men are like grass, and all their glory is like the flowers of the field; the grass withers and the flowers fall*' (that pattern of tragedy expressed in so much of our greatest art: the sadness at the root of our fallen universe that is in 'bondage to decay' (Rom 8:20-21), where there is no beauty that does not finally age and disintegrate, no glory that finally does not turn to dust....)

'*But*' – within this decaying universe there is something radically different – '*the Word of the Lord stands forever.*' When everything around is perishing, the seed of God's Word is the presence of the alternative; in a world dominated by death it embodies what is 'living and enduring'.[25] (*Thankyou, Lord!*) And it is 'through the Word' that we have been 'born again' (v23), through the springing up into our lives of this incorruptible firstfruits of the alternative universe. These ideas were evidently standard in the early Church. James says, 'He chose to give us birth through the Word of faith, that we might be a kind of firstfruits of all he created' (1:18)[26]; and 'firstfruits' is the word Paul uses to describe the Church as the bridgehead of the new creation in Romans 8:20-23. (As we pioneer, the Epistles illuminate each other.) The vision of 'kingdom now', embodied in the Word, is vital even in an Epistle focusing on the kingdom to come.

But all this about the Word is not merely mystical. Peter is not just speaking philosophically, nor only about the time when Christ was on earth. He turns straight round and adds, 'And *this* is the Word that was preached unto *you*.' The preaching that first drew us to new birth: unpolished maybe, full of mixed metaphors and jumbled thoughts maybe, and yet through the weakness of the messenger we caught sight of salvation; that was this 'living word' in contemporary reality.[27] (It is with reason that Peter later gives an awesome, yet deeply encouraging, charge to preachers: 'If anyone speaks, he should do it as one speaking the very words of God' (4:11).)

We have, within us now, the Word that embodies the powers of the 'imperishable' universe. And so Peter rounds off the message of this section with two linked commands. First, '*Crave*' (that theme of desire again) the 'pure spiritual milk' – what NASB translates as 'the pure milk of the Word'[28] – for through that 'living' Word, and our desire for it, we will 'grow up in our salvation'. (*Lord, thankyou for your Word! Please guard that desire in me, help me keep that intake flowing...*) How shall we foster that desire? Crave the Word, says Peter, 'now that you have tasted that the Lord is good': as if that 'taste', and its recollection, motivates the longing to feed further in the Word. Where then do I recall the taste of the *goodness* of the Lord? Through reflecting, via the Word, on his cross (cf.1:18-19)? Through reading in the Gospels about his life on earth? Through listing all the good things he has done in my life, turning that into praise (as proof of Romans 8:32) and seeking to learn from his Word to recognize more of his goodness?

Oliver Barclay was once asked why the student Christian Unions retained spiritual vibrancy over many decades, while some other spiritual movements drifted and dwindled. He replied by pointing to this 'craving' for the 'full biblical diet that is really taken into our minds and lives'[29] – the triple intake of the Word through personal quiet times, small-group Bible study and large-group exposition. It's what we need.

As this Word comes to saturate our being, says Peter, it becomes the power for holiness, for 'growing up in your salvation' (2:2).[30]

And so the 'heavenly vision' leads straight into issues of holy lifestyle now. There is a decay-oriented, 'empty way' of relationships that m. ches this tragically decaying universe (v18). But there is also a radical force within us since the new birth, a power extending beyond all human probability, 'imperishable', 'living and abiding'. How then is holiness to be achieved? 'You have purified yourselves by obeying the truth' (v22), says Peter, that is, 'you have been born again'(v23). As the past tenses make clear, the crucial transformation has already taken place, 'so that you *have*', now, 'sincere love for your brothers'(v22). Or as Paul puts it, God '*has* poured out his love into our hearts by the Holy Spirit' (Rom 5:5).

So act on it, Peter says (1:22,1:25-2:1)! For a community of 'aliens' in exile, 'loving one another deeply' is essential[31]; and new birth has put within us the power to make it happen. (*I believe it. Thankyou, Father...*) John calls us similarly to love, and uses the same 'seed' image as in v23 here: 'No-one who has been born of God will continue to sin, because God's seed remains in him; he cannot go on sinning, because he has been born of God' (cf.1 John 3:9-10). It is also the argument we find Paul waxing enthusiastic over in Romans 6-8: new birth involves inner transformation that must, in the end, result in changed behaviour.

Therefore *do it!*, says Peter, in terms that imply real seriousness of commitment: 'Love one another *deeply, from the heart*' (v22, cf.4:8). We are reminded of Paul's '*make every effort* to keep the unity of the Spirit' in Ephesians 4:3. Peter warns carefully against love that is hypocritical (2:1); unreality is always a danger if we are not building on the real regeneration that he is invoking here. Humanly speaking, the result of his exhortation should be forced smiles, insincere affection. But that is the importance of what he's written about the new birth, and the power of the Word. There is something in you that is real, he says, the seed of genuine love; as you feed on the Word, you will find it grows to change your behaviour.

Isn't this reality? 'Love is a decision,' writes Gary Smalley. Loving those who might naturally be (and have acted as) our enemies scarcely starts with a feeling of affection. Instead, it begins with a deliberate, repentant choice (often in response to the Word) to act out the reality of love: setting out (reluctantly?) to 'rid ourselves' of the tangible specifics of 'malice and all deceit...slander of every kind' (2:1); then in deliberate (reluctant?) affirmation and encouragement, in thanksgiving and prayer for the other person. And we set out on this road, not from any confidence to do it ourselves (that might well lead to hypocrisy), but because we know this is the Spirit's agenda; and the Spirit reigns in our deepest self, no matter what our emotions say. We try ('crave') to soak ourselves in the Word, and slowly the bitterness is eclipsed, seeps out, as the Word seeps in. And one day – maybe after weeks, maybe months – suddenly the presence of the kingdom's power becomes apparent to us; we glimpse a feeling towards that person that we recognize as affection. God's transformation has spread slowly right through to our emotions.

Lord, these words are all too easy to write, and I don't trust myself at all; but I do trust your Word, and your Spirit. Thankyou; help me to learn your ways of getting my relationships right...

A home in the wilderness (2:4-10)

Pioneering – following the taste, the desire, for the 'pure milk of the Word' – will lead different people into different discoveries.

It is always risky to say we've found *the* theme of a book. It may be what God has for us now; but as time goes on we may see that, though it was certainly in the passage, there are

other themes that matter equally, or more. Only through
going on rereading, and listening to other believers (indeed
believers from other cultures, other biblically-minded
traditions, other eras), do we start to see the full picture. And,
thank God, we will never exhaust it on earth!

So there are various ways in to every Bible book.
Nonetheless, as we speed-read ahead, it's useful to make a list
of what seem the prominent themes – what the writer
emphasizes, or repeats. Of course our personality and
background make us alert to some rather than others. But we
have everything to gain by starting searching; and God will
find ways to open us up to what else we need as time goes on.

This chapter of our study is an example. We began by
viewing Peter through the theme of exile, of believers as
'strangers in the world', on our way to our promised
inheritance but, as of now, still away from home. The fact
that Peter opens his Epistle with this theme (1:1, but cf. also
1:4, 1:17, 2:11) suggests it is worthy of attention. We intend
no claim that it is *the* key to 1 Peter; books usually don't
work that way. Rather, we're exploring a possibility that
may be fruitful in illuminating, unifying, enlivening different
parts of the book for us.

And one question it may illuminate is this: As we read 1
Peter, don't we keep on hearing echoes of Exodus?

It is not surprising if we do. Could a Jew like Peter view
us as strangers on our way to our inheritance without thinking
of the Exodus story? It was central to his nation's identity,
and celebrated each year in the joyful festival of Passover.
The echoes seem plain: the 'sprinkling of Christ's blood' in
1:2, echoing the liberating blood on the Passover doorposts
(Ex 12:7) and the blood ratifying the basic old testament
covenant (Ex 24:7-8); the reference to our 'redemption'
through the blood of Christ as the Passover lamb 'without
defect' in 1:18-19, echoing Ex 6:6 and 12:5[32]; probably the
command in 1:13 (literally 'gird up the loins of your mind'
(AV)), echoing the Passover arrangements that included dressing

in conscious preparation for the tough journey ahead (Ex 12:11). Plus, obviously, the references to our 'inheritance' to come (e.g. 1:4), that key idea underlying the Exodus story from Genesis 15 through to Joshua 1:6; and to the establishment of a priesthood to offer sacrifices (2:5,9, quoting Ex 19:6). Indeed, Exodus themes would be unusually meaningful for Peter personally. He had seen Moses with his own eyes at the transfiguration; and he had heard Christ discussing his approaching departure as, precisely, his 'exodus' (cf. the Greek of Luke 9:31).[33]

So now, says Peter, we follow in Christ's footsteps. We are on the long journey home from captivity, through the wilderness. Exodus becomes an illuminating image for the salvation-process that is on Peter's heart. To see our experience in terms of Exodus helps us understand our 'exile' (cf. 4:12). The 'salvation' from Egypt was spectacular, but it led into a tough sojourn in the desert. So it may be for us. Unemployment, singleness, bereavement: how could these 'wilderness experiences' be happening now that we are children of God? And yet with the obsolescence of Christendom, the dominant experience of the Western Church as a whole may soon be 'wilderness'.

The issue is how we handle the wilderness; and it's an important issue, basic to our entire calling on earth. 'If you suffer for doing good and you endure it, this is commendable before God. *To this you were called,*' says Peter in 2:21, 'because Christ suffered for you, leaving you an example, that you should follow his steps.' And again in 3:9: 'Do not repay evil with evil or insult with insult, but with blessing, because *to this you were called so that you may inherit a blessing.*' The 'suffering-and-glory process' is God's way to 'blessing', to our 'inheritance', to Christ-likeness. ('We must go through many hardships to enter the kingdom of God,' Paul told the Iconium believers.[34]) The cross was the ultimate 'exodus'; so for us too there are times when the wilderness process, the way of the cross, is the way of discipleship to Jesus (cf. 4:1).

So let's read into the next section, 2:4-10. How do we cope with the wilderness journey?

First, we do not do it alone. Exodus gives us another clue for this passage. In one sense, wilderness means being away from home; but in another, vital sense, Israel were not entirely 'homeless'. The book of Exodus isn't just about God delivering Israel from Egypt and leading them towards Palestine; it is also, centrally, about his desire to live among them on the way. Its close presents exactly that, with the completion of God's 'dwelling-place'[35], the tabernacle, and his glory descending to fill it (Exodus 40). Is this in Peter's mind here? At any rate, we have a home in the wilderness, and Peter tells us about it in 2:5. God is building a 'spiritual house' for himself; and as we saw in Ephesians, we as individuals are its components, the 'living stones' from which the master-builder creates his home.[36] (And great is his patience and creativity. Can we imagine building a house out of 'living stones', each with their own minds on the subject? All sorts of humorous possibilities present themselves!) The Church is precious because it is God's dwelling-place, not only in eternity, but now. And amid all the stresses of the wilderness journey, it is our home too.

Second, our experiences of 'exile' aren't meaningless: they are what we were told to expect. In fact, says Peter in vv 4 and 7-8, our experiences of rejection mirror, and share, the experience of Christ. (Hebrews tells us the same; look at 13:13-14.) And if we as his people find ourselves 'rejected' now as Christ was, we rejoice that we are lovingly 'chosen' by the One who really matters, just as Christ was (2:9, cf. vv4,6). *(Thankyou, Lord!)*

Third, we are not lost in the wilderness; we are there because we are 'called' by our Father (v9). Peter's mind often turns to this idea of calling (1:15, 2:21, 3:9, 5:10), and at least two of these instances are about our calling to the suffering-and-glory process. Ultimately, our journey is under God's direction. (Indeed, says Peter, even Christ's rejection by the Jews was foreseen in God's plan (v8, cf. Acts 4:27-28).) During 'exile experiences', we can be tempted to start thinking of ourselves as doomed to a tragic fate. But there is no 'tragic fatality' about the purposes of God; he is the one who rescues us from tragedy, taking those who were 'not a people' and turning them into the 'people of God' (v10).[37] We've been 'called out of darkness into his marvellous light' (v9); we may be exiles, but we are on our way to an assured inheritance. *(Thankyou, Lord!)* That sense of God's loving, almighty direction is vital for our survival in the wilderness.

Fourth, we have a purpose (a specific calling) during our wilderness travel: to be a 'holy priesthood' offering 'spiritual sacrifices... that you may declare the praises of him who called you out of darkness' (vv5,9). ('Priesthood' is, we note, a calling for all believers on the journey, not for some special caste among them.) As Paul says in 1 Thessalonians 5:18, praise is the purpose of our existence; we are, says God, 'the people I formed for myself, that they may proclaim my praise' (Isaiah 43:21). *(Lord, please teach me to praise you!)*

In the wilderness we might seem to have lost our identity. We don't fit any longer among the people we used to belong to (cf. 4:4) – and we've not fully come 'home' either. But Peter shows us reality: the scattered, rejected exiles have received a glorious identity, a home, a calling and a purpose. Grasp this vision, Peter challenges us *(Father, please help me)*; then you can be proud to belong to the wilderness Church!

After this, vv.11-12 will take us a step further. As priests we each declare God's praise; but that must be through our lifestyle as well as by our words. (Just as we evangelize through our transformed relationships as much as by our message; see, for example, 3:1 (or John 17:20-23).) This emphasis on the meaning of our 'good deeds' (cf. also 2:15, 3:1,16) is a theme throughout the next section.

Wilderness relationships (2:11-3:22)

2:11 reintroduces the concerns for holiness of 1:14-15: 'Dear
friends' ('Dearly beloved' in the warmer earlier version![38]), 'I
urge you, as aliens and strangers in the world, to abstain from
sinful desires, which war against the soul. Live such good lives
among the pagans that...they may see your good deeds.' We
saw in chapter 1 that Peter's prime interest with regard to
holiness had to do with the transformation of our
relationships. So it is here; holiness is expressed above all in
our love.

And the next section is especially concerned with handling
relationships that have gone wrong, that have become
wilderness relationships. How do we set about that? It's
advice we all will need from time to time.

The first example is our relationship with the authorities
(vv13-15). We may be 'aliens and strangers', but we have a
role in the land of our exile, as Jeremiah reminded the Jewish
exiles in Jeremiah 29:7. Our attitude is the issue here. Peter
calls us to a stance of respect for our rulers rather than scorn
or hatred, because if a community loses all respect for its leaders
the result will soon be loss of respect for its laws, and then
anarchy.[39] Of course the need to 'submit' and 'honour' the
authorities did not prevent Peter challenging them
prophetically in Acts 4:19, any more than it did Amos or
John the Baptist. So for us too: the 'heavenly vision' that we
don't belong here, and are on our way home, must not
preclude active concern about abortion, about two-thirds-
world debt, the arms trade, the degradations of media
pornography and consumerism, the needs of the inner cities,
the defiling of the environment.

But Peter's readers' relationship with the authorities of their
time was clearly a 'wilderness relationship', judging by the
persecution they were undergoing (e.g. 4:12). 'Wilderness'
also marks the other relationships he addresses: wrong
working relationships characterized by slavery and the 'pain

of unjust suffering' (2:19), by the hurling of insults and threats (cf. 2:23); marital relationships with unbelievers, marked not by love but by fear (3:6); relationships within the church itself that are not free from evil and insult, where 'living in harmony' has to be a matter of deliberate choice (3:8-9).

I have to say that, for myself personally, these are some of the more difficult passages in the Bible. It is true, as Davids observes, that for Peter to address himself directly to slaves would have seemed 'remarkable' to his contemporary readers, and that to address wives directly was 'revolutionary'.[40] Yet in its 'non-liberationist' stance, its apparent lack of critique of slavery or male-dominated marriage, it runs against our deep-rooted instincts.

But to say this is to raise the wrong question. Peter is not presenting a broad theology either of social justice or of marriage (God gives us these elsewhere, and it was that input that historically brought the slavery system down). Rather, he is guiding his readers in handling specific 'wilderness relationships' that have clearly gone wrong. Secondly, our problem here as contemporary readers is in fact the overall 'problem of suffering', raised in a specific context: there is an enormous amount of evil in the world, and God seems to allow it to continue, for the time being at least. God gives us no simple 'answer' to this question; for the time being we are called to live by faith in his goodness (cf. 1:7). But perhaps the partial answers we have to the overall problem are relevant here also: that domination has resulted from our rebellion at the Fall, and our ceaseless attempts to run our relationships outside his direct reign (cf. Gen 3:16); that Christ has entered into our situation at Calvary, and dealt with its root causes; that deliverance is coming; that meanwhile God is in the anguish with us, working there for good, making us like Jesus (cf. Rom 8:28-29).

And here we find an issue possibly even more challenging for men than for women. What God develops in women through these 'wilderness experiences', says Peter, is the 'unfading beauty of a gentle and quiet spirit, which is of great worth in God's sight' (3:4). That 'unfading' takes us back to chapter 1; here is something else of eternal value, in a wilderness of transience and decay. But what should catch our attention is surely the potential to attain a quality 'of great worth in God's sight'. Not that this is of concern to the male sex – or is it? Patience, goodness and gentleness are 'fruit of the Spirit', precisely what God wants to shape in us (Gal 5:22-23). They run counter both to the spirit of egoism intrinsic to the Fall, and the lures of power and status in the classic temptation of Matthew 4. Might it be that the pain women often undergo in a fallen society creates environments where such fruit can develop; while men – in fact to their lasting impoverishment – have fewer such experiences? We might recall Christ himself spending thirty years living out a 'gentle and quiet spirit', entirely out of the limelight. Psalm 131 comes to mind: 'My heart is not proud, O Lord, my eyes are not haughty... I have stilled and quietened my soul; like a weaned child with its mother, like a weaned child is my soul within me. O Israel, put your hope in the Lord...' Are there reasons here why there are many more women than men in the church? Does our male experience make it harder to develop Christ-likeness? If it's 'of great worth in God's sight', may men have to learn it by passing through other 'wilderness experiences'?[41] And what are the implications for men seeking a truly Christ-like spirituality?

What more do we find in this section to help us 'journey through' these 'wilderness relationships'? Peter gives us at least four further 'life-sustaining' insights to apply in our own situation.

Firstly, the thought-provoking phrase in 2:19: someone bears up under the pain of unjust suffering 'because they are *conscious of God*'. (How do I train myself to be 'conscious of God'– in the phrase of Brother Lawrence, always 'practising the presence of God'? Is a deliberate, regular mental focusing on Christ as Lord the point also of 3:15?) Second, there is the emphasis on maintaining hope (see 3:5,15,9: 'Do not repay evil with evil or insult with insult, because to this you were called *so that you may inherit a blessing.*') (How am I 'maintaining my hope'?) Third, there is a recurring challenge to keep the evangelistic vision burning through these experiences: thinking what will cause pagans to glorify God when the right time comes (2:12), thinking how unbelieving husbands can be 'won over without words' (3:1), being prepared always to explain our hope (3:15). As Jesus emphasized (Matt 5:16), some of the crucial tools in evangelism are behavioural: Peter summarizes them here as 'purity and reverence' (3:2). To that end he reverses his (and our) culture's priorities of image against character, of looking good against doing good (3:3-4) – with all the expense of time and effort that our choice of priorities involves.[42]

But most obviously, life comes to us for these phases of the journey through the grasp of Calvary. Twice in this section, Peter turns our minds carefully to the Christ who took the form of a slave (cf. Phil 2:7): 'Christ suffered for you, leaving you an example, that you should follow in his steps' (2:21). 'It is better, if it is God's will, to suffer for doing good than for doing evil. For Christ died for sins once for all, the righteous for the unrighteous' (3:18, cf. 4:1,13). The cross was how God responded to the evil of the wilderness; and Calvary, Christ's own 'exodus' experience, becomes our example in wilderness relationships (cf. also Hebrews 5:7-8, 12:2-4).

At the cross, says the French Christian sociologist Ellul, God absorbed the evil out of the world as with a sponge; and that pattern is repeated as the people of the cross in turn 'forgive each other, just as in Christ God forgave you' (cf. Eph 4:32). Instead of responding to evil with evil (3:9) and prolonging a repetitive vendetta, forgiveness means letting go of the evil, handing it over to God,[43] confident in his loving sovereignty. ('He made no threats. Instead, he entrusted himself to him that judges justly' (2:23).) And thereby, incidentally, becoming free from evil ourselves. *(Lord, this is all so easy to write, and to read. Please help me see, and give me your grace to act, when the times come to do it...)*

John F. Alexander was a leader in the left-wing 'radical evangelical' movement that developed a strong evangelical politics in the 1970s. His book *The Secular Squeeze* is a powerful statement of the church's central calling to be a community of forgiveness. He makes his point by presenting what Peter might have written in 2:20-24: 'What credit is it to you if you suffer unjustly and don't rebel? For to this you have been called, because Christ also fought for his rights, leaving you an example that you should follow in his steps. When he was abused, he returned abuse; when he suffered, he fought back; he didn't simply entrust himself to the one who judges justly. By his rights campaign you have been healed.' (The idea of submissiveness to bad masters is 'outrageous to any right-thinking, freedom-loving American', Alexander adds wryly; Peter 'actually says that God approves of people suffering patiently, though to us it's clear that people have not just a right but a duty to defend themselves.... His evidence is that Jesus did it, and he's our example. Suppressing these teachings is the root of the failure of the church... We have no intention of living the way Jesus did. And without that, we can't live in reconciliation.'[44])

We understand here why communion, 'remembering the Lord's death' in worship, has a central place for spirituality. It is our model for understanding our experience, and for deciding our response. Sharing in his suffering in wilderness relationships is central to our *calling* (2:21). We are called to participate in Christ's ministry of absorbing evil from the world; to Christ-likeness, and so, ultimately, to resurrection glory. 'I want to know Christ,' said Paul, 'and the power of his resurrection and the fellowship of sharing in his sufferings' (Phil 3:10).

Briefly back to Noah…(3:17-4:1)

The chapter's closing verses are some of the obscurest in the new testament. That's why we're putting these five paragraphs in small print, and some readers may prefer to skip across to the next section. But they have their own value. Space allows us only a quick glance. But if we write down their sequence of ideas, it seems to be something like this:

(i)   Our example is Christ suffering for us and then being vindicated, vv17-18;

(ii)   in the same Spirit, preaching was made in connection with another 'exile' occasion when God's judgment had not yet been revealed because God was 'waiting patiently', namely the time before the flood (vv19-20, compare 2 Peter 3:9,15, 3-7);

(iii)   that judgment, when it came, became part of the salvation-process (v20; compare 4:17-18);

(iv)   the flood parallels water-baptism which has a similar role in our salvation-process, cutting us off likewise from a 'drowned world' and bringing us through to a new world (v21);

(v)   baptism is linked to the resurrection, whereby, after his suffering, Christ likewise passed triumphantly into the other world (v21-22);

(vi)   'Therefore, arm yourselves with the same attitude' (4:1).

Now the question for us is 'Why is all this here?'; that is, how do these verses add to the letter's overall flow of thought?

This question seems hardest if we see in vv 19-20 Jesus proclaiming his triumph, between his death and resurrection, to those spirits of the dead who had opposed the preaching in Noah's time.[45]   That's quite a common interpretation, and the logical sequence of allusion to Christ's dying, preaching, rising and ascending makes it attractive; plus 'preaching in prison' would be all too relevant to Peter's audience, as Michael Griffiths points out. But, to this reader at any rate, it is hard to see why Peter should suddenly bring this up (why spirits from Noah's time in particular?), and harder still to summarize his thought-flow in a way that makes the illustration integral, and then leads naturally on to baptism.

The alternative is to see Peter as giving us a whole series of God's witnesses who underwent Spirit-empowered suffering (cf. 3:13-17), that led them further into the salvation-process and to ultimate vindication. Then Christ is the first of these, and Noah the second. (Peter was interested in Noah's preaching, cf. 2 Peter 2:5.) Christ was the ultimate example (v18); and, by the same Spirit, he also preached[46] through Noah in Noah's time.[47] Noah too was rejected by the people of the old world ('only a few' were saved there, v20); but his apparent rejection resulted – as ours will too (vv14-16) – in his being 'saved', passing through to the new world.[48] Then Peter moves on. This salvation-process is what baptism is about, he says.[49] It's a total breaking with the drowned old world[50] that parallels ('symbolizes', v21) Noah's; and baptism also reflects (cf. Rom 6:3-5) Christ's own resurrection into the new world (his 'exodus'). Therefore, he concludes, 'Arm yourselves with the same attitude' of determined faithfulness as Christ and Noah demonstrated (4:1), and set your hearts upon radical distinctiveness from the world around you (4:2-4). *(Lord, help me – for I know this is not just an intellectual puzzle, but a matter of my ongoing 'salvation'!)*

This approach seems to fit the passage's ideas into the book's overall flow. Still, with such a complex section we may feel it is simplest to focus on the flow of thought that is expressed clearly in 3:18 and then 'emerges into the open again' in 4:1, because the intervening verses don't seem to have changed it significantly.

The vision that arms us (4:1-11)

Studying 1 Peter could save our lives.

We're only on this planet for a few decades; we're in heaven for eternity. But the 'wilderness times' are the times when we're most likely to give up on discipleship. If we do, however, we turn our whole earthly existence into something we will one day look back on with desperate regret. Quite seriously, working carefully through this book could make a difference to us for the next million years.

As we move on into chapter 4, we'll notice that it's something of a reprise; time and again, Peter reworks the central ideas of chapter 1. We should skip this chapter then? Not at all! First, because seeing what Peter re-emphasises helps us grasp what is most on his heart. But it's deeply valuable

for a far more personal reason. What will save us in the
wilderness is not just the ideas we've read, but the truths that
have burrowed deeply into our hearts. Peter – and the Holy
Spirit who inspired him – wants us to re-absorb these life-
giving insights, because this increases our chances of really
grasping them. It's the repeated exposure that can drive them
deeply enough into our hearts to make the vital difference
when the wilderness comes upon us.

So what are these ideas that Peter takes such care to
highlight? Let's list what we find here:

(i)   Our sufferings are not meaningless or fruitless, 4:1 –
an affirmation repeated from 1:6-7;

(ii) but we need an 'arming vision', the adoption of a
deliberate mental stance, 4:1 cf. 1:13 (in chapter 4 this 'arming
vision' is primarily of Christ's cross, as in chapter 3);

(iii) 'as a result', we make the vital choice of desires, 4:2
cf. 1:13-14;

(iv) radical, holy distinctiveness in view of the coming
judgment, 4:3-6 cf. 1:17 – deliberately focusing our minds on
the 'End', 4:7 cf. 1:13;

(v)   as a result of that 'focusing', grounding our
distinctiveness by learning self-control, 4:7 cf. 1:13;

(vi) 'above all', at the heart of holiness, fervent mutual love,
4:8-9 cf. 1:22;

(vii) love leads into the deliberate use of all our 'gifts' for
others, 4:10; pre-eminent among these is sharing the Word,
which is in fact nothing less than 'speaking the very words of
God', 4:11 cf. 1:25.[51]

(We need to take time here to pray our way through these!)

These issues seem very personal to Peter. 'Arm yourselves
with the same attitude', he writes; was he remembering his
own failure to 'arm' himself at the crucial moment? Recalling,
perhaps, how in his self-confidence he failed to take seriously
Christ's command (and example) to 'Watch and pray so that
you will not fall into temptation' (Matt 26:33,41-42)– and how,
when the conflict came, he was 'armed' only with a useless

physical[52] sword, rather than with the necessary mind-set from
Christ's Word (26:51-56, John 18:10-11), and ended up denying
his Lord?

So what do we learn here about this vital 'arming vision'?

First, it is in our *'attitude'* (NIV), our *'mind'* (AV), that the
'arming' for the wilderness occurs. If our spirituality grows
'mindless', we will be disarmed for experiences of the
wilderness. (There are churches where this can happen: that
almost seem to cultivate a spirituality of the empty skull. It
can be a costly mistake.) We become 'armed' as God's
concerns get a grip, ahead of time, on our thinking: Christ's
cross[53], and (1:13) the 'grace to be given you when Jesus Christ
is revealed'. Here again is where communion is important
for our spirituality: these twin insights are 'refreshed' in our
minds as we take bread and wine and remember 'the Lord's
death, until he comes' (1 Cor 11:26). 'Let us fix our eyes on
Jesus... who *for the joy set before him endured the cross*, scorning
its shame... so that you will not grow weary and lose heart.
In the struggle against sin you have not yet resisted to the
point of shedding your blood' (Heb 12:2-4). *Lord, help me
arm myself for holy faithfulness, with this vision of your faithful
suffering caused by sin; I worship you...*

Second, we sense the *seriousness of Peter's demands for
radicalism* in the 'struggle against sin' (4:3). We are 'aliens
and strangers in the world' (cf. 2:11). So we must embrace a
willingness to be dramatically different from the 'empty way
of life' around us (cf. 1:18), which he sees as marked by
'debauchery, lust, drunkenness' – like all too many parts of
the contemporary clubbing scene. They 'think it strange' that
you do not plunge in alongside them, Peter writes to his readers
here (v4); in our own day, the media make it seem doubly
peculiar. Yet our calling is to be radical, 'aliens and strangers'
if necessary, when club culture and kingdom culture clash.
'If anyone loves the world, the love of the Father is not in
him', says John[54]; as Jesus taught us, the passion for holiness
is indispensable ('If your right hand, causes you to sin, cut it

off'). But then the issue will be which has become more real for our minds, the presence and example of the Lord or the approval of our peers who may indeed 'heap abuse' on us (vv4-6).[55] (I am finding, more and more, that when I slip into sin it isn't just the sin itself I need to repent of, but a prior casualness about holiness – a lack of concern as to whether I grieve God or not.) What matters, again, is whether we are 'conscious of God' (2:19), and how firmly we have grasped that soon 'each of us will give an account of himself to God'[56] (cf. v5). The 'fear of the Lord' is the 'beginning of wisdom': lose this and triviality and carelessness about sin will soon follow.[57] *(Lord, I indeed believe that soon I shall give account of my life to you; please keep that reality at the forefront of my consciousness...)*

(Isn't this the reason why Peter now emphasizes again that the 'end of all things is near' (v7)? As in his second letter (especially 3:1-4, 8-14), it is awareness of this reality that empowers us to holy resistance and choice; it's people who have lost this prophetic awareness that end up 'following their own evil desires.' 'Prepare your minds for action,' Peter had said in 1:13, 'be self-controlled; set your hope fully on the grace to be given you when Jesus Christ is revealed.' The same group of ideas belong together here.)

This radicalism, affirms Peter, is indispensable for two reasons. First, our holiness (being 'clear-minded and self-controlled') matters if the Holy Spirit's power is to be released in answer to our prayers (v7). The insight parallels that in 3:7, where he stressed that if the holiness of husbands was deficient in considerateness and respect for their wives, then their prayers would unavoidably be hindered. (That assumes, of course, that our prayer lives are alive enough for us to sense the difference.)

Secondly, life in exile depends on our learning the radical holiness where we 'above all, love each other deeply'(v8). The spirit that 'always protects, always trusts, always hopes, always endures'[58] is indispensable for a community seeking to make it together across the wilderness; the spirit that shares 'without grumbling'(v9) – where every resource we have is available, according to God's command, to 'serve others'(v10).

This may be crucial for us in these coming decades, unless 'the end' indeed comes with the Lord's return.[59] We very probably face a situation where the results of the 'loss of God' continue to multiply; where Western civilization continues to disintegrate, with speeding erosion both of its foundations for anything but selfishness, and of its protective legal and social 'safety nets' for anyone weak or in need. If current trends continue – that is, unless God sends 'revival' – the only way to survive the darkness of post-postmodern Britain may be in local communities taught and empowered by God to be deeply committed to each other in just this way. *(Lord, help me see where I need to learn more of this right now.)*

What then is it, we might ask from these verses, that survives in exile? Peter answers us in v11, as his thought seemingly comes to climax: a community of unselfish (Christ-like) mutual support, empowered by supernatural strength; through the preached Word of God, through self-giving service, and through devotion to God's glory...

The way ahead (4:12-5:11)

Peter is someone for whom contemplation of these realities turns into actual acts of worship; and so should we be. Here in v11 his teaching blossoms into an outbreak of praise to Jesus: *'To him be the glory for ever and ever! Amen!'*

After that we almost expect to hear the closing hymn! But God has one page more to bless us with. It's as if Peter felt that the experiences his beloved readers faced were such an urgent challenge that he couldn't resist asking his secretary (5:12) to make a few last insights absolutely crystal clear.

What then are the issues highlighted in this final, culminating section? There are four at least: about the Spirit, the Father, the Church and the devil.

Don't be surprised when these things happen, he says as he recommences, but rejoice. Suffering and glory go together like the two sides of a coin; it's as we share in Christ's sufferings (what a bizarre notion!) that we will share in his glory (vv13-14, cf. 5:1).[60] And these are the moments (this should intrigue his more charismatic readers!) when *'the Spirit of glory and of God rests on you'* (v14). *(Father, help me believe that...)*

He moves on. The Spirit of glory, we know, is the Holy Spirit who sanctifies (1:2); growth in glory is growth into holiness. So Peter goes on to underline that our sufferings are a refining judgment on God's family (v17). (Compare the sense of refining in 1:7: 'All kinds of trials... have come so that your faith... may be proved genuine and may result in praise, glory and honour.'[61]) The purpose of the wilderness journey is to ready us for glory; we find meaning in it as we hold on to faith that it has some Godward dimension (v19), that somewhere in it God is 'working for good' for and in us (cf. Rom 8:28). So what in particular is the 'arming insight' here? Surely, that our Father is a *'faithful Creator'* (v19).

It's yet another thought-provoking, unusual phrase. But Jesus had talked the same way in Matthew (6:25-33, 10:29-31),[62] and we can feed here on the lesson Peter had heard him draw: we can be at peace in this world because we are worth so very much to the Father (Matt 10:31). The Father made us, he loves us, he is sovereign in all that happens, and he can be trusted in what he is doing. *(Lord, I worship you; please help me put my faith in you and 'continue to do good' (v19)...)* In wilderness situations, our calling is just to trust him, day by day and step by step. Overall, yes, it's important to think strategically; Christ calls us (Acts 1:8) to a mindset looking continually for the 'next step' in evangelism God has for us, Judaea then Samaria and towards the ends of the earth. But at those points when we're really experiencing the wilderness, there are just two 'times' that matter: the present moment, trusting and obeying the Father, step by step; and the 'end', when we will stand in glory before him. These are what we

must focus on, rather than the cares of the unforeseeable future.
As the Russian writer Solovyov observes, in the Sermon on
the Mount we are instructed to pray for our bread for 'today'.
'Tomorrow' we entrust to God (Matt 6:11,34).

But such 'faith' isn't easy. To maintain it we need the
help of others; we need love and good food to make it through
the wilderness (cf. 2:2). So, thirdly, Peter now turns to the
shepherds, those whose task it is to keep the foodchain going
(5:1-4, cf. 2 Peter 1:12-15, 3:1-2). (Behind these verses we surely
sense his final, repeated commission from Jesus: 'Feed my
sheep' (John 21:15-17).)

Peter himself is an example of a good 'shepherd' in his
humility here; we notice he describes himself not as an apostle
but as a 'fellow-elder'. Does this reflect his own 'wilderness
experiences'? He calls himself a *'witness'* (not 'participant' as
in 4:13) 'of Christ's sufferings, and one who will *share* in the
glory to be revealed'; remembering, perhaps, that he indeed
'witnessed' Christ's sufferings, but evaded 'sharing' them,
despite his earlier boasts (Luke 22:33). Such a realism, a
humble, self-revealing honesty, sitting loose to status and
(because it's secure in Christ's love) able to admit what God
knows about us, is a mark of the true 'shepherd'. It is fuelled,
too, by the certainty that even we who have failed can 'share
in the glory to be revealed'.

In 5:2-3, therefore, Peter focuses on three key issues that
can ruin the leaders who must shepherd God's flock through
the wilderness: resentment, money, and control. Peter
responds to these by highlighting three things leaders need to
keep in mind: for resentment, the will of a loving God who
'cares for you'(cf. v7); for greed, the calling to eager servant-
leadership[63]; for our 'control-mentality', the calling to be
examples of Christ-likeness.[64] Then he turns also to the
younger believers, whose Christ-likeness will be equally vital
if the 'wilderness community' is to move forward together
through pressure and change (something doubly true, we
might add, when the world is changing as rapidly as in

postmodernity): 'Young men, in the same way be submissive to those who are older.' He doesn't make the point explicitly, but we might recall (cf.3:4) that this kind of process is how humility, the fruit of the Spirit, is fostered, and God needs to take us all that way from time to time. 'God opposes' (an alarming notion!) 'the proud, but gives grace to the humble,' Peter continues. 'Humble yourselves, therefore, under God's mighty hand, that he may lift you up in due time.' Then he adds, 'Cast all your anxiety on him, because' – the essential thing to hold on to in the wilderness[65] – 'he cares for you.' We have to focus on our trust in God, 'living by faith', and not on the outward circumstances (cf. Matthew 10:28-31).

One November Sunday afternoon I was watching the golden leaves drop from the trees behind our house, as more and more of the branches became blackened and denuded. Winter was coming, and it was one of those moments when you feel old. And then I thought: But the presence of God within us is the guarantee, eventually, of new life: of resurrection, pentecost, glory. So it is here. 'Humble yourselves under God's mighty hand, that he may lift you up in due time.' In God's purposes there are Novembers, but springs will come also; there are 'dark nights of the soul', because only so can full rejuvenation be brought to pass. So 'standing firm in the faith' (v9) is the anchor. 'Cast all your anxiety on him, because he cares for you.' Some lessons have to be learnt in winter, in the wilderness, because there is no other way.

Fourthly, then, Peter presents one final motive for being 'self-controlled and alert', one particularly relevant to the 'winter months': spiritual warfare (v8). The devil is more active than many of us imagine, and, as Jesus had warned Peter in Gethsemane, we need to genuinely 'watch and pray' to recognize the attack when it comes. The choice of a wrong priority, the nursing of a grudge, the welcoming of depression rather than deliberate thanksgiving: any of these can mark the subtle incursion of satanic influence. (*Lord, please help me bother to 'watch and pray': help me be alert – and holy and obedient....)* Still, Peter's overall tone here is confident and not paranoid: God is in control! As Nigel Lee has put it, there is 'nothing Satan can do that has not already been filtered through the loving hands of your Father God'. 'Cast all your anxiety on him; he cares for you!' *(Thankyou, Lord!)*

Thus in his triumphant conclusion (vv10-11), Peter points again to the salvation-process that we must discern in the wilderness ('God... after you have suffered a little while, will himself make you strong, firm and steadfast'); to the inseparable pairing of wilderness sufferings with 'eternal glory'; and to the power of God undergirding it all. We are not in the wilderness because God is powerless; rather, we stay alive there only because we are 'shielded by God's power'(1:5). 'To him be the power for ever and ever!', for he knows what he is doing. *Lord, Amen!*

PS: Grace is the meaning (5:12-14)

It's striking to see how Peter closes his letter with a further image of exile – Babylon, the old testament city of exile *par excellence*, presumably symbolizing Rome in this case. 'She who is in Babylon, chosen together with you, sends you her greetings': even in exile in Babylon, God's church is chosen and loved by the Father. 'And so does my son Mark' – this beloved Mark being someone else who had experienced the process of wilderness, failure and growth very personally, as we know from Acts.[66]

But then, even as he signs off, Peter throws in one final, fascinating remark. 'I have written to you briefly, encouraging you and testifying that this is the true grace of God. Stand fast in it.'

If we want to grasp 1 Peter's concerns, we should latch onto this apparent summary. Looking back over his letter, grace has been the point of it all, says Peter: to set out what grace is, and what it means to stand firm in it. So what has Peter told us about grace?

'Grace be yours in abundance' was how he began his letter (1:2). But he didn't mean this traditional greeting to be empty, unconsidered 'Christianese'. Grace, God's overwhelming, undeserved love for us, is what we must hold on to if we are to survive the wilderness journey; and grace is the hallmark of God's entire salvation-process (1:10). Peter has given us at least three specific examples: through sharing the gifts of the Spirit we pass on more of God's kindness, 'God's grace in its various forms' (4:9-11); by building Christ-like relationships we act as fellow-sharers in the 'gracious gift of (eternal) life' (3:7); and thus we can stand in the place where that grace is flowing most freely ('God... gives grace to the humble', 5:5).[67] Grace is what the enormous kindness of Christ has done and is doing in our lives; grace is what his kindness will do (1:13). In case his wilderness readers might be tempted to doubt that kindness (4:12), he points to its purest revelation at Calvary (1:18-19, the theme he returns to throughout chapters 2 and 3), and challenges them, 'Set your hope fully on the grace to be given you when Jesus Christ is revealed'(1:13). God is the 'God of all grace'; his Fatherly love is the element in which we live, and that endless love will surely see us through (5:10, cf. 5:7). This 'grace-process' was what the whole old testament had pointed to; grace, God's unstinting, astonishing kindness, *is* salvation (1:10-11). *(Thankyou, loving Father! Please help me trust you, and share this vision...)*

So this, above all, we need to hold on to. 'I have written to you briefly, encouraging you' – refreshing your vision of grace – 'and testifying that this is the true grace of God. Stand fast in it.' God has created a world where 'seasons' of 'ordinary' wilderness, of trials unrelieved by miracle, are integral to our growth in faith; where even Jesus submitted himself to 'learn obedience from what he suffered' (Heb 5:7-8).[68] The wilderness can be a tough place; and our calling there is to trust and obey, and having done all, as Ephesians 6:13

says, to stand. And we stand because indeed we have 'tasted
the kindness of the Lord' (2:3 NASB), tasted just a little of the
'goodness of the Word of God and the powers of the coming
age' (cf. Heb 6:5); and that foretaste of God's grace, his
kingdom in our hearts, can take us through exile to glory.
Life that survives through the wilderness marks the reality of
God's reign in our deepest being;[69] and that reign, ultimately,
is the presence of his grace, and of his glorious kingdom.

Notes

[1] Of course the kingdom focuses on God's house, the Church,
in the new testament too.

[2] This 'being put right' appears most frequently in the old
testament as a focus of longing and promise; of desire for 'judgment',
for a time when things will be put back in order, when Israel will
see that 'our God reigns'; a time that will fulfil the promises of
God's blessing from Genesis 12 onwards. God's acts in the old
testament give hints of how that can be; even if the old testament
sets out more often the vital lesson that sin leads, by God's law, to
tragedy, disharmony and death. But ever and again it looks
longingly towards the saving coming(s) of Messiah.

[3] And the fall of Jerusalem isn't the end of the story. After that
stark revelation of sin's tragic consequences, there begin to be
equally clear expressions of God's power in deliverance, leading
finally to the return from exile.

[4] Job 13:15. Or as Bonhoeffer wrote: 'Before God and with
God we live without God.'

[5] He is referring to when he sent them out to 'preach the
kingdom' in Luke 9:1-6.

[6] Peter apparently misunderstood this, and the result was the
violence of vv49-51. Jesus' point was surely the need to be armed
spiritually, in the way Paul spells out in Ephesians 6:13: 'Put on
the full armour of God so that when the day of evil comes you
may be able to stand your ground, and after you have done
everything, to stand.'

[7] But there is a mystery here, helpfully expressed by Henri
Nouwen: 'In prayer the distinction between God's presence and
God's absence no longer distinguishes... God's presence is so much

beyond the human experience of being together that it quite easily is perceived as absence. God's absence, on the other hand, is often so deeply felt that it leads to a new sense of God's presence.' (*Seeds of Hope* (1998 edition), pp.125-26.) Psalm 42 is a moving example of this.

[8] In Numbers 1-13 they are in the wilderness because God has chosen to put them there (cf. Ex 13:17-18; Deut 8:2 also states how God has led them in the desert 'to humble you and to test you in order to know what was in your heart'). But from Numbers 14 onwards it is more because of their own sin and failure to live by faith. Numbers educates us, we may say, in both aspects.

[9] Look too at Jesus' charge to Peter in John 21:17 and Luke 22:32, and the way he responds in 2 Peter 1:12-15.

[10] Once again we see here the way the Word and the Spirit belong together. We are 'born again through the ... Word of God' (1:23), the 'Word that was preached to you' (1:25), but also through the 'sanctifying work of the Spirit'(1:2).

[11] 'Salvation' can even refer specifically to the journey's heavenly culmination, e.g. in 1:5. So can 'grace', e.g. in 1:13. If (as we will suggest) the Exodus is in Peter's mind as he writes, then it becomes important that the central 'Exodus-moment' of deliverance had meaning insofar as it was the beginning of a journey, a process.

[12] It's striking to see how instantly Peter's mind goes to the 'new birth'. Sometimes the older type of liberal churchman or religious journalist talks as if being 'born again' was merely a concern for 'fringe fundamentalists'. It isn't; it is as central to the Christianity of Peter (see also 1:23) as it was to the message of Jesus (John 3:3-8).

[13] Job would be the classic old testament example. And we see how very greatly God values the faith that is 'proved genuine', since he doesn't explain to Job that his calamities are caused by Satan. Rather (can we say?) God trusts Job to trust him 'in the dark'; our process of learning faith is evidently of enormous worth.

[14] As Michael Griffiths has put it, we are not hanging on by our own power, we are kept by the power of God (v5) – and that is what people need to know in persecution. As we noted earlier, God's power is actually as central to 'exile' as to 'kingdom'.

[15] Cf. Phil 3:20-4:1: 'Our citizenship is in heaven. And we *eagerly await* a Saviour from there... *That* is how you should stand firm in the Lord, dear friends!'

[16] As David Gooding observes, Peter had Jesus' word for this: cf. Luke 10:24. The idea here(vv10-12), that the prophets themselves were trying to understand what they had written, implies that sometimes at least the revelation they received had meanings beyond what they were able to comprehend. That is important for how we interpret their words - and Revelation too: its meaning is not limited by 'what a first-century reader could fully understand'.

[17] Is his mind going to Daniel 12:5-10?

[18] When Peter writes that the prophets' revelation was primarily 'not serving themselves but you', we can imagine his thoughts going back to Pentecost, and the staggering realization that the wonders he and his fellow-believers were seeing were the fulfilment of Joel's ancient prophecy. '*This*', he would recall declaring – this astounding outpouring on '*all*' flesh' of the Spirit's presence, which for previous millennia had been the preserve of so very few – 'is what was spoken by the prophet Joel.'

[19] But cf. also James 1:14-15.

[20] Note that it is 'through' the promises that we escape; cf.'recall the words' in 3:2. It is in part because the 'promises' matter so much that 2 Peter puts such emphasis on the reliability of the Word (1:16-21); only if the Word is fully trustworthy can we receive with confidence its life-changing promises. Hence also the catastrophic consequences of the false prophets, whose activities nullify the promises' effect by 'bringing the way of truth into disrepute' (1:20-2:2).

[21] The same choice is underlined by Paul in Colossians 3 as an alternative to wrong desire both sexual and materialistic ('greed, which is idolatry', v5): 'Set your minds' (AV has 'affections') 'on things above, not on earthly things'(v2), because, again, of the 'glory' to be revealed (v4). Cf. also Phil 3:18-20.

[22] For example, in *The Screwtape Letters*, the preface to *The Pilgrim's Regress,* and 'The Weight of Glory' in *Screwtape Proposes a Toast.*

[23] Michael Griffiths observes that much in this passage is set up to give security to people under pressure; for example, the repeated emphasis that we are 'called'(v15). This is true of v21 especially: it is through Christ's own power that we believe, and what we have believed in is a God who has already proved in history his utter

trustworthiness (cf. Rom 8:11); 'and so your faith and hope are in God'.

[24] Above all, it is Jesus who is 'precious', as the next chapter will emphasize (2:4,6,7).

[25] It is interesting that for Peter the 'imperishable' bridgehead of the other world is found firstly in the Word rather than the Church.

[26] And in contrast James presents, again in language very close to Peter's, the rich man who 'will pass away like a wild flower. For the sun rises with scorching heat and withers the plant; its blossom falls and its beauty is destroyed. In the same way, the rich man will fade away'(1:11).

[27] We saw something similar in 2 Corinthians 4:4-6. We might note too how Jesus presents the self-authenticating, supernatural power of the preached Word as itself a reason for our faith (Matt 12:38-42). Jesus alludes particularly to the wisdom of Solomon, in whose glory the presence of God was revealed in one of the climaxes of the old testament. In Solomon's story the supernatural spoken 'wisdom' God had given (1 Kings 3:5-12) becomes the 'apologetic' that most impresses the queen of Sheba (2 Chron 9:3,5,6,7), the evident presence of the supernatural on earth. The embodiment of that wisdom, that Word, is of course one reason why Proverbs is in the Bible.

[28] 'Logikos', translated 'spiritual' by NIV, surely relates to 'logos', the Word. It is odd that the NIV does not offer this alternative even in a marginal note.

[29] In a perceptive article on what keeps spiritual movements healthy long-term, in the IFES magazine *In Touch*, 1979-1.

[30] Peter Davids points out that Peter's alternative to the vices listed in 2:1 is not the pursuit of a parallel list of virtues. Instead, it is the self-saturation in the power of God through his Word. In fact 'crave' in 2:2 is the only direct command in the whole passage – that is, the prime thing that Peter summons us to do; the other imperatives in these verses are all dependent clauses. (New International Commentary on the New Testament, *First Epistle of Peter* (Grand Rapids, 1990), p.81.)

[31] Ron Sider cites sociologist Peter Berger to the effect that any community intent on a radical (or 'alien') lifestyle will preserve it amid the surrounding pressures only through a 'strong sense of

solidarity' and by 'huddling together' with 'like-minded fellow deviants very closely indeed. Only in a counter-community of considerable strength does cognitive deviance have a chance to maintain itself.' (Peter Berger, *A Rumour of Angels* (1976), quoted in Ron Sider, *Rich Christians in an Age of Hunger* (1977), p.166.)

[32] Cf. 1 Cor 5:7 for a parallel comparison of Christ to the Passover lamb.

[33] That whole experience was very formative for Peter's subsequent life: cf. 2 Peter 1:16-18. We should note too the Exodus-like image of our body as a temporary 'tent' in 2 Peter 1:13.

[34] Acts 13:22.

[35] Ex 25:8.

[36] Again we sense the personal reference; 'stone' is the meaning of Peter's own name, given him by Jesus.

[37] Surely there is an echo here of God's unending love as acted out in Hosea 1 and 2 (eg Hosea 1:10, 2:23).

[38] Davids observes that this is a common greeting in Christian letters, but relatively rare elsewhere in the period (p.94).

[39] Which, conversely, places a responsibility on rulers to rule in a way that creates an atmosphere where 'godliness and honesty' can flourish (cf. 1 Tim 2:2) - a major issue in some post-communist countries.

[40] Davids, pp.105,115-16. 'The church was drawn from the disenfranchised levels of society, and it offended society by appealing to these people directly rather than through their masters/husbands. It was this adoption of an independent lifestyle that as much as anything brought on persecution' (p.22). Jewish and stoic writers on similar topics do not do anything of the kind. Paul does, of course.

[41] The whole passage reminds us that 'theology', in its widest sense, is learnt as much in relationships as in the lecture-theatre. That is a lesson also of Ephesians 5:25-33 and 1 Timothy 3:4-5 (and possibly 2:15?).

[42] Proverbs 31 offers useful sidelights here. Davids observes that Peter's approach to the cultivation of image would have lessened class distinctions within the Church; released money for ministry; and expressed a radical, unworldly simplicity that has often marked the Church in times of revival (p.118). This remains the case.

[43] In fact this is not a position of total powerlessness. Because

blessing (3:9) has real power, we have a concrete way of actually doing good to those who hurt us (Davids, p.129).

[44] John F. Alexander's *The Secular Squeeze* (Downers Grove, 1993), pp.209,147. Alexander used to edit *The Other Side*. He expounds this theme further from Romans 12 and 13: 'Reconciliation depends on humbly accepting a limited view of your gifts and allowing yourself to be wronged. In my experience, a church (or a marriage, for that matter) can never be at peace if the partners are concerned about their rights. You can only be reconciled if you accept the sins of others in your body, as Jesus did. Everything else is talk. Peace is not benign intentions but a cross with nails' (pp.147-48).

[45] A variant is to see the 'spirits in prison' to whom Christ proclaims his triumph (cf. Col 2:15) as fallen angels; cf. 2 Peter 2:4.

[46] Compare Christ's preaching through others in Acts 3:26 or Ephesians 2:17, and the preaching through the Spirit in 1:12 and indeed Genesis 6:3.

[47] Is the point also that because Noah stood out, refusing to join the 'flood' of debauchery around him (cf. 1 Peter 4:4), he was saved when that flood turned into the flood of judgment?

[49] This assumes that 'baptism now saves you' is not presenting baptism as that moment of new birth that is central to the biblical gospel. That seems clear from other parts of Scripture; we are saved through repentance and faith (Acts 20:21), and Paul makes it very clear that baptism does not form part of his 'gospel' (1 Cor 1:17). Rather, we understand 'saves' here as referring to the ongoing salvational process that is so much a theme for Peter. (Paul sometimes uses 'salvation' this way too; cf. 1 Tim 4:16.) And indeed what saves here in baptism, as Davids notes (pp.144-45), is not the outward washing, but the verbalized pledge made at the time from the conscience; cf. Rom 10:9-10.

[50] The Chinese writer Watchman Nee has a perceptive chapter on this section in *Love Not the World* (1970 edition), pp.27-36.

[51] While writing this section I've been reading the remarkable Russian preacher Alexander Men. Each of his sermons begins: 'In the name of the Father and of the Son and of the Holy Spirit!'

[52] As we noted above, it isn't unreasonable to think of that incident alongside Paul's comments about arming for spiritual conflict in Ephesians 6:13,17. Part of Peter's problem was perhaps

misunderstanding Christ's words in Luke 22:36-38; we need to use our minds, because Scripture doesn't 'arm' us if we misunderstand it.

[53] The last part of 1 Peter 4:1 is difficult. Interpretations include: that freedom from sin comes from full identification with Christ's cross, as in Romans 6 (expressed e.g. in baptism, the theme of Rom 6:1-7 and 1 Peter 3:21); that the person who chooses to follow Christ at all costs, even when it involves suffering, has a mind set free from the rebellion against God that is the root of sin (but cf. 1 Cor 13:3); that to suffer to the point of death means not loss but victory, full freedom from sin, just as Christ our example, by suffering to death, completed his 'exodus' (cf. 3:22) and finished with the effects of sin once and for all.

[54] 1 John 2:15, cf. James 4:4.

[55] Cf. Jesus' comments in Matt 10:26-28.

[56] Paul's wording, in Rom 14:12.

[57] Proverbs 9:10.

[58] 1 Cor 13:7. Both Paul and Peter feel the need to stress the priority of love 'above all' as they discuss spiritual gifts.

[59] It has to be said that the Great Commission does now seem to be not very far from completion, and that is a crucial sign of 'the end'; see Matthew 24:14.

[60] Is there underlying this an echo of Peter's final, climactic conversation with Christ, and its reference (no doubt never far from his mind) to how Peter's martyrdom would '*glorify* God' (John 21:18-19)?

[61] Paul presents a very similar idea in 2 Thessalonians 1:4-5.

[62] As Davids observes, p.174.

[63] Cf. Matthew 20:20-28, 1 Corinthians 9:19-24, John 13:1-15.

[64] Cf. 1 Corinthians 11:1.

[65] Cf. the movement in Habakkuk 3 from the biblically-transmitted vision of God at work in the past (v2ff) to the mindset of faith and praise (v18) in the wilderness of the present (v17).

[66] Acts 12:25, 13:13, 15:37-39, 2 Timothy 4:11.

[67] Cf. 2 Peter 3:18: 'Grow in the grace and knowledge of our Lord and Saviour Jesus Christ.'

[68] And cf. Heb 2:10. Jesus' submission to our experience of ordinary, un-miraculous, 'exile', his self-restraint from using kingdom power, marks such periods as Matthew 4:2-7, 12:39 or

26:53. There is a fascinating interplay between the 'seasons' of 'wilderness' and 'kingdom' in Jesus' ministry: the 'wilderness' time of his self-restraint in Matthew 4:3-7 leads into the glorious outburst of kingdom power in 4:17-25; in contrast, the 'classic' kingdom sign of the feeding of the five thousand (John 6:1-15) leads to his refusal to show his power in 6:30ff, and this 'un-miraculous phase' becomes a crucial test of his followers' faith (v66). (At these times Jesus emphasizes the Word as our permanent source of grace and life: Matthew 4:4, John 6:63.)

[69]'It is comparatively easy...to engage in the service of God when He intervenes in power to sustain His servants and to secure results,' wrote Edward Denny over a century ago. 'But it is only the man of faith who can labour on amid discouragements of every kind, who can trust to a power not seen to uphold and prosper, and is assured that the Spirit, who is invisible in His working to the natural eye, is even more mighty than manifested power...' That is true faith for the wilderness!

Interlude:
A Spirituality for the Twenty-First Century
(2)

What kind of spirituality will give us depth for the new millennium?

It may well not be an easy time. For years the West has lived as if it doesn't matter whether there is a God or not. Slowly, the inheritance of centuries of Christian underpinning to society has eroded. The Christian concepts of the individual's value, of love, of truth, of freedom: all are fast dwindling as the new millennium begins. We may soon be radicals again – possibly a despised and hated kind of radical at that. What roots will give us the strength to survive?

Or to put the other side of the question: what kind of spirituality can offer the genuine profundity that the postmodern world – nauseated by its own dazzling images, sickened by its own shallowness – is yearning for? Where do we find depth?

A spirituality with roots (1)

Jesus' answer is clear. 'Everyone who hears these words of mine, and puts them into practice, is like a wise man who built his house on the rock. The rain came down, the streams rose, and the wind blew and beat against that house; yet it did not fall, because it had its foundation on the rock.'[1] One foundation only; no alternatives; all else is sand.

Recently I've been listening to Grace Morillo, a Colombian IFES staff worker who was hijacked by rebels and held for sixty-eight days. How had God forearmed her to cope, she was asked? By being 'formed in a context shaped by study of the Word', she replied; 'That's how I believe God prepared me for this experience.'

For all of us, if not so dramatically, the storms come; times of 'exile' come. 'Sometimes it is winter', a woman shared at a Lithuanian church I visited recently; 'The cold kills the evil things in our lives; we cannot smile at those times, but we can thank God, and move forward.' But how to live through winter, through the storms? 'My prayer is not that you take them out of the world, but that you protect them from the evil one', Jesus prays to his Father just before the cross; but how? 'Sanctify them by the truth; your Word is truth.'[2] This was certainly his own approach to spiritual conflict; confronted by the 'evil one' in the desert (Matthew 4), he wards him off with three key passages from Deuteronomy. (Some of us would be hard-pressed to make use of one!) For him as for Paul, the 'sword of the Spirit' is 'the Word of God' (Eph 6:17). When many of the disciples buckle under the pressure, it is again the Word that we see keeping Peter alive. '"You do not want to leave too, do you?" Jesus asks the twelve. Simon Peter answers him, "Lord, to whom shall we go? You have the words of eternal life."'[3]

'Words of eternal life.' Central to our spiritual growth is the realization that the Bible is not like any other book. It is alive with its own supernatural life. 'The words I have spoken to you are Spirit, and they are life,' Jesus told us.[4] As Anfin Skaaheim of Norway expounds this: the words are not merely symbolic expressions for the presence of God, they *are* the presence of God.

So it is that the growth of the Church and the spread of the Spirit are one and the same as the spread of the Word. The fruit of being 'filled with the Spirit' is precisely the same as of 'letting the Word of Christ dwell in you richly' (compare Ephesians 5:18-20 with Colossians 3:16-17); the words are Spirit, and they are life. It is striking in Acts to see how Luke closes a phase in his narrative[5]: sometimes he says 'The churches grew' (cf.9:31,16:5), but more commonly it's 'So the Word of God spread' (6:7), 'The Word of God continued to increase and spread' (12:24) or 'The Word of the Lord spread widely and grew in power' (19:20); the two mean the same. We saw in Ephesians how Christ transforms and fosters his Church collectively, making it 'radiant', 'by the washing with water through the Word'[6]; and in 2 Corinthians 3, the Word and Spirit were the supernatural power behind our individual transformation. In every sense, then, the growth of the Church is inseparable from the spread of the Word: as we read it personally, as we gossip about it, as we feed on it in home groups, in public exposition and proclamation. This is depth; this is power; this is spirituality.

A spirituality with roots (2)

Surely, then, a spirituality for the coming century must be rooted in what is most *central* to the Word.[7] That is to say: spiritual depth comes through an ever-deepening grasp of the gospel, in its truest sense.[8] That is not how it works with more 'technical' branches of knowledge, and we are so shaped by the mentality of technique that it is easy to feel spiritual growth will somehow lead us 'beyond' the first principles. It isn't so, because developing (or recovering?) spiritual depth is less like mastering a technique than about deepening (or rekindling?) a relationship. To use Jesus' own image, it is about recovering our first love.[9]

Where do we find this 'heart of the Word', that the Word is most centrally 'about'? An obvious place to look is Paul's summaries of the core of Christian faith. The shortest are at the start of 1 Corinthians: 'We preach *Christ, crucified*... I resolved to know nothing while I was with you except *Jesus Christ, and him crucified.*'[10] Or, at slightly greater length, in 1 Corinthians 15: 'Now, brothers, I want to remind you of the gospel I preached to you... By this gospel you are saved, if you hold firmly to the Word I preached to you... For what I received I passed on to you as of first importance: that Christ died for our sins according to the Scriptures, that he was buried, that he was raised on the third day according to the Scriptures.'[11]

We need a subjective side too, of course: how does God want us to respond to these realities? We're answered in another twin-sided 'crystallization', this time Acts 20:21: 'I have declared to both Jews and Greeks that they must turn to God in *repentance* and have *faith* in our Lord Jesus,' says Paul. Repentance is turning to God, turning from self-rule and our own sinful ways: turning to live a Christ-centred life and do his will, to love the Lord passionately with all our heart, soul and mind and our neighbours as ourselves.[12] And faith: staking everything we are on the Gospel – that Christ has died to pay for our sins and restore us to God, and that now he will live within us as our Lord, bringing new life. (Repentance and faith in the gospel were the heart of Christ's own proclamation, as we saw in Mark 1.)

We might view other aspects as almost equally 'core'. I would turn to Jesus' life as God's self-revelation, and his definition of authentic Christian lifestyle in the Sermon on the Mount; or to Pentecost, and its aftermath in the life of the Church. But what Christ instructed us to remember in the central celebration of communion (and indeed in baptism) is neither the Sermon on the Mount nor Pentecost, but the cross and resurrection. Jesus' body broken, his blood poured out; this is the heart of the matter, this is what we are called to 'proclaim until he comes'.[13] The Messiah and his cross, and the response he desires in thankful repentance and faith, are the core of the new testament, and the consummation of the old. Ephesians is, ultimately, a book about Christ, as we have seen; so is Revelation. At the heart of 2 Corinthians or 1 Peter stands the cross. Books like 1 John, or Mark, point us toward the meaning of repentance expressed in love, and of faith.

Of course there is far more besides, waiting for us as we read the Bible. But what can be more foundational than the realities central to God's dealings with us? So what better starting-point, as we study his Word, than to ask (turning the questions into prayer): Lord, why is this passage in the Bible? What does it tell me about God, about you, Jesus? about your cross and resurrection? What does it tell me about the life shaped by repentance – that is, of ever-deepening holiness under the Lordship of Christ, of love for God and for anyone who can be viewed as my neighbour? What does it teach me about a life shaped by faith, by a vision of the world, that is 'according to the Scriptures'?

The gospel's applications will surely prove far richer than the understanding we start with. But these simple starting-points integrate all we read with the deepest fundamentals. And this could be of increasing importance in the new, 'de-Christianized' millennium. The gospel, after all, is for everybody – but especially, it would seem, for the poor[14], and for children.[15] That explains its character, 'both simple and profound... a pool in which a child may wade and an elephant can swim'.[16] At least in the West, our 'postmodern' generation seems increasingly bad at coping with complex idea-structures. But biblical spirituality presents us with very few foundational issues: if these are in place, everything else makes sense too. It is these few things we absolutely have to keep our hold on, to keep alive and central in our own and the Church's spirituality. (It isn't easy, and it doesn't happen without struggle.) We will always need to return to the roots, the sources; that is why communion is designed to bring us back to them – to Christ, crucified according to the Scriptures, and to renewed, grateful response in repentance, and in faith. These are the realities at the heart of existence; and it is these that we must retain an ever-deepening grasp of, an ever-growing passion for – or else backslide.

Built upon these core concerns, however, our spirituality can spiral out to take in the universe, like the arms of a colossal galaxy. The gospel's implications extend to infinity, and it will take not just this lifetime but eternity to explore and

absorb them. Repentance that commits to loving my
neighbour as myself leads (given Jesus' redefinition of my
'neighbour'[17]) into unlimited commitment to evangelism and
to justice. And we rejoice because, in a culture full of
meaninglessly unrelated information, we can integrate all these
aspects upon a robust, consistent foundation in God's Word.

'I long to see you that I may impart to you some spiritual
gift to make you strong', wrote Paul to the Romans; '...That
is why I am so eager to preach the *gospel* also to you who are
at Rome' (1;11,15). The gospel, he continues, 'is the power of
God'; and 'preach the gospel to you' (the Roman believers!) is
precisely what he does, with all its implications, in this the
longest of his books. Then he concludes in worship to 'him
who is able to establish you by my gospel and the proclamation
of Jesus Christ' (16:25). A spirituality with roots is grounded
in the 'gospel, and the proclamation of Jesus'!

Holistic spirituality – (1) Jesus-centred, energizing prayer

What then makes for a truly holistic spirituality built on the
Word? We can focus on at least seven aspects:

- *It is Jesus-centred, and it energizes our worship and prayer.*
- *It is outward-bound – it equips and empowers us to share our faith in Christ.*
- *It brings us to true and deep perceptions of the real issues in our world.*
- *It demands and empowers biblical action.*
- *It energizes and integrates with our life in the Spirit.*
- *It integrates the physical, symbolic and emotional aspects of our faith.*
- *It gives the only possible foundation for Jesus-style radicalism.*

Emphasis on the Word has its dangers. Western Protestantism has fallen into them head first. We've developed (albeit by talking about the Word rather than feeding on it) something the Word was never meant to foster: a spirituality that goes nowhere beyond the academic, arid and sterile. Paul warned us: 'Knowledge puffs up, but love builds up.' He was right. He went on to make clear what really matters: 'The man who thinks he knows something does not yet know as he ought to know. But the man who loves God is known by God.'[18]

That is what everything is for: that we may love God and be known by God. A Word-based spirituality must always be a Jesus-centred spirituality[19]: focusing us on Christ, helping us to know him, teaching us to follow him, energizing us to love and worship him. We can test our own discipleship by these criteria. 'Just as you received Christ Jesus as Lord, continue to live in him,' writes Paul, 'rooted and built up in him'; on that basis we can be 'strengthened in the faith as you were taught, and overflowing with thankfulness'.[20] It is never wise to spend too long away from learning to know Jesus through encounter with his Spirit-empowered depictions in the Gospels[21] – and encounter that leads directly into worship.

More and more, our Bible reading should turn into praise and intercession. Theology fossilizes when divorced from worship and action – as it too often is. A spirituality for the next century must be 'holistic' in this regard. That is why we have included expressions of prayer and thanksgiving in these studies; such responses are integral to true 'Bible study'.[22] The point of it must be to foster a deepening sense of – or participation in – the glory and love of God, the wonder of Christ and his life, death and resurrection. As Paul summarized his life's passion in Philippians 3: 'I want to know Christ and the power of his resurrection and the fellowship of his sufferings, becoming like him in his death; and so, somehow, to attain to the resurrection from the dead.' This is why we were given the Word at all!

Prayer and worship consummate our thankfulness and love for Jesus, so giving fresh energies for our exploration of the Word. How in turn does the Word energize our prayer and worship?

Probably in at least four ways. First, and crucially, *motivation*. Our culture is one hypnotized by the visible, and by the power of human technique. But a vision for prayer depends on our grasping imaginatively that the real powers in this world are invisible; that what 'makes things happen' is not human skill or resources, but God's power released in response to prayer[23] – 'not by might, nor by power, but by my Spirit'. The Church seems to grow fastest in the two-thirds world (countries like Nigeria) and in 'recently emergent' societies (e.g. Korea or Brazil) – cultures not yet so brainwashed by our media humanism. I was astonished in Nigeria, for example, to see student fellowships holding half nights or whole nights of prayer each week, attended by four hundred students from just one university. Despite real problems, these fellowships are among the world's largest, sometimes numbering a thousand on one campus: dwarfing their counterparts in Europe. Prayer goes with supernatural power! We learn the same from the Korean church and elsewhere.

To recover such prayerfulness, we Westerners need a spirituality that can reverse the brainwashing of the all-encompassing media, and its obsession with the visible. That means we need the Word; both because its way of presenting events prioritizes God's underlying purposes; and also because of its specific passages (Exodus 17:8-16, or 1 Samuel 12:23, or Colossians 4:12-13, or James 4:2; or the priority of prayer in the life of Jesus, Paul or Daniel) that burn into our minds the indispensability of prayer.

How else does the Word energize our prayer lives? Perhaps by giving us *images of the Lord to focus our attention* as we seek to slow down for prayer.

For years my own way of starting to pray was to turn abruptly from the flood of everyday tasks, and rush into God's presence with a stream of requests. It wasn't very satisfying. But it wasn't till my thirties that I learned the value of stopping first, of coming into stillness; focusing worshipfully, perhaps, on the life-giving pictures the Lord has given of his nature: the shepherd finding his lost sheep (Luke 15); 'the King of kings who alone is immortal and who lives in unapproachable light' (1 Tim 6:16); the Father running to meet us (Luke 15 again); the 'sun of righteousness', by whose life alone I live (in Malachi 4); the rescuer in the story of the Good Samaritan; the 'Servant King', coming to cleanse and refresh us in John 13. (And, with them, the Word's pictures of my situation: the lost sheep; the lost son; the traveller helpless at the side of the Jericho road; the disciple, being cleansed by the Lord; or perhaps the tree sinking its roots down into God's refreshment, in Psalm 1.) As we 'pioneer' into fresh parts of the Word, the Lord gives us more and fresh images of himself. Bible reading turns into conversation as we focus thankfully on the aspects of his nature highlighted in what we're reading: the love with which he initiates relationship – that same love which alone has drawn us into his presence now; the holiness in the light of which we examine our hearts as we come to prayer now, in repentance and faith.[24]

But it is also in the Word that we learn *what to pray for*. Our prayer life grows stale when we lose the sense of what needs our prayers. As we learn to 'pioneer' in the Word, however, we learn more of the Father's heart for the Church and the world, and can turn those insights into specific prayer. Soon, there will be far more things that we see need prayer than we can possibly find time for; and our 'prayer lists', like our evangelism, become tied to sensing God's specific callings for our lives. For example: the prayer concerns of Paul that we saw in Ephesians 1 – and the related, but different, concerns in Philippians 1:9 or Colossians 1:9 – apply to the individuals we know, particularly as we see in the Word our surprising power to 'bless', to release God's goodness for each other. And the more we learn from the Word about how mission works[25], or how the church should be, or of God's concerns for justice[26], the more we have to pray about for our own church, for every other church we are acquainted with, for our own country and all others; like Paul, 'wrestling in prayer' for those he has never met.[27]   We begin to sense the astonishing thing God has done, giving into our hands the key that opens the channels of his power into our workplace, our family, our surroundings; we start to commit to the lifelong process of being his 'co-workers' in releasing goodness into the world. The Word energizes such a vision.

Still more does the Word empower our *collective worship*. We grow so tired of the invertebrate triviality sometimes offered us under this heading: the uninspired thoughts, the occasional mindlessness. Yet real praise, real thanksgiving, are essential to energize our collective life, including our collective prayer. So where does depth come from? Isn't it true that both open worship and worship-leading have 'guts', have robustness, directly insofar as they embody fresh insights about God from his Word, that have really passed through the worship leader's heart? This isn't a matter of the leader quoting the odd verse to introduce a song. Rather, it's an issue of storing up life-giving insights, grasped through a 'pioneering spirituality'; continually impacted by fresh discoveries of God's glory, and ready now to channel them onward to the wider blessing of the Church.

Such worship will then energize us in other directions too. 'If you love me, you will obey what I command,'[28] said Jesus. To worship from God's Word in God's presence will focus us on expressing the two great commandments as we come to perceive them, ever more deeply, in that Word. True spirituality expresses its love for the Lord, and then its love for its innumerable neighbours, in creating channels for God's loving power on earth by serious prayer. And then, by other forms of ministry and action.

Holistic spirituality – (2) The Word energizing witness

True spirituality bears fruit or it is meaningless.

In the four preceding chapters we have seen the importance of the vision of heaven and of cosmic transformation to the books we've examined. One of the many things Scripture does is to give our visible world a supernatural context. Our culture needs that; we are little people, and we need the big picture to give our existence meaning.

The twenty-first century will need it still more. As we have observed, the barrenness of the late twentieth century has made clear that we must find a way out of the sterility of the materialist ghetto. Hence the rise of New Age, the bottomless fascination of horoscopes, tarot, feng shui; or at a more exalted level, the triumph of 'magic realist' novelists – Gabriel Garcia Marquez, Ben Okri, Salman Rushdie. But the false promises of transformation with which New Age seduces its adherents are truly fulfilled only in Christ. The hunger will remain in this new century – but it can only be met by a mysticism grounded in reality, in truth, in rationality, in history: in the Word. Twenty-first century spirituality must not be 'over-mystical' (in the sense of losing its base in Scripture) nor 'over-pietistic' (to the exclusion of social or intellectual concerns); but it must make room for the mystical, and it must be pietistic.[29]   Often the gateways to profundity are in what the Word reveals to us of the supernatural. These can be precisely the passages that send theological liberals gibbering to their beds! But we live now in a postmodern culture that has lost profundity and meaning, and is desperately hungry for it. It is there, in truth, in the Word.

The Bible's 'big picture' is about heaven, and the whole of earth. As we saw in Ephesians, 2 Corinthians and 1 Peter, the mysticism leads straight into practical discipleship. Twenty-first century spirituality needs to be both practical and deeply-grounded, both heavenly-minded and streetwise; true spirituality is a radiant unity. 'Growing in Christ', being 'transformed into his likeness with ever-increasing glory', is meaningless unless it bears fruit in passion for those things for which Jesus lived and died. This necessitates a life lived always, consciously, on the frontier: aware that our own bodies are the frontier of the kingdom, that we are empowered by God to be the bridgehead through which heaven's love, truth and power flow out into the world.

This work of outreach was, after all, the point of Jesus' last weeks of teaching. Matthew felt the whole forty days' teaching after the resurrection could be boiled down into three verses: 'All authority in heaven and on earth has been given to me. *Therefore go and make disciples...* and surely I am with you always!' What Luke records from this period has the same thrust: 'You will be my witnesses in Jerusalem, and in all Judaea, and in Samaria, and to the ends of the earth.' Evangelism is what Christ emphasizes here (Acts 1:8) as the single prime consequence[30] of the Spirit coming in power on his Church:[31] an ever-widening gospel commitment to individuals around us, to our whole country, to our whole world.

If this commitment is so indispensable to spirituality, what difference does it make that true spirituality is Word-centred? We have seen the unity above: Luke's way of saying 'The Church grew' is frequently 'So the Word of God spread'(Acts 6:7), 'The Word of God continued to increase and spread' (12:24) or 'The Word of the Lord spread widely and grew in power' (19:20). The two mean the same. But what might this imply in practice? How does the Word-centredness of spirituality impact our evangelism?

First, it again impacts our biggest problem-area: it *motivates*. Believers who desire, deeply and passionately, to reach out to their friends daily with the love of Christ, will find a good way to do it sooner or later.[32] Indeed, the love itself will attract, no matter how flawed the methods. But we live in a system that erodes that desire, brainwashing us to consider the eternal world unimportant. (We never read about it in the papers.) Immersion in the Word's 'alternative input' is needed to 'refresh' our grasp of eternity, our sense that the eternal issues are the crucial ones. It also renews our passion to pray for others; and our witness is powerless until that is happening, because Satan's power has 'blinded the minds' of those who don't yet know God[33], and no amount of talk achieves anything until that barrier has been broken through by the grace of God.

It *empowers*. 'Our struggle is not against flesh and blood, but against... the powers of this dark world and against the spiritual forces of evil in the heavenly realms' (Eph 6:12). Paul's point is not limited to witness, but is surely applicable there; and in his classic treatment of arming for spiritual warfare he presents just two offensive weapons, prayer and the 'sword of the Spirit, which is the Word of God'. We see in practice that the Bible's own words have particular power in our dialoguing;[34] 'Thus says the Lord' has a greater felt[35] authority than do our own opinions!

It empowers us in a broader way too. In the end, we are to be '*my* witnesses', Christ said; it is to Christ that our friends must respond, not merely to a set of ideas. How better, then, than through encounter with the revelation of Jesus in the Gospels that are inspired, and empowered, by the Spirit himself? In the student scene worldwide, we see that creating opportunities for not-yet-Christians to encounter God's presentation of Christ in small-group study of the Gospels is central to fruitful outreach. (Gospel exposition can have the same effect.) Whether initially they 'believe in' the Gospels is unimportant; the point is that they are encountering them, and the Spirit will do his own powerful work through his Word. Our task is to find ways of bringing people to those encounters. ('Practising the presence of God' in our lives, expectantly, may well mean we carry a Gospel with us that we can leave behind after a meaningful conversation.)

Thirdly, the Word gives our witness *precision*. What is our message? Inevitably our way of thinking about what matters

in life grows shaped by the media bombardment around us.
And our way of presenting the gospel can come to be shaped
by those priorities. Up to a point, it has to: the 'felt needs' of
not-yet-Christians we share with are also shaped by that
brainwashing. But in the end that isn't enough, otherwise we
slip from expressing true, radical Christianity into offering
mere socially-conditioned 'religion'. We need to be speaking
to the real needs, not just the ones our culture keeps on the
surface.[36]   I must be reminded by continual re-immersion in
Scripture of what these 'real needs' are: our alienation from
God and his response; emptiness and heaven; forgiveness in
view of the impending judgment, to name a few. Also, I need
my gospel to be biblically 're-balanced'. Some of us, like
myself, are non-confrontational by nature, and re-immersion
into Scripture's priorities is essential to bring back into our
witness the more 'confrontational' aspects of the gospel.
Others are quite 'confrontational' enough already, and need
to be reminded of the enormous, unstinting love of the Father,
the love we see in, say, the story of the lost son in Luke 15.
We need, as Nigel Lee says, a biblical 'illumination of the
whole mind to see things as God sees them'; immersion in the
Word is essential if our gospel is to be *true*.

Re-immersion in the Word is crucial for a fourth reason: it
gives our witness *relevance*. Not many people want to talk
about 'religion'. Our whole culture has been set against it: it
is intrusive, infringing on the privatized space of others. But
there is a way round this. Often what will be meaningful to
others will be what has gripped our own hearts in our
prayerful[37] Bible-reading that week – our fresh source of
enthusiasm about Jesus, about God, about his purposes. In
one sense it is easier: our enthusing about what we've read in
a particular chapter is less threatening than an obviously-
targeted gospel presentation (which we hope will follow later!).
But it also blasts a hole in our friends' prejudices about the
tepidity, the uninteresting nature, of 'religion', as they sense
that we have experienced something real of the glory of God

and the wonder of Jesus. What we enthuse about doesn't have to be related directly to the 'way of salvation'; the important point is that it is genuinely fresh bread. So our regular re-immersion in the Word gives us something to share that may be the first step in 'setting the juices running' for our friends. Real encounter with the Word gives fresh power in our witness.

Lee makes a further point here, that immersion in Scripture equips us to move more simply to the issues as Scripture sees them. In our witness we so often get sidetracked; the more we are soaked in the Bible, the easier it is to (think and) say, 'You know, I was reading a passage in one of the Gospels that I found fascinating on that', or 'Actually, Jesus had something very interesting to say about that'. 'Often they will be willing to follow you into the heart of the thicket where you found the answers,' says Lee. 'The net effect isn't instant conversion, it's rather that folk are more willing to go looking where they will find answers.'

And the Word empowers us in a fifth way too. We grasp in it the reality of God, and we are *strengthened* to take risky steps in witness in our everyday lives; as we grasp God's glory there comes a confident faithfulness about the long-term results of what we do. To step out on the basis of what we have read and take risks in God's service is to learn to live by faith; that experience sends us back to the Word with fresh hunger, and the Word gives us 'backbone' and sends us out again. The Word leads to a faithfulness that sends us back to the Word; we grasp that trust in God's words is justified; we develop what Nee calls a 'history with God'.

Holistic spirituality – (3) The Word grounding understanding

As the twentieth century has drawn to a close, there has been an increasing sense of discontent with the narrowness of individualism: a hunger for a broader, more global vision. Scripture meets that hunger, magnificently.

For this writer's own life, that has been crucial. I grew up in a good church that was deeply committed to the Bible, but had a rather restricted view of its gospel. Sunday evenings saw virtually the same message preached faithfully, week after week. 'Tell me the old, old story', we sang; spirituality seemed to involve being able to hear almost identical things every Sunday and feel enthusiastic about them. And outside, a whole complex world went by. Then I went away to study – and began to glimpse how *wide* the Bible was. There were huge issues at stake in our society: it spoke to them. It had something to say to the central issues in the media, in politics, in culture, in the arts: to Derrida, to Marx, to the music on the cutting edge. In fact, if there was anything really important in the world, then by definition the Bible spoke to it. It made me proud of the Bible, and still more of the God who had given it! That has been vital for my commitment ever since. In science, the best theory is one that can integrate and make sense of the maximum amount of data. Such is God's Word – providing we truly practise a pioneering spirituality, exposing ourselves to all it has to give us. I thank God for that Word!

Postmodern culture faces a vast overload of data; but its denial of values leaves us no path through it. The sheer flood of information makes it hard to know what to focus on, how to tell the superficial from the significant. Ultimately, only a Bible-shaped worldview can integrate it all. 'Give me a long enough lever and a place to stand, and I will move the world', declared Archimedes; the Bible is that place to stand. Postmodern culture can no longer handle the big questions. It is the woman or man soaked in the Word's priorities who can be a 'free thinker', able to start to integrate each issue into a worldview shaped by the way God sees things, and to find a path through the flood of data.

Oliver Barclay offers a perception I have found fruitful: 'We must adopt the priorities of the Bible. Since nothing is as important as the things that the Bible regards as important, the *balance* of Scripture is a part of its comprehensive nature.'[38] That is: We must see what issues Scripture prioritizes, and then learn to prioritize them too.[39] Truly life-giving spirituality depends on 'keeping the fundamentals fundamental', and keeping lesser matters secondary to the Word's – or God's – 'core concerns'. (We touched on this issue three sections earlier in this chapter.) These priorities help us discern what is significant among all the experiences bombarding us; they become reinforced as our thinking blends into our worship. Further, there is a 'fully-roundedness' about what the Word gives us: 'All Scripture is God-breathed... so that the man of God may be *thoroughly* equipped for *every* good work,' says Paul.[40] If we have read, pioneered and meditated widely enough in the Word to have our minds significantly reshaped, we will be 'thoroughly' equipped for what we have to do; no truly major aspect will be missing. Thus 'truth-full' thinking depends on ensuring that our intake of Scripture, and its 'digestion' in prayer, worship and obedience, are sufficient to have as deep an impact on us as the other input we receive.

This process cannot be individualistic; it is only 'together with all the saints' that we will grasp God's truth (Eph 3:18, 4:11-16). That will help us listen suspiciously to the issues we prioritize for application; *are* those really Scripture's priorities? Nor does it mean we have nothing to learn from anywhere else. It means that the Word defines our central agenda, and stands supreme over all other input. But thereafter, can there truly be anyone anywhere from whom we can really learn nothing? The Church is called to stand with the Bible in one hand and the newspaper (or Web-mouse) in the other; keeping our hearts and minds full of the Word, then expressing that Word prophetically in terms of the world's realities.

What a 'pioneering', Word-centred spirituality brings is an imagination shaped by Scripture's priorities, and by sufficient time spent in prayer to sense God applying them

around us. Some of the best interpretative keys for a preacher
are found in the newspaper.[41] We don't want to be moulded
by our environment (Rom 12:2), but we must be able to
respond to its real issues, and to those intuitions of truth it
already possesses. That isn't the full story: we recall the
barrenness that came from liberal assertions last century that
'the world must set the agenda'. Ultimately the questions
that matter are those on God's agenda; if they 'seem not to
matter' to the contemporary world, then we have to pray
and communicate till they do. But the Spirit has been working
at that long before we get there. So where is our world facing
its need, its lostness? Where is it sensing the possibility of
righteousness (Christ-likeness) in the fullest sense, and even
of judgment (John 16:8ff)? These questions show us points
where the Spirit might be opening the way for us; prayerful
absorption – first of the Bible on the widest scale, then of the
newspaper and our neighbours' conversations – can guide us
to them.

There is something self-defeating here about the way
Western theological education trains our leaders-to-be.
Claiming a desire for relevance, for 'merging the biblical and
contemporary horizons', it cloisters its adepts away from their
neighbours, and (too often) trains them to think in jargon
meaningful to ever-decreasing numbers.[42] If we really wish
to 'merge the horizons', then surely our goal will be to create
mindsets skilled at building the shortest possible bridges by
which Jesus'– the Word's – concerns can speak into the realities
of not-yet-Christians around us. For a leader-to-be, that means
firstly being reshaped by the widest possible range of Scripture:
digging deeply into the Word, and into the best Bible teaching
we can find. And then it means getting our fingers close to
the pulse of what matters on the contemporary 'horizon'.

Where do we learn that? To some extent in reflecting,
prayerfully, on the newspapers, the ads, soaps and MTV: still
more, through deep relationships with enough not-yet-
Christians to sense what is really on their hearts.[43] So true

'leadership training', of the kind that helps churches grow, should be passionately biblical, and thoroughly streetwise. Can that be attained in monastic retreat from our neighbours? Logically, shouldn't we expect to learn it through the prayerful listening and relating involved in walking the world with Christ, learning slowly how to bring his life where it is needed? Isn't prophetic relevance – 'biblical and streetwise'– learned in prayer and in evangelism, and in reflection on ministry through minds being reshaped by the Word? Such breadth comes from a prayerful, actively obedient and biblically 'pioneering' spirituality; there is no alternative.

So the development of a Bible-soaked worldview, relating to the whole of human reality, is not merely the acquisition of knowledge, though it includes that; it is 'growth in Christ', learning to see the whole world through the eyes of his Word. 'Knowledge puffs up, but love builds up.' Above all it is Jesus-centred, soaking ourselves in the Word for the sake of his glory and gospel; loving the Lord with all our hearts, minds and strength, and our neighbours, passionately, as ourselves; Bible-based, gospel-focused, grassroots-oriented. Love builds; a biblical worldview is given us not as a hobby or an 'academic field', but to bear fruit[44] practically for the kingdom of God: Jesus' reign growing in my life, Jesus' reign growing across the nations. And then it grows broad enough to make sense of the entire world.

I am deeply thankful for two of the authors who did most to shape my earlier faith, the American guru Francis Schaeffer and the Chinese teacher Watchman Nee. How utterly different they are, and how fiercely they might have argued had they met! But God used their equal devotion to Christ enormously in my life. Schaeffer taught me that biblical faith had breadth.[45] It was almost a saving realization: the 'old, old story' wasn't something shrunken, narrow and marginal, rather it speaks life, to the arts, the media, history, politics, to every sphere of human activity. Reformed thinking at its best! Nee taught me that biblical faith had depth; that in the Word's revelation there are heights and depths, grandeurs and glories of which I had caught only the smallest glimpse.[46]   Heaven and earth, the depth and the breadth, pietism and activism: a twenty-first century spirituality will need it all.

Holistic spirituality – (4) The Word energizing action

A Word-based spirituality isn't an alternative, or competitor, to other aspects of the spiritual life. ('You're into the Bible, but I'm into contemplation.')   Bible reading isn't a total spirituality; there is prayer, mission, fellowship and far more besides.   But what a Word-based spirituality does is provide a profound foundation on which other components can be integrated into a radiant whole, built on the revealed purposes of God.

Sociopolitical action is an example. If we're committed to the Word, we will desire passionately that its life and power be released into the real issues of our world. Within the local contexts of Western fellowships, our instincts are usually to apply the Word to very personal issues, because these are the ones most pressing for most of us. And that is right. But there is far more. We're living in a global village now, where if we trouble to listen we will learn that many sisters and brothers struggle on the very edge of survival.

19,000 African children die each day from hunger- and poverty-related causes. Children of our brothers, our sisters; surely that is the Word's, and our, concern. ('Who then is my neighbour?' the lawyer asked Jesus; anyone whose life you can affect, answered Jesus in the story of the Good Samaritan.) I care passionately about the health and growth of my children. If I were living in sub-Saharan Africa, I would care passionately if my children faced major health risks because my country was planting crops primarily for export: if it was bleeding money from its ill-equipped hospitals, and massively increasing their charges, all to service its huge debts to Western institutions and satisfy the IMF's demands.

('Economic crisis for Westerners means not being able to afford a second car or a holiday in the Caribbean,' Vinoth Ramachandra challenged a recent IFES conference. 'For many of us in the two-thirds world, it means that tomorrow our children are dead.')

Does the Word speak here in terms of hope or justice? Such applications would surely be primary for me if it was my wife, my child, my mother who was going to die, and not just my 'neighbour's'.[47] But this is exactly what is happening this day for my sister or brother in, say, rural Zimbabwe. True religion, states James unequivocally, is about looking after the defenceless (orphans and widows are his example) in their distress (Jam 1:27). Does this not become, therefore, an essential[48] application of the Word for me in London too?

Many of us in the West are incredibly poor at releasing God's Word into these situations. We have scarcely learned where to start. The issues seem so vast. With global poverty, for example, we have been seeking for years to collect money charitably for the world's poor, and then began to realize that our countries' financial institutions were bleeding £9 out of the health and education systems of the poorest countries for every £1 the charities send in. Does Scripture say nothing to that? Most surely it does: in Amos, Isaiah, Habakkuk, James. But how do we apply the Word, what must we do?

Hopefully the next decades will see local churches growing much more adept in targeting practical issues for biblically-minded action. This will include making better use of the World Wide Web. Part of our problem has been that the solutions aren't always clear: we need web sites where biblically-minded believers of differing perspectives can debate the causes and possible steps forward. Another problem is that such issues often need collective action at short notice: we need web sites well known across the evangelical world, where can be posted updated suggestions (in forms easily reproducible for local congregations) of actions that are needed – for example, in poverty-related issues on which congregations throughout the affluent lands should bring the Word to their legislators before meetings of the G8 ministers.[49] This would enable those with shared biblical understanding to respond rapidly in concert across the world. (I mention global poverty as a key example here, but the same need exists for better enabling of rapid, concrete biblical obedience in issues related to abortion law, to pornography, to crises in religious freedom, to the arms trade, or to flashpoints on the ecological front.)

All this is part of a Word-based spirituality for our time; as we allow ourselves to be reshaped by the old testament, we learn plenty about the need for such obedience. At the same time, a Word-based spirituality helps us keep the true priorities central; and that's vital too. Sociopolitical action is essential obedience – yet it is still not the most central issue of all. We have watched liberalism make that mistake, and self-defeat was the consequence. By deifying the social dimensions of faith, they created religious groupings marked by impeccably orthodox manifestos (in political terms), but with smaller and smaller active memberships. Their disregard of the Word's core priorities, the gospel, even of worshipping Jesus, meant, in the end, that their sociopolitical clout became minimal too. (Who in politics listens when the big liberal theologians speak?) One sees a similar pattern threaten the evangelical left when the Word, as a whole, gets neglected.

And finally, if our social action has teeth, it will lead us into situations of conflict and hostility. But what kind of spirituality strengthens God's people for faithfulness when the going gets tough? How can we avoid being infected by the hatred or communal selfishness endemic in some of these issues? And where do we find power for radical distinctiveness in the first place? What fosters the development of people willing to go 'over the top' in their professions for the sake of kingdom values? 'It is Christians who had kept the vibrancy in their faith that you could use, people with a very deep spiritual faith', I recall Filipino evangelical activist Melba Maggay remarking. 'When you have to pay the price, it's your spirituality that counts.' But where do such roots come from? We saw God's answer at the start of this chapter: from the Word – and not just from those passages that speak to sociopolitical issues.[50] So the core, the Word-base, is vital for social action with real impact.

Holistic spirituality – (5) The Word energizing life in the Spirit

To repeat: a Word-based spirituality isn't an alternative, or competitor, to other aspects of the spiritual life. The Word-based spirituality gives a basis upon which other aspects can be integrated into a living whole. So, as we have seen repeatedly, the Word and the Spirit go together in the Bible's spirituality.

Yet this life-giving unity has become seriously fractured in much contemporary church life; what the Bible unites, all too often we have allowed to split asunder.

In Britain, for example, evangelical spirituality is often viewed as a spectrum stretching from the 'reformed' at one end to the 'charismatic' at the other.[51] It isn't entirely caricature to say that a danger at the 'reformed' end is of deep concern for the Word (or at least for 'biblical doctrine') that has little interest in the Spirit; and that the corresponding temptation at the 'charismatic' end is of deep concern for the Spirit (or at least for 'the gifts') that has lost interest in the Word.

This should not be. A pressing concern in the next decade will be what happens to the charismatic movement. Undoubtedly there are all too many places where personal Bible reading seems neglected, little serious Bible study happens in cell groups, thorough exposition is absent and the Bible is allowed to be seen as a little bit dull and sombre. For those of us who have glimpsed how passionate, full-blooded and colourful a Word-based spirituality can be, this is nothing short of tragic; it means the roots are shrivelling. Already one senses parts of the charismatic movement petering out in disillusionment with an occasional flash of sparks ('After renewal, what?'). A month before writing this I listened to a leader of the healthiest charismatic churches in one Eastern European country bemoaning their loss of fire and impact. He went on to say he thought their church members were putting little effort into personal Bible study, and declared his determination to 'start again and make the Bible central'. Recovering a love and a deep grasp of Scripture, a Bible-soaked 'pioneering spirituality', is surely among the most vital challenges facing many contemporary charismatic 'streams'.

But there is much to learn at the other end too. My prayer would be that twenty-first century evangelical spirituality will be one 'filled' with both the Word and the Spirit. In Britain at least we have benefited enormously from cross-fertilization of the spectrum's two ends. The recovery from the tragic years of the early twentieth century, when liberalism strangled so much of our church life, was fuelled by the unshakeable commitment to the Word of (for example) InterVarsity Fellowship (later UCCF), and giants linked with it such as John Stott and Martyn Lloyd Jones: heroes of the faith, men passionately committed to the Word and with links to the 'reformed' end. Yet surely, more recently, what has brought us out of our ghettoes, fuelling evangelicalism's increasing ability to challenge the entire nation's consciousness, has been impulses from the charismatic side: the colourful confidence of the 1970s Jesus Movement; the vigorous commitment to evangelism of men like David Watson, Michael Green and Roger Forster; the fruitful spread of small-group 'Alpha' evangelism inspired by the Anglican charismatics at Holy Trinity Brompton. We should thank God for ministries like the Evangelical Alliance, and UCCF, that have fostered this cross-fertilization. One thinks in contrast of parts of Europe where the gulf between non-charismatic and charismatic evangelicals remains abysmal: where charismatics are not held accountable by non-charismatic friends for capitulation to fads with no basis in Scripture[52]; and where the non-charismatics have not been encouraged by charismatic fire and prayerfulness, and remain huddled in defeatist ghettoes while their charismatic sisters and brothers are out on the streets.

A Word-based spirituality certainly doesn't mean a spirituality disinterested in the Spirit's power! As we've seen in the preceding chapters, the two belong together. Perhaps I can illustrate from my own pilgrimage, as someone from a non-charismatic background. I grew up in a context deeply committed to the Word. I cannot thank God enough for it: those 'roots' have kept me alive! But it taught me to be not just non- but even anti-charismatic. I went to university, found myself in the student Christian Union alongside thoroughgoing charismatics. When we weren't evangelizing together, we were arguing for hours about the things of the Spirit. But they were people of prayer; they loved praying in tongues, but they also prayed more in English than the Christians I had been reared among. I came to see that, whatever minor flaws I could find in their ideas, they were strong in things that mattered. (Meanwhile, some of them were on the move too, hungry for greater depth in the Word.) I came to see that their sheer adventurousness was finding answers to the questions I was asking, about how to evangelize relevantly, how to live church life and the life of the kingdom relevantly, in the contemporary situation. I came to see the point Packer makes, that whatever criticisms can be levelled at charismatic spirituality, by a number of criteria it 'becomes plain at once that God is in it'; for example, in its effects in deepening prayerfulness, evangelistic zeal, generous giving and wholehearted worship (scarcely results one would expect from a work of the devil!).[53]

Later, my wife and I were involved in pioneer student evangelism both in Holland and in Russia. I remember one evening my wife returned from a meeting to set up a witnessing student fellowship. She was deeply frustrated: 'The charismatics all want to pray and get started, but the reformed folk just have lots of questions.'   In one part of Russia I'd found the same.   Because of my background, as we sought partners for student outreach I headed first for non-charismatic churches - some of whose leaders, I must say, had stood firm with massive heroism through the darkest days of persecution. But too often the fears, and questioning, were endless, and fruitless.[54]   In contrast, our first visit to a city where we knew only charismatics (of a somewhat 'suspect' variety) brought a different reaction: 'Well then, we must start praying for the students, and we must plan for an outreach.' Now, to this day I remain totally unconvinced either that Scripture teaches a 'second blessing' or that tongues are for everybody.[55] But we began to feel that in practice, whatever minor criticisms one might make, there was something about charismatic church life that got evangelism and worship started naturally.[56] Also, as we interacted with colleagues from other continents, it was evident that commitment to the Spirit's power marked the majority of the world's fastest-growing churches, for example in Brazil or Nigeria.[57]

There is an extraordinary paradox about contemporary evangelicalism. On the one hand, theoretically at least many pentecostal churches believe that the majority of their members have already, once and for all, been 'filled with the Spirit'. But when Pentecost Sunday comes round, they will be crying out to the gates of heaven for God to fill them afresh. In contrast, many non-charismatic churches see the filling of the Spirit as something continuous, something needing continually to be renewed. And the Word teaches us – in Galatians 3:14, for example – that this was what Christ died to bring us.[58] Logically, then, one would expect seeking the fullness of the Spirit to be a regular passion in the life of non-charismatic churches. Instead, in many congregations, it never gets mentioned. Hasn't something gone wrong here? And what should we do about it?

A further vital issue arises from what we've said earlier about heaven now and heaven to come: about 'kingdom' (the power and reign of God expressed in our world) and 'exile' (the situations where God withholds his power, where we live with the Fall's anarchic consequences). Both of these are realities. Many Western evangelicals need to be reminded of the power of the 'kingdom': that God is not limited by sociological probabilities, that the norm is for prayer to get answered, that God is entirely capable of doing more than we can ask or think. At the same time, many charismatics need to be reminded that God is God; that he doesn't always heal, he doesn't always do what we want; and that this isn't (at least not necessarily) a matter of our lack of faith, but rather of his wisdom. Both sides need to be preached from the Word in the new millennium. My observation, working in a trans-denominational movement, is that if you get a charismatic speaker you tend to get an emphasis on what God can do; while if you get a non-charismatic speaker, you're somewhat more likely to get an emphasis on coping with what God in his wisdom may not do.[59] Both need saying, though at this time in the West one suspects we need a little more expectancy of the former, because of the way the media brainwash us to assume the opposite. But really we must have both; 'kingdom' and 'exile' are both biblical realities we need to understand. We must learn to expect God's strength and power to come into our own situation as we trust him. And yet it's also okay, and sometimes even essential, to feel weak in the wilderness times, as Paul does in 2 Corinthians. We must live by both sets of insights.

It may be we should look back a century to the time before many evangelicals grew nervous even to mention the Spirit for fear of being associated with extreme pentecostalism. Personally I suspect we should look more carefully at the passion for the Spirit expressed by many nineteenth-century evangelicals – giants like Oswald Chambers, D.L.Moody, Andrew Murray, H.C.G.Moule, Charles Finney, Jonathan Goforth, A.J.Gordon, S.D.Gordon, F.B.Meyer, C.H.Spurgeon or Hudson Taylor. About the details (particularly the meaning of 'baptism in the Spirit') they differed; but what unites them all is a passion, based on the Word, for ensuring the filling of the Spirit.[60] Their era laid the foundations for so many of the strongest aspects of modern evangelicalism, and saw the explosion of the modern missionary movement – so probably they were doing something right! (There is in Acts 1:8 a clear connection between the fullness of the Spirit and the missionary spread of the gospel, of course.)

Far more could be said. The point here is that Word-based spirituality in no way involves insensitivity to our need for the Spirit's power. Indeed, let us go further – for the above is not intended merely as a paean to the charismatic movement. The Word is indispensable if, long-term, the life of the Spirit is to flourish. Too many churches with a passion for the Spirit neglect to give their members the roots that would come from equal passion for the Word. In various parts of the world, charismatic church life is sputtering as a result, with impressive rhetoric masking significant dropout rates. Partly for historical reasons, many of our continent's most creative and adventurous leaders are active in charismatic churches; their non-charismatic brothers need to learn from them, and in many ways are doing so. What is unclear is whether the newest generation of charismatic leaders have the grasp of the Word and the gospel that galvanized their predecessors. A crucial, revealing test of the health of specific expressions of charismatic spirituality is how far they are willing, genuinely and seriously, to test new developments by the Word (cf.1 Thess 5:19-22). If this is missing, their movements will not stay vibrant in the coming century; for it is the Word that energizes the life of the Spirit, and wards off counterfeits. (And it is the Word that must energize the Spirit's life in the non-charismatic churches, too. Our experience of ineffective non-charismatic churches has often been of doctrinal commitment that lacks a live tradition of relevant, thorough, wide-ranging – 'pioneering'! – Bible exposition.)

May God grant us a twenty-first century spirituality that is passionate about the Word, and (however it views the details) longing for more of the Spirit!

Holistic spirituality – (6) The whole Word for the whole person

With the charismatic dimensions of faith, then, as with the sociopolitical ones, our Word-based spirituality can integrate all God has to give us, while empowering an overall harmony: keeping the core where it should be, and where it can ensure life to all the rest...

Let's now take another important element (and be a bit more controversial!). A key challenge for twenty-first century spirituality will be our culture's 'postmodern' loss of confidence in rational thought. Without doubt this will bring far more harm than good. But it will mean that spirituality for the coming century cannot function at a purely cerebral level. It will need the imaginative, the symbolic, the emotional, the physical; it will need to know how to 'love the Lord with all your heart, soul, mind *and* strength'.

One of the most intelligent groups of non-Christian students I have encountered in Russia was an astronomical society meeting in St. Petersburg's Palace of Railwaymen. The first time I spoke there, I employed the full battery of apologetics arguments one would use in the West: if this, then that. Afterwards some students said to me, 'You English think much more logically than we do.' It really set me thinking. How does one communicate in a 'less logical' context? By sharing more about our experience of the supernatural, or about the symbolic in Scripture? On my next visit I preached the symbolic aspects of Jesus turning the water into wine in John 2; and it seemed to open windows my earlier presentation could not. Which wasn't ideal, of course: without the rational we can't tell the true from the fake in the mystical realm (and Russia is full of spiritual counterfeits). But I needed to broaden out if I wanted to communicate. And our postmodern Western culture is moving in this same direction; where the merely rational no longer has power, on its own, to convince.

Here, then, is the glory of the Word, and of a Word-based spirituality. It speaks at every level; it offers the rational, but also the mystical, the historical, the symbolic. The Gospels give us historical facts on which to base our faith in the deity of Christ; Romans expounds the gospel in a (relatively) sequential manner. But at the same time there is the poetry of the Psalms, the drama of Job; there is the passionate symbolism of Daniel and Revelation, bringing violent colour into our spirituality. The coming century needs to draw on all the levels of the Word.

It needs to respond to the Word *emotionally*. To understand God truly involves choosing to feel, and to worship, in response to his Word. Some of us have been taught to close off this whole area; it was suspect – too charismatic, or too un-masculine, or too un-scholarly. (I wonder even if some readers feel the prayers in this volume shouldn't be set alongside serious attempts at exegesis. 'Ephesians 1 is glorious!' isn't a comment one expects to find in the cloistered pages of most academic commentaries.) Yet can we really hope to interpret the Bible aright if we're blocking off the response God designed it to evoke? It is, at the least, deeply ungrateful to the Spirit who inspired it then and must open it up to us now.[61] Just as, for a marriage to work, a certain type of husband has to learn, or permit, himself to say 'I love you!', so spiritually we will stay cold until we learn to say, 'God, this is wonderful, I worship you!' (And in a church, when a few people learn to respond like that, the contagion spreads...) This isn't instead of the rational, of course; there must be no either-or here. Liberals' unwillingness to trust the Bible's 'truth-content' has led them to use passages (or creeds) they don't actually believe, for the sake of their 'resonance' to the hearers. That is simply emotional manipulation. In true spirituality the emotional expression must converge with the truth we believe; mind and heart must go together.

But the Bible speaks to, evokes, our response on all these levels. God didn't choose to inspire his Word in the form of a systematic theology. He gave us vast quantities of life-giving doctrine, but nearly always embedded it in specific life-contexts (the Gospels, Paul's letters aimed at very specific situations), where we can watch what the doctrine means in concrete terms.

A spirituality for the coming century will also need to respond to the Word on the *physical* level. Over recent decades British culture has moved away from the its over-cerebral state in Victorian times, and we've begun to listen again to the Word's encouragements: 'I want men everywhere to lift up holy hands in prayer'[62]; 'Praise him with the sounding of the trumpet, praise him with the harp and lyre, praise him with tambourine and dancing, praise him with the clash of cymbals!'[63]; 'Let us shout aloud to the rock of our salvation... Come, let us bow down in worship, let us kneel before the Lord our Maker!'[64]; 'Clap your hands, all you nations; shout to God with cries of joy!'[65] Of course these are specifics of the biblical culture, and nobody's sinning if they aren't into lifting their hands or kneeling. Some of us just aren't built that way. But it seems that more and more people are (a cultural change resulting from our saturation in physically-oriented music, one suspects). And isn't it likely that God chose to reveal his Word in a more holistic culture, and we may often benefit as we listen to it more closely?

More important, though, is the way a Word-based spirituality, paying careful attention to Scripture, helps us see *how* to employ the physical. Music is an example.

Human religion often confuses purely aesthetic uplift (a string quartet in a service, for example) with genuine spiritual experience.[66] A Word-based spirituality helps us grasp the issues here. Music can indeed be an act of 'worship', 'service', in a broad sense (just like any other activity done to God's glory); and such a sense of uplift can be consciously turned into praise; but musical experience that isn't focused on Christ isn't 'spiritual' *in itself*. It's a vital distinction, in an era famished for anything it can call spirituality. Yet there is a real link between musical and spiritual uplift – despite the complaints one hears of music being used 'to get people going'.

If we've dug into the Word, we'll have picked up some insights about this. The Bible makes clear that music does affect our responsiveness to spiritual influences (even if it doesn't explain how); see, for example, 2 Kings 3:15, or 1 Samuel 16:23.[67] And this matches our experience. A set of powerful worship-choruses, or a Wesley hymn with a passionate Welsh tune, leaves us with a sense of elevation, ready and waiting for the (or a) Word.[68] Getting up to preach at such a moment is like surfing on a wave that's already rolling! And that's what we want in the church – but the issue is what comes next. The musical, physical act of worship opens up our hearts; it's meant to, because we're 'whole people'. What's bad is when it's garbage (or candyfloss) that then gets shovelled in! A Word-based spirituality helps us build with the music in a life-giving way.

But thirdly, a holistic, Word-based spirituality needs a place for the *sacraments*.

Now, we can face a serious pitfall here. When evangelicals rediscover the sacraments, they often slip into carelessness about the seriousness of the error that crippled the medieval Church, and had tragic repercussions on so many continents: the idea that to be baptized is to be regenerate, whether or not there is personal faith and repentance. Only eternity will show the tragic consequences of this error in innumerable lives. Or there's the equally crippling variant, that if (and only if) you can keep up your sacramental observance right through to life's closing seconds, then you might make it to heaven; but the sacramental emphasis leaves no assurance, with all the consequences of guilt, uncertainty and frustration (rebounding often into carelessness about sin) that one sees in lands where the dominant faith still talks this way. Our postmodern culture is weak at thinking doctrinally, and easily slips into clutching at something tangible for its hope; one notes astounding naivete among some evangelicals on these issues. The consequences could be heavy in twenty years' time, if those we disciple never grasp their need to set their faith, once for all, on what Christ did on the cross, and to know that they are therefore born again. Such a spirituality stands distinct from the sacramental process of (say) traditional Catholicism, where forgiveness comes by ongoing participation in baptism and the mass, rather than once-for-all repentance and faith.[69] Scripture is clear about all this. In Romans 4, Paul goes to some length to show that faith comes first and the sacramental sign (of circumcision in this case) second; in Acts 20:21, he makes clear what his *gospel* is (repentance and faith); in 1 Corinthians 1:17, he makes clear what it isn't (baptism).

But that's not the end of the story. We must be clear what the gospel is. But then it becomes obvious from Scripture that baptism and communion (like good works) are essential responses to the gospel. For too many of us they have become marginalized.

This has much to do with our history. We owe the gospel's rediscovery, in Britain, to Reformers who were often in reaction to Catholicism's overemphasis on the sacraments. Again, the present health of British evangelicalism owes much to alliances built in a spirit of interdenominational brotherhood, that have focused on our unity in the gospel and downplayed secondary issues. And clearly (1 Cor 1:17) baptism is such a secondary issue. So, for example, we 'Baptists' have downplayed our private concern that, biblically, baptism is for believers confessing their new birth, and hence, ultimately, God's will hasn't been obeyed in its deepest sense by an unbaptized believer. (Obviously that doesn't involve doubting our Anglican friends' regeneration. We know many of them walk far more closely with God than we do![70]) This 'downplaying' has been essential for the unity we've needed as biblical faith has fought for survival in a hostile climate. But as a result the whole matter can become marginalized, in our own thinking and our local church's. And that's bad. It is utterly wrong for believers to ignore Christ's command to be baptized as they (on reflection) understand the term; but that can often be the consequence.

It won't do. The coming century will need that element in a truly Word-based spirituality that the sacraments provide. If evangelicals don't figure this out, people will be drawn to where they find sacramental experience, even with some highly unbiblical baggage hidden beneath it. Baptism and communion matter because in them faith is expressed in physical, material terms. We need such 'symbols' to help us to a truly holistic discipleship. (The word 'symbol' is too weak if it sounds merely like a communication tool. Calvin and Luther weren't wrong in trying to express the sense of God at work as we partake in faith of the sacraments.)   If all we have is ideas – vital though these are: 'the words that I have spoken to you are Spirit and they are life'– there is a danger that our faith will be purely cerebral. In postmodernity especially, we need symbolic expressions that impact us on a physical, emotional level, because our faith has to be lived out on a physical, emotional level.

Take baptism. (I ask the forgiveness of my paedobaptist reader and offer these next three paragraphs to him/her as an expression of how things look from the other side of the fence.) Biblically, baptism involves a deep *submergence* (the Greek word means 'dip' or 'sink') in water symbolizing our total identification with the death of Christ. We are as dead to the old world as he was.[71] (Cf. Romans 6:3-11.) And that 'deep, devout drench in the pool' operates at so many levels. Faith suddenly ceases to be discreet, private and safe. Everybody sees you (because the baptismal confession is public; many of us invite our not-yet-Christian friends and family to watch). It is very physical and very embarrassing; you do get very wet, you do come out looking very odd. ('Who would have thought the boss would let himself be seen in public like that?') It is often profoundly emotional, deeply cathartic.

It's meant to be; that catharsis often leads to a new level of commitment (and sometimes, it seems, of spiritual warfare too). If we take them seriously, passages like Galatians 3:26-27, or Acts 2:37-38, Romans 6:3-4 or Colossians 2:12 underline how very, very close, for the new testament, is the link between inward faith and outward confession in baptism. '*All of you who were baptized into Christ have clothed yourselves with Christ*'; '*having been buried with him in baptism and raised with him through your faith...*' For many of us, a truly Word-governed spirituality will lead us to confess that we wouldn't have mentioned baptism here! Now, these verses don't force us to say that water baptism is identical with the moment of new birth. Such a position leads to impossibilities[72]; plus we face the overwhelming majority of texts when the Bible identifies believing faith as the gospel's heart,[73] and the coming of that faith almost never coincides with the act of baptism. But a Word-governed spirituality must take that minority of 'odd texts' seriously, rather than just reading them as saying what we already know from elsewhere. And they do show that, for the biblical writers, to have faith and to be baptized are *almost* synonymous. Those who have put their faith in Christ, and those who have been baptized, are, for the new testament, the same groups of people.[74]

Plus, as 1 Peter 3:21 says unmistakably, 'Baptism saves you.' As we'll see when we look at Romans, 'salvation' in the new testament by no means always refers to our receiving forgiveness at new birth; it can also refer to the ongoing salvation that is spreading out across our personalities. (See, for example, Philippians 2:12, or 1 Timothy 4:16.[75]) So it is in the broader sense that, as Peter observes, this 'pledge of a good conscience' which we express in the cathartic act of baptism contributes vitally to our ongoing salvation. It does make a real difference. That is why, if we pay attention to Matthew 28, we find that 'making disciples' in the Great

Commission leads first of all into our baptizing people.[76] To say this may be to go beyond what our sometimes over-cerebral tradition is comfortable with; we distrust the emotional, communal gesture[77], preferring (and with some reason) the mental step taken alone in privacy. But, as so often, we need them both here; and a truly Word-based spirituality, one that listens carefully to the verses we 'wouldn't have phrased quite like that', leads us beyond our inherent biases, and delivers us from the merely cerebral. It leads us to give to physical, emotional expressions of faith an importance greater than our cultural background might choose; it recognizes them, indeed, as means of (in the broadest sense) *salvation*.

The bread and wine, again, are central to the practice of a biblically holistic spirituality. Having focused our hearts and minds on the meaning of the cross and resurrection, we take the bread and wine: 'This is Jesus' body.' 'This is Jesus' blood.' The smell of the fresh bread, the flavour on the tongue of the richness of the wine: 'This is my body, which is for you. *Do this*, in remembrance of me.'[78] Moments of silence to think, to reflect, to worship in the light of the Word; to assess our relationships, to confess our sins; to re-examine and reaffirm our discipleship in the light of the revelation of the cross.[79] This is holistic – Word, sacrament and personal action building on and reinforcing each other.

I find it tragic to visit strong evangelical churches where communion has become marginalized. The Word is preached; a closing hymn is sung. And then most of the congregation melts away (for coffee, which embodies fellowship in the way the communion bread should do?). Meanwhile a few of the stalwarts – may the Lord help us, mostly the elderly – remain for communion, tacked on for five minutes at the end, led by a weary pastor whose adrenalin has dropped sharply after an insightful and passionate sermon. It should not be so. 'This is Jesus' body.' 'This is Jesus' blood.' These are holy, climactic moments; it is Christ himself who called us to 'do this in remembrance of me'. At every level in our being we interact in this moment of communion with the cross that stands at the centre of the universe. We need to gaze on it, and gaze on it.

I grew up in a church whose spirituality centred on weekly communion, and know only too well how that can sometimes go wrong. There is a world-denying negativity (and repetitiveness) that can result when Calvary is stressed without the exultant joy of the resurrection; a shrunken faith that results if the full input of the Word is lost, seeing only the aspect of redemption from judgment, rather than unpacking all the glorious facets of the cross, resurrection and pentecost. Yet our habit kept in focus an essential reality: this, even more than, say, the Sermon on the Mount, is and must always remain 'the heart of the matter'. We drift so easily: so many valuable but secondary issues– organizational, doctrinal and spiritual – usurp the centre of our vision that belongs to Christ, and the cross and empty tomb where his glory was supremely revealed. We need to think hard how to keep central the experience of what that bread and wine and that cathartic baptismal water signify: not instead of the Word, but acting out, responding with our entire being to, the gospel revealed in the Word. We need it at the heart of a 'whole-person' spirituality for the coming, increasingly de-verbalized century.

In these varying ways, then, we find that a sensitively Word-based spirituality isn't an alternative or competitor to other aspects of spiritual life. Rather, it's the only possible base on which the physical, emotional aspects of spirituality can be wisely and harmoniously integrated. The Word is what holds everything together. Praise God for his Word!

Holistic spirituality – (7) A radicalism with foundations

Around the turn of the century there has been a sense of ecumenical carelessness in the evangelical world. The postmodern mood makes it so difficult to think with doctrinal precision; it acts as a kind of narcotic, making it hard to care about those issues of the Word's authority which mark out evangelicalism (charismatic or non-) from its alternatives.[80] But we must, if our spirituality is to remain rooted in the Word and full of life.

Three historical factors may render this particularly important.

First, as we've suggested, it may be that the charismatic movement is at a turning-point. Did it owe something to– did the Spirit use – the social characteristics of the baby-boomer generation?[81] And is it now, in turn, swimming against the tide with Generation X and their successors – generations much more cautious, stressed, sceptical, much more inhibited about self-expression? At any rate one senses a search for new impulses; and sometimes (as in many parts of our culture) a retreat into the safety of a 'tradition'.[82] But among Christendom's traditions are some very weak in the Word, having discouraged its circulation for centuries: traditions that preserve both strengths and errors from the ancient past. All traditions (including, most definitely, evangelical and charismatic traditions) need continual re-examination in the light of the Word.

There is a second factor, for which we have a grim historical example. Just a century ago, vast swathes of Western Protestantism drifted into a liberal theology uncommitted to the Bible.[83] Within a few decades the results were obvious: those churches and denominations lost their spiritual energy and dwindled (at great cost to their nations), while – in time – churches and movements receiving life from the Word grew and became established. But then a further shift occurred: people who would never have worked with 'evangelicals' earlier (when the term had the ugly overtones of 'fundamentalist' today) began to seek roles within the evangelical institutions – so diluting their positions until Bible-oriented spirituality often becomes regarded merely as 'one of the great Christian traditions', one of the options on offer for the religious-minded. For ourselves there are real attractions in this respectability, in no longer facing the scorn that was heaped on our predecessors. But it comes at a heavy price when it involves politely refraining from 'contending for the faith', as Jude puts it, and when the word 'evangelical' becomes diluted to have little concrete meaning. Arguably, that is where we are now (especially, perhaps, in many Western seminaries).[84] The need to 'contend for the faith' might well seem as acute as ever, except that a 'tolerant' postmodern climate is one in which it is terribly bad manners[85] to do any such thing. We have a grim warning in the catastrophe of a century back, when vast numbers of churches lost all their impact through the careless acceptance of influences which watered down the Word's reliability. It's all too easy to see how we might repeat that mistake.

There is a third factor, also linked to our postmodern climate. Sometimes we're told that the struggle for the trustworthiness of Scripture is safely over: 'The battleground has moved from whether we're "Bible-believing" to whether we're "Bible-practising"... What marks us out as Christians isn't our distinctive belief but our distinctive practice.' It's a false either-or, and, again, potentially calamitous. If we know Genesis we'll know that a central question from the very outset of spiritual conflict was, 'Did God really say..?' (Gen 3:1). That question will never stop being thrown at us – whether openly or covertly. We'll recall, too, that Jesus' approach to spiritual warfare was centred on the repeated affirmation 'It is written...'; if that confidence in the Word is so central for our survival, it is sure to face continual attack. Right belief and right practice are inseparable; as we have seen in Ephesians and 2 Corinthians, biblical ethics build directly on biblical doctrine. Both, therefore, will remain unending battlegrounds. Our postmodern environment trains us to think that the specifics of what we believe are no longer important; all that matters is our actions. But one flows from the other. If we grow careless about the Bible's authority we leave ourselves unarmed at the level of thought, and undermined at the level of action also.

Yet there is an even bigger issue at stake. The real issue in our commitment to the Word is about *truly following Jesus.* 'The Lord Jesus did not only cherish a high view of Scripture; he submitted to it himself as the ultimate authority in his life and ministry, with certain conviction that "What Scripture says, God says",' writes Ghanaian leader Gottfried Osei-Mensah.[86] 'When therefore we affirm the divine inspiration, truthfulness and authority of both the old and new testament Scriptures... we do so on Jesus Christ's authority.'

Following Jesus in this way has been crucial for the Church's life at various points this century. The story of the student Christian Unions is a classic example. In the late nineteenth century, there arose a vibrant group called the Student Christian Movement. It spread rapidly around the world, sharing the biblical gospel with enthusiasm and mobilizing mission wherever it went. Almost the only major difference between the SCMs and today's Christian Unions was that the older SCM leadership were anxious to include Christians of all persuasions in their enterprise; they refused to insist on any doctrinal basis ensuring that leaders were committed to the Bible. Within a decade of the foundation of WSCF (the worldwide SCM), the results were obvious. The British movement, for example, decided by 1906 to 'adopt frankly the modern position about the Bible' and 'shake itself free' from its former commitment to the Word's authority. A paralysis of evangelism and Bible-based devotion and thinking followed; within a further twenty years it no longer expected its leaders to affirm even the Trinity or the deity of Christ. The consequences have been exactly what one would expect. Across Europe today the SCMs are heavily liberal in theology, and have minimal impact on the universities.

But God had his alternative. There was a crucial moment in Cambridge in 1910 that would have massive results in the student scene. In direct opposition to the trends fostered by the SCM establishment, the local CU leaders reaffirmed radical commitment to the Bible and the gospel, and withdrew from the national SCM. The issue at stake, for them, was obedience to Jesus: it was, they argued, 'sufficiently reasonable' to hold that view of the Bible 'which Christ himself held'. This was a very lonely position to take; they were labelled 'old-fashioned', and they faced almost universal criticism. But because they held their ground, it was from Cambridge (and the London medical schools) that there arose, twenty years later, the CU movement which has had such enormous impact for church growth this century; and from Britain and Norway (which saw a similar turning-point in 1924) arose the international movement known as IFES, which impacts the universities with the gospel in 140 countries today. Those students' determination to hold to the Bible's full trustworthiness, centrality and authority was to have incalculable significance worldwide.

History shows us many similar examples; holding fast to the Word means, ultimately, holding fast to life. And the central issue here is the way Jesus looked to the Bible.[87] As we read the Gospels, we find Christ responding to Pharisee traditionalism or Sadducee anti-supernaturalism with that repeated, radical challenge: 'Haven't you *read*...?' (Matthew 12:3,5; 19:4-5[88], 21:16,42, Mark 12:26). We find him setting God's Word authoritatively against human tradition, even that of the chosen people (Mark 7:6-13); we find him challenging the rebellious Jewish theologians with 'Are you not in error *because you do not know the Scriptures?*' (Mark 12:24). (As Stott has observed, Jesus was clearly unafraid to be a controversialist!)

Again, Christ's teaching frequently – deliberately?! – builds on those very parts of old testament history that would make later, theologically liberal, academics squirm with embarrassment: Sodom, Noah, Cain and Abel, even Jonah! (Matthew 11:23-24; 12:41; 23:35; 24:37[89]). Jesus confirmed

that the old testament law contains no mistakes. 'Until the
heaven and earth disappear, not the smallest letter... will by
any means disappear from the Law until everything is
accomplished', he says in the Sermon on the Mount; 'Anyone
who breaks one of the least of these commandments and
teaches others to do the same will be called least in the kingdom
of heaven' (Matt 5:18-19). Biblical prophecy is, for Christ,
again God's entirely trustworthy Word, the fulfilment of
which governed the future, even his own – evidently with no
capacity for error. Continually he shows how his life, death
and resurrection are in total conformity with old testament
prophecy. (For example: Matthew 26:24,54; Mark 12:9-12;
Luke 4:18-21; 18:31-34; 22:37; 24:25-27, 44-47.) As his
followers, we must take careful note of how Jesus operates
here. His attitude to the Bible clearly wasn't some minor
accommodation to his culture and surroundings. Rather, the
dependability and authority of the old testament and its ancient
prophecies were basic to his whole self-understanding.

It is as Jesus' followers, therefore, that we now make the
crucial refusal to correct Scripture by contemporary opinion,
preferring rather to allow our own decade's limited
conclusions to be corrected by the eternal Word.[90] (Ultimately,
this choice – what finally shall we base upon, God's Word or
this decade's opinions? – may be the fundamental difference
between the 'evangelical' and the 'liberal'.) It is on Christ's
authority, too, that we look to the Word as our final criterion,
supreme even over the tradition of the Church, and are willing
to 'contend for the faith',[91] just as Paul was willing to stand
up to Peter at Antioch when the nature of the *gospel* was at
stake.[92] We know these are not just esoteric philosophical
debating-points. Rather, the refusal to commit to the Word's
final authority leads in time to a different message, and an
entirely different approach to Christian life and discipleship.[93]
Only if God has clearly spoken can we share the good news
with certainty as 'Thus says the Lord'; if we do not have a
trustworthy Word from heaven, our liberating gospel

proclamation will dwindle, in time, into mere religious exchange of views that never comes close to 'conversion'. (And we certainly see that happen.)

Likewise, it is only if our teaching and ethics are founded on a trustworthy Word from God that we can be certain they are more than our own bright ideas, and so be able to march with confidence against the fashions of our own particular decade. Prophetic critique and radical holiness build on the certainty that 'This is the Word of the Lord!' Ultimately, indeed, a full-blooded, Word-governed spirituality is the only true radicalism. In our thirst to follow Christ we must be, as Stott puts it, *'radical conservatives'*: unshakeably committed to the trustworthiness of the whole Bible and all it teaches, then radically, creatively consistent in all its applications to personal and communal lifestyle and mission. But any other 'radicalism', choosing what biblical passages it prefers to obey and believe, will in the end be moulded by the various changes of fashion in its culture's thinking.

'What Scripture says, God says.' Robust commitment to the Word's authority is the essential backbone for vibrant spirituality. In affirming it we are treading in Paul's footsteps: as when he challenged the Corinthians regarding what was 'of first importance', insisting that the gospel he preached was 'according to the Scriptures'.[94]

But most important, when we set our hearts on such a spirituality we are following Jesus. He shaped his life in unqualified commitment to his Father's flawless Word. As his followers, we cannot do otherwise.

Growing a life-giving spirituality

The twenty-first century urgently needs a holistic, Christ-centred, 'pioneering spirituality', with its foundations deeply grounded in the Word. How then, finally, shall we cultivate it?

The first step is to decide – individually and collectively – that we want it!

So, if our working day permits, we will set aside some fixed time daily for absorbing the Bible personally. If it doesn't, we will train ourselves in the habit that, each day, as soon as we have some disposable time, we give it to Christ and his Word: at any rate, deciding each day when we will meet with God tomorrow, and then protecting that time. (We can say we are busy then! We have, in truth, a highly important meeting![95]) Easy to suggest, of course. This habit of meeting God daily is perhaps the most important thing a young believer can learn; and families particularly need to affirm each other in it. Since it is so crucial, it will be a constant area of satanic attack. We win some weeks, we lose some, particularly when there is stress at work or in the family, or at times of lifestyle change. The thing is never to give up. Learning to use fifteen minutes daily on a train is far better than nothing. To miss a time with God isn't a deadly sin; we simply try to get it right the next day. Failing to have a real talk with my wife for a day or two isn't a deadly sin either, and it doesn't mean the marriage is over. But, if I am wise, I'll ensure it doesn't happen too often. Otherwise the relationship will suffer as we begin to feel like strangers to each other – precisely the problem we sometimes feel with God.

And how shall we use our time absorbing the Word? We vary it, because there are at least two styles of Bible study. In one we speed-read a book, getting the overall idea, passing over the difficulties for now: three chapters a day perhaps (that takes less time than to go through a good newspaper). Three chapters a day takes us through the whole Bible each year; and by the fourth year, even the obscurer books will be feeling familiar, as we have some sense of their direction. (Some books, Jeremiah for example, are not so nourishing at lower speeds!) But we need the other style too, where we read each verse carefully, listening out for the unexpected, chewing away at the difficult parts.

We pioneer, we explore. We venture into the Bible books we haven't read before. We know the Lord has nourishment for us throughout his Word, and that for a balanced diet we need the whole of it. Sometimes our pioneering will need the backup of a good commentary (even if George Muller was right, that it's best first to read a new book with God's help only; the commentary comes afterward). A German friend decided to 'pioneer' in the minor prophets. It gave her, she said, a 'broader vision of God. It never struck me so much before – God's amazing love, in Hosea, and to think that he loves us like in a marriage. And then Amos: God's seriousness about our behaviour and what we call our minor sins. It's true, each book has its own special message.' But these aren't the easiest books, and she found she needed a practical commentary: or at least a Bible study guide 'with some questions just to give you a few rough ideas what the issues are – otherwise I wouldn't have got all these things out of it'.[96] We're laying up treasure for heaven as we invest in a library of such aids (and as we lend them to others!).

We pioneer, we explore. As we do so, we know that God foreknows both what we will read and what will happen to us that month, and has planned for the one to meet the needs of the other. We venture into new parts of the Bible, confident that the Spirit goes with us to teach us, because it is his Book. We ask him about it, trusting him to put his answers into our minds: 'Holy Spirit, what is this doing here in your book? What is this passage really about?'

We respond. It is a real conversation: God speaks to us through that day's specific passage from his Word; we respond to him equally specifically in worship and in prayer.

Maybe we carry one verse or idea with us, to chew on during the day. 'Do not let this book of the law depart from your mouth,' God told Joshua, 'meditate on it day and night... Then you will be prosperous and successful!'[97] (The 'book' in which Joshua was called to meditate day and night was presumably Genesis through Deuteronomy – a somewhat

tougher diet than faces us today!) 'Meditating day and night'
sounds a little like Paul's challenge to 'pray without ceasing':
having something from God running at the back of our minds
throughout the day, and bringing it to the front occasionally,
so that his presence is the background to whatever we're doing.
(Some people find a Bible memorization scheme helpful
here.[98])

Maybe we can pass it on. 'Give, and it will be given to
you', said Jesus; an essential part of pioneering is learning to
share what we've seen with not-yet-Christian friends, with
fellow-believers, in our church. ('The most loving thing you
can do is teach people this Book,' says Rico Tice.) Often the
freshest insights we've received from God will carry the most
vibrancy as we talk with friends who are not yet believers.
They may not quite fit into our 'gospel outline', but they will
carry the scent of God's presence. They may even broaden
horizons for a jaded homegroup. It may take boldness to step
through an unwritten rule that to share a new discovery from
Scripture is to sound naive or super-spiritual... or, more likely,
arrogant. But the mutual exchange of what God is giving us
('Hey, I read this on Monday, didn't quite understand it,
but...') is meant to be basic to Christian communal life. When
you come together, says Paul, *everyone* has something to give
(1 Cor 14:26)...

Vision for pioneering is also a communal matter.
'Spirituality' can be an area swayed by fashion; yesterday we
'caught the fire', today we go Celtic. That's not entirely
wrong, providing the options are all truly grounded in the
Word. There is more to God than we will ever grasp at any
one time, and at different stages he may steer us towards
different input, to give us a broader sense of himself and of his
will for us. But as we saw in Ephesians 4, not 'every wind of
teaching' is beneficial, and the gifts of the Spirit are given to
ward some of them off. There are fashions that displace or
eclipse the hunger for God's Word. Or there are fashions that
offer a uselessly 'easy way', the spiritual equivalent of junk

food. The Bible was designed to be difficult in parts, to 'take some chewing'; otherwise it couldn't continue to give us nourishment over a whole lifetime. But because of that, our collective church life needs to reinforce for us the encouragement to keep on pioneering in it.

Above all this involves the hearts of a church's leadership. If they themselves are not digging into Scripture, they will create an atmosphere in which it grows rare to do so – where it sounds 'super-spiritual' when (say) a woman comes to church bubbling over with lessons she's learnt in Isaiah. Every church leader should be 'able to teach', Paul instructed Timothy, even though only some would have 'preaching and teaching' as their special work.[99] That is: every church leader, whether gifted in public teaching or not, should be 'able to teach' in the sense of drawing nourishment from exploring the Word, and passing that Word on, one way or another, to other sisters and brothers. If church leaders aren't doing that, they soon become merely 'managers' – and we see that happen often enough. The Church grows as the Word spreads, we have seen; leaders may not have a gift for public teaching, but they must surely have a hunger for learning God through his Word.

Thus their concern will be to set the whole church 'pioneering': to create an atmosphere where everyone is learning to explore the Bible for themselves. Their teaching programme will include specific sessions at regular intervals on how to do this. They will teach Ephesians 4, that the Body 'grows and builds itself up in love as *each* part does its work... joined and held together by *every* supporting ligament'; because the whole church needs the discoveries that each of its members should be making, whatever their age-group, education, gender or years in the faith. They will encourage house groups to be places where people are sharing, and praying through, their discoveries from week to week – and their questions. They will discuss Scripture informally among themselves, for its own sake. And they will model the humility of seeking to learn from each fellow-believer, rather than allowing any sense that pioneering into the less well-known sections of Scripture is only for the academic or theologically trained.

I've watched it being done. In my student time, we often had Sunday lunch with a church leader and his wife. Margaret is an excellent cook. And halfway through the meal, one of them might suddenly say (setting a Bible between the sprouts and the gravy), 'I've been reading Timothy this week, listen – what do you make of that?' And a new Christian present might respond (accurately or not), 'It sounds like what I've been reading for the first time, and it's brilliant...' Then across the table someone finds the courage to ask, 'Yes but I never understood that next bit...' It happened, not once nor twice; and by the end of the meal everyone present had caught some new reminder of the glory of God and his ways.

A leadership concerned for a spirituality with roots will foster this atmosphere of discovery. They will ensure that worship has a solid backbone of biblical input. They will be praying how to give the church a feel for the overall sweep of Scripture, over a period of time in the church's teaching plan. Nor is this merely the business of the leadership! It is for all church members to pray for their preachers and worship leaders, that God will anoint them with his Spirit and his message. We all suffer if cynicism replaces expectancy in this regard. It is tragic to see a congregation where people don't bring their Bibles: it says a lot about our expectations! But a congregation 'living by faith' in the Spirit's desire to teach them will be bringing notepads too, if we believe God Almighty has something for us that he wants remembered beyond lunch... Members of black churches both in Britain and America will often comment verbally – or even pray for the preacher – as the teaching proceeds. It's a good idea; even a dull sermon can be made meaningful to a listener who prays or thanks God silently every few minutes for something that is being said. (We are, after all, in God's presence, no matter how apparently weak is his messenger.) And it is striking – as

at a Welsh church we visited recently – to watch a whole
congregation silent in prayer for a couple of minutes as the
service closes: God's gift is being put to use, the message is
being internalized and responded to in prayer; conversation
is happening with God.

Thus the Word 'increases and spreads' in a church as it is
absorbed at three levels. Fostering the habit of personal Bible
exploration throughout the fellowship is the foundation. Then
the small-group Bible study and large-group exposition
complement each other. Both do what the other cannot. In
the home group, questions can be safely asked, difficulties can
be raised and explored, and the whole thing is earthed in an
atmosphere of mutual caring, and responded to in specific
prayer. But the large-group exposition has its place too, when
the Word is explored systematically and with a power
impossible in any other context. Out of that flows a sense of
unified vision, of a community glad to be together and going
somewhere with God.   The Church in Acts grew as 'the
Word of the Lord spread widely and grew in power': the more
the Word flows into the church, the more there is to flow
out.

We need to learn from each other, because none of us
knows the whole story. If Scripture is indeed the living,
undiluted Word of God, we must 'keep our windows open'
for it to surprise us with fresh insights, the passages we 'would
not have put quite like that'. It's all too easy to domesticate
them into the shapes of what we already know – so learning
nothing. Listening for the unexpected is the only (gradual)
way out of what is called the 'hermeneutic circle': the trap
where we only find in the Bible what we came expecting to
see. Somehow, that circle must become a spiral. It is true
that, as we read, we tend to find what we expected; but little
by little we can learn to welcome the unexpected, which in
turn, under God, transforms our approach to the Word for
the future. We must allow God, in his majesty, to teach us
(for we have hardly begun) things greater than we have

expected, thought or dreamed. Only such spirituality is truly submitted to Scripture as the authority over our thinking.

There is, then, an adventurous open-endedness about pioneering biblical spirituality that speaks to the open-endedness of postmodernity. We recognize, as Jude did, an authentic 'faith' that must be 'contended for' against alternatives, un-contemporary though that will be; we know, as Paul affirmed, that there is a core gospel (the things 1 Corinthians 15:3 terms 'of first importance') that must at all costs be maintained, in the face of deceptively similar substitutes. (Paul doesn't greet the false teachers of Acts 15 as 'friends from a different tradition from whom we can learn a lot', even though they too were evidently 'Christ-followers' in some sense: his 'contending for the faith' is clear and uncompromising.) The 'doctrinal bases' that define the foundational gospel understandings of the Evangelical Alliance, or of IFES and UCCF, serve precisely to define this core biblical faith; 'liberating truths', as Samuel Escobar writes, 'dynamic elements within movements of renewal that God has used to keep his Church alive';[100] affirmations ensuring we stay aligned with the true sources of life, and the realities of the life and salvation of God. But beyond these central certainties, we do well to be humble about our possession of every jot of truth. 'God still has more light to break forth from his holy Word,' as one of the Pilgrim Fathers said. In postmodernity that is a healthy note to strike. 'Now we see but a poor reflection as in a mirror; then we shall see face to face' (1 Cor 13:12). We cannot imagine how much we have still to learn.

So our pioneering must be hungry, and open, for more of God: hungry for a deeper grasp of the central realities, hungry too for all he has for us as we go on pioneering, and learning via the rich breadth of the Bible-believing community. The person who stops growing is a backslider; the person who stops pursuing the Way has lost it almost as much as if (s)he had turned aside. And that's the point of the impressions in the previous chapters, and the ones that follow. God has far more for us in his Word; and we've tried to capture a little of the way that, day by day, 'unreached' parts of Scripture can be a source of roots and of regeneration to a 'pioneering' spirituality. And beyond that, how they can be sources of active love for our neighbour, and for the world: above all, of active, worshipping love for Christ.

That's our hope now, therefore, as we look at parts[101] of three further books. 'Come farther up and farther in!'[102]

Notes

[1] Matthew 7:24-25. Cf. Psalm 1's blessing on the man who 'does not walk in the counsel of the wicked... His delight is in the law of the Lord, and in his law he meditates day and night. He is like a tree planted by streams of water, which yields its fruit in season, and whose leaf does not wither' – having roots, unlike the wicked whom 'the wind blows away'.

[2] John 17:15,17. In the toughest period hitherto of my own life, Hebrews became incredibly meaningful as a source of insights that were 'roots', holding me firm, keeping me from falling away. So much so that, after working through it twice, I found myself almost afraid to move on into another book!

[3] John 6:67-68. Cf. 1 John 2:14: 'I write to you, young men, because you are strong, and the Word of God lives in you.'

[4] John 6:63. See also Matt 4:4.

[5] Cf. David Gooding's excellent commentary, *True to the Faith* (1990).

[6] Eph 5:26.

[7] This 'centrality' isn't a very postmodernist way to think about a text; but postmodernist interpretation arose precisely from a denial of a God who guarantees interpretation (e.g. Derrida's *Of Grammatology*). Paul is obviously comfortable with crystallizing his message into pungent summaries – he could never have been a great communicator otherwise; writers like Derrida and Baudrillard clearly aren't.

[8] Of course the term 'evangelical' means, literally, someone whose spirituality centres on the biblical gospel, the *evangelion*. It is because this gospel is 'according to the Scriptures' (1 Cor 15:1-4)

that commitment to the Bible's authority is at the heart of evangelicalism, as against liberal theologies that are comfortable about correcting Scripture by contemporary opinion.

[9] Rev 2:4.

[10] 1 Cor 1:23, 2:2. It is good to check if this is truly the heart and centre of our message. It isn't, in much theological liberalism; and it isn't in cults such as Jehovah's Witnesses, whose message on the doorstep is invariably not about Jesus but about reaching paradise by keeping the law. (Romans 1-7 are clearly out to show that that's impossible; the question, then, is why the thrust of the JWs' message is so different from Paul's.) But evangelicals can lose the centre too.

[11] The other comparable 'summary' in Paul is Colossians 1:27, where (having defined the 'gospel that you heard' in vv21-23 in terms of our reconciliation to God through Christ's cross) he summarizes the 'mystery' he is preaching as 'Christ in you, the hope of glory'.

[12] If repentance involves turning from our own ways to do God's will, then surely these two commandments are its supreme expression? For Jesus, they embodied God's entire revelation to that point ('All the Law and the Prophets hang on these two commandments' (Matt 23:37-40)).

[13] 1 Cor 11:23-26.

[14] Luke 4:18.

[15] Mark 10:14-15.

[16] From Leon Morris' introduction to his commentary on John in the New International series (1971), p.7. Morris is referring to that Gospel in particular, but his words hold good for the Bible as a whole.

[17] Luke 10:29-37.

[18] 1 Corinthians 8:1-3.

[19] Some writers have sought to drive a wedge between a Christ-centred and a Word-centred spirituality. This is meaningless; the two are inseparable. It is Jesus himself who taught us to ground our lives in his Word. Further, without the Word we cannot know what Jesus was and is like; and we end up conveniently constructing our 'own personal Jesus'. This study approaches our spirituality from the aspect of its basis in the Word; but Christ, and Christ only, must be its heart and its goal.

[20] Col 2:6-7.

[21] This book has focused on some of the Epistles, because these seem less well known to many people, that is, more 'pioneering'. But there is grave danger in losing touch with the 'image of Christ' in the Gospels (and doubly so when their narrative speaks so directly to our 'story-oriented' postmodern culture).

[22] Colossians 3:16 would seem to be saying that 'singing psalms, hymns and spiritual songs with gratitude' is basic to 'letting the word of Christ dwell in you richly'.

[23] If we're 'pioneering' in Genesis, we might find chapters 18 and 19 relevant here. Lot does his best to maintain justice in Sodom (cf. 2 Peter 2:7-8), but what ultimately determines the city's fate isn't his actions but Abraham's prayers (18:23-32).

[24] Books that have helped me in this area have been Ray Mayhew, *Spirituality at Street Level* (1988), particularly chapter 9, and Joyce Huggett, *Listening to God* (1986), particularly chapters 5 and 6. But a key issue is how biblical our images are. Lossky, from the Orthodox contemplative tradition, makes central the image of Moses' ascent of Sinai to meet with God (*The Mystical Theology of the Eastern Church* (tr.ed.of 1957), p.25). But what does this image bring to our prayers? 'One must... scale the most sublime heights of sanctity,' says Lossky; '...It is only thus that one may penetrate to the darkness wherein He who is beyond all created things makes his dwelling.' There is much power in Lossky's writing, and some real truth. But surely the result here is to focus our hearts on our own self-sanctifying efforts; and biblically, the whole point of what follows from Sinai throughout the old testament is that the human attempt to ascend to God by our own efforts is doomed to failure, and we desperately need God's loving, self-revealing grace to come down to us, as it did in Jesus. From the old testament we learn we cannot 'get up there' by ourselves; then in the new, God comes down. (Sinclair Ferguson points to the relevance of Romans 10:6-8 to how we approach God: 'The righteousness that is by faith says: "Do not say in your heart, 'Who will ascend into heaven?'" (that is, to bring Christ down)... But what does it say? "The Word is near you..."' (*Christian Spirituality*, ed. Donald L. Alexander, 1988, p.194). So the wrong, biblically uninformed contemplative image can actually send our longing for God off in an unfruitful direction.

[25] Cf. Paul's sense of his own dependence on the prayers of others (Rom 15:30-31).

[26] See, for example, Paul's priority that we pray for our rulers and the moral and spiritual climate that they generate (1 Timothy 2:2); or Hebrews' emphasis on 'remembering' the persecuted and ill-treated (13:3); to say nothing of the broader canvas of Amos and Habakkuk.

[27] Colossians 2:1-2, cf. 4:12-13.

[28] John 14:15.

[29] 'It is unfortunate that the term "pietism" has become derogatory,' Peruvian Samuel Escobar has written. 'In light of history and human need, we have to recover this dimension and recognise that intense personal piety in no way needs to be divorced from serious theological reflection, or from committed social and missionary action.' When this dimension is abandoned, he adds, the whole life of a spiritual movement becomes weakened. ('Our Evangelical Heritage', *IFES Review* 1983-1.) Cf. Martyn Lloyd-Jones: 'The evangelical... is not merely interested in the need for life and power, he emphasizes it with the whole of his being... The true evangelical is always pietistic and it is the thing that differentiates him from dead orthodoxy.' (*What is an Evangelical?* (reprint ed. of 1992), p.57.)

[30] There is a selflessness about evangelism and mission that makes sense of its being given a certain primacy in our activities, such as this verse implies. In my experience, a group that is really committed to evangelism becomes more serious about prayer, probably more serious about learning, and usually more serious about fellowship; as we encounter real conflict, we sense we need each other. So putting Christ's commission to witness first brings many other good things with it. (Cf. Philemon 6: 'I pray that you may be active in sharing your faith, *so that* you will have a full understanding of every good thing we have in Christ.')

[31] Cf. also Luke 4:18: 'The Spirit of the Lord is on me, because he has anointed me' – for what, above all?: 'to preach good news to the poor.'

[32] Once again, the Word and the Spirit belong together here, because the Spirit is central to the keeping aflame of that 'desire'. Acts 1:8 is clear: it is the reign of the Spirit in and through us that is the starting-point to our being Christ's witnesses.

[33] 2 Corinthians 4:4.

[34] The same can sometimes be true in counselling.

[35] British university evangelist Nigel Lee observes that in a curious sense a postmodern audience may sense the 'weight' of the authority of what God has spoken, when the speaker has clearly internalized it, more than they might a ten-point case for its truth.

[36] As Lee observes, one of the things the Spirit is doing in an evangelistic situation is moving someone from what they thought were their needs to the realization of the real needs as God declares them to be: from the symptoms to the true causes.

[37] In my own experience, it is often when I come to respond in worship and prayer to the passage that I grasp what 'the point' is.

[38] Oliver Barclay, 'The Comprehensive Word', reprinted in *IFES Review* 1979-2.

[39] Again, at the mention of priorities there looms a head-on clash with postmodern hermeneutics. But evidently God is a God to whom certain things do matter enormously! As we have suggested at various points in this book, there are priorities in the biblical text, even though we need to be humbly suspicious about the way we are conditioned to impose our own priorities on it. But to trust the Spirit is to believe in the possibility of a 'hermeneutic spiral'. If we truly seek God's mind, listening prayerfully, pioneering into as much of Scripture as possible, interacting with others, the Spirit will lead us, step by step, beyond our first impressions and into what is truly on his heart.

[40] 2 Tim 3:16-17.

[41] I'm not advocating the 'infallibility' of the newspaper's concerns! The priorities of the media are shaped by (and so reinforce) those underlying an increasingly godless culture. Issues of personal holiness will obviously not feature much on their agenda.

[42] This isn't the place to go into the matter in depth, but there is an inevitable problem of two only partly-compatible agendas competing in our theological education. One comes from the demands of accreditation in an academic system (either of the state or of a doctrinally-confused denomination) that is far from being ideologically neutral and is shaped by the priorities of a highly secularized academic tradition; inevitably, it demands immersion in a liberal scholarship now utterly irrelevant outside the mainline

denominational hierarchies and self-perpetuating academic theology. (Pick a few key figures – the Bultmanns of our own day – and then try to find anyone on the street, or even the pew, to whom they are significant.) On the other hand there is an agenda of spiritual growth as a future leader, shaped by hunger for the Bible, the gospel, and their priorities and vision ('biblical and streetwise'); the things an evangelist or Bible expositor might most want someone immersed in who was to follow in their footsteps; a mindset and spirituality that is shaped by the Word rather than critiquing it. Of course the two agendas are by no means always divergent. However, many seminaries have no choice but to tread an uneasy path between the two; and we have to ask what price is paid in the leadership training that results. (Particularly for the two-thirds world, to which the Western liberal agenda is still more damagingly irrelevant.) The academic world has its own social patterns, partly arising from its isolation, in which status can too easily be defined in the terms of the secularized system; and the resulting mindset can steadily drift away from that of a Bible-soaked spirituality passionate for Jesus and the gospel.

[43] In our 'global village', leadership training should include some exposure to the realities of not-yet-Christians in other countries too. ('Who then is my neighbour?', as the man asked Jesus.) Can we responsibly train a leader for a large church in a Western city without expecting them to gain at least some limited exposure to the realities of the mission field and the poverty of the two-thirds world? Often this can be far more 'ministry-changing' than an entire course of lectures.

[44] Cf. Matt 7:15-21. The parable of the talents is highly relevant here to the issue of what we do with what we learn (Matt 25:14-30).

[45] Most obviously in the brilliant if sometimes frustrating *The God Who is There* (1968).

[46] Not all of Nee can be commended without reservation. I am thinking here primarily of the fine books published by Kingsway: *Changed into His Likeness*, *Sit Walk Stand*, *The Normal Christian Life*, *Love Not the World* (a fascinating book to feed into a neo-marxist critique of the media), and especially *What Shall This Man Do?*, which Richard Foster selected for his *Devotional Classics* collection. Elsewhere in his work, however, Nee's 'one locality, one church' principle can tend, as Foster observes, to a divisive

Interlude 211

separatism; he has also been criticized for making too sharp a distinction between body, soul and spirit, and equating the lesser 'soul' with the mind or intellect. (See Macaulay and Barrs' critique in *Being Human*, 1978), Nee remains, however, one of evangelicalism's profoundest non-Western teachers.

[47] The book that first opened my eyes to these essential aspects of true, biblical spirituality was Ronald Sider, *Rich Christians in an Age of Hunger* (1977).

[48] Vital for ourselves and our own prayer lives too, incidentally: 'If anyone shuts his ears to the cry of the poor, he too will cry out and not be answered' (Prov 21:13).

[49] A good beginning is the site maintained by SPEAK on www.speak.org.uk. We've focused here on global concerns; good starting-points for growing in involvement with more local needs are Fred Catherwood's brief, inspiring *It Can Be Done* (2000) and Fran Beckett's *Called to Action* (1989).

[50] I remember one visit to South Africa where many of my white colleagues were preaching the political applications of Amos to apartheid. This was indeed vitally relevant. But I wondered whether their hearers might lose sight of Christ himself, if that was all they heard – and then how long their spirituality would be robust enough for true distinctiveness.

[51] This isn't an ideal model. It doesn't for example do justice to the little-known but distinctive and rich spirituality of the 'Brethren' tradition, as expressed in writers like William Kelly or George Muller, and reflected in, say, John White; this has affinities with the 'reformed' commitment to biblical doctrine and the 'charismatic' reliance on the Spirit, but also something unique and significant of its own. Nor does it adequately reflect aspects of Anglican evangelicalism that are not really either 'reformed' or 'charismatic' – the spirituality represented by a book like C.S. Lewis' helpful *Prayer: Letters to Malcolm*, or the more biblical aspects of the contemplative tradition.

[52] That is to say: when non-charismatics complain that charismatics in their city are 'all way off the rails', it may well be their own fault, if the prayerful and loving friendships have not been cultivated where brother can challenge brother on how far their church life matches Scripture.

[53] J.I.Packer, *Keep in Step with the Spirit* (1984), p.185. Packer's whole assessment in chs.5 and 6 is controversial in parts but well worth reading.

[54] But only sometimes! To this day, many of my deepest and most respected Russian colleagues are non-charismatic.

[55] To put my own cards on the table, the most helpful study of the biblical and doctrinal issues seems to me to be D.A.Carson's *Showing the Spirit* (1995).

[56] Others whose pilgrimage has led them in this direction might be stimulated by Rick Nathan and Ken Wilson's brilliant book *Empowered Evangelicals* (1995), or Tony Campolo's *How to be Pentecostal without Speaking in Tongues* (1991).

[57] A helpful book for me in this regard was missiologist Peter Wagner's *Look Out! The Pentecostals are Coming* (1973; reissued in a revised form as *Spiritual Power and Church Growth* (1986)). It is Wagner who makes the thought-provoking point that 'no other non-political, non-militaristic human movement in history has grown as rapidly as the Pentecostal/charismatic movement has over the past forty years'. (*How to Have a Healing Ministry without Making your Church Sick* (1988), p.69 - another very interesting book for those of us keen to learn from the full evangelical spectrum.) There is a remarkable dynamic here, and it might well seem more than merely human.

[58] Note, too, the way the promise of the Spirit feels rather like the culminating point of Luke's narrative in Luke 24:49, and is also the end-point of Peter's message in Acts 2:38. Lloyd-Jones' words are again relevant: 'The evangelical... is not merely interested in the need for life and power, he emphasizes it with the whole of his being.' (*What is an Evangelical?*, p.57.)

[59] And trebly so, of course, with liberals, who tend to be awestruck by writers that emphasize the silence of God.

[60] A fascinating study is Leona Choy's *Powerlines: What Great Evangelicals Believed about the Holy Spirit, 1850-1930* (Camp Hill, Pennsylvania, 1990). It is unfortunate that Choy has chosen to paraphrase rather than quote, leaving the reader to take on trust her interpretations of those she writes about. But it remains a most helpful volume.

[61] This is actually a serious 'hermeneutical' issue. The divorce from worship is surely one reason why so much 'professional' exegesis brings forth fruit that is so arid and life-denying.

[62] 1 Tim 2:8.

[63] Psalm 150:3-5.

[64] Psalm 95:1,6.

[65] Psalm 47:1.

[66] This is a mistake often made in New Age circles. An experience of peace resulting from soothing music by candlelight isn't 'spiritual' if it has nothing to do with acceptance by God and closeness to him.

[67] Hence the advice often given about the value of singing to start our prayer time on those occasions when we're 'not in the mood': 'If I can't pray, I sing.'

[68] That's not what it's *for;* praise must by definition be for God, not for ourselves. But it is (as a by-product) what it *does*.

[69] In case this sounds too anti-Catholic, we should note that there is a segment of the Catholic charismatic movement whose proclamation can be close to that of evangelicals. See, for example, Ralph Martin, *Hungry for God* (1975).

[70] And we rejoice in an 'infant baptism' as a believing family's act of commitment, of claiming God's grace and presence. What the more 'radical evangelicals' suggest is simply that baptism is the wrong word for it, because, in the absence of faith in the infant, it cannot lead to 'salvation' in the broad senses that the new testament links with baptism. Thus, if a believer is 're-baptised', (s)he doesn't deny what happened as an infant, but rather expresses gratefully for him/herself that identification with Christ prayed for in hope by the parents. We know, too, that the (somewhat more cerebral!) act of 'confirmation' can embody much that a 'radical evangelical' would express in baptism. But we have a discomfort about saying, 'Lord, I knew the way you wanted this done, but I thought this might do instead!'

[71] Some of us would feel, therefore, that traditions which neglect believer's baptism often tend to be weak precisely on the 'death to the world' that it embodies, blurring fatally that crucial line between the world and the Church.

[72] If we see infant baptism as biblical baptism, then identifying baptism with new birth would mean viewing the large numbers of

people who are 'baptized' in believing families but then grow up total non-believers, as being born again, regenerate and forgiven, despite all the signs to the contrary. (Or, as having been briefly regenerate and then fallen away – but then Hebrews 6:4-6 would seem to rule out their ever being re-converted.) If, on the other hand, we view biblical baptism only as believer's baptism, then to identify baptism and new birth means writing off most believers in the Lutheran, Anglican and Reformed confessions as unregenerate. Clearly, however close the link, baptism cannot be identical with that new birth after which one is fully a child of God, after which conversion is no longer an issue, and after which 'no man shall pluck them out of my hands'?

[73] Note the centrality of 'believing' and 'faith' to the gospel in: Acts 13:38-39, 15:7-9, 16:31 (though here baptism follows immediately, we should note), 20:21, John 1:12, 3:14-18,36, 5:24, 6:28-29,35,40,47, 7:39, 20:31, Romans 1:16-17, 3:22,25-31, 4:5,9-16,24-5:2, 10:8-11, 13-14; 1 Corinthians 1:21, Galatians 2:16, 3:2,5-9,22-24, Ephesians 1:13, 2:8, 1 John 5:1. In many of these the term 'baptism' could easily have been used instead of 'believing' or 'faith', if baptism were indeed the means of new birth. These are well worth looking up, and many more could be cited, e.g.: Mark 1:14-15; Luke 8:11-12, John 9:35-38, Acts 10:43,26:18, Rom 9:30,32, 10:4, Phil 3:9, 1 Tim 1:16, 4:9-10, Heb 4:2-3, 11:7, 1 John 3:23, 5:13 (where it is noteworthy that assurance of salvation is *not* located in the attractively tangible act of baptism).

[74] We should take seriously the view that holds being 'baptized (submerged) into Christ' (Rom 6:3) as referring not to water baptism itself but to our internal baptism or submergence or union with Christ that occurred at new birth, when we repented and so were permanently 'submerged' or baptised in the Spirit and into his Body (1 Cor 12:13). Even so, the connection between the inward 'baptism' and the outward expression must be close, if the same word is used for them together; and any approach that weakens this link must be doing some violence to the new testament vision. (Which is also one of the snags with 'infant baptism'.)

[75] Or even to its culmination in the transformation of everything we are, physical body included, at the End (e.g. Rom 13:11, Heb 9:28).

[76] Matthew 28:19. We need to note how automatically baptism flows out of the gospel's acceptance in, say, Acts 8:35-36, 9:17-18 or 16:31-33. In Acts 2:38, Peter's answer to the question 'What shall we do?' is 'Repent, and be baptized!'

[77] The Russian evangelical tradition, operating in a much more communally-oriented culture, puts a far higher emphasis on, first, the public confession of repentance in the church, and the act of baptism.

[78] 1 Cor 11:24.

[79] Cf. 1 Cor 11:28-29.

[80] For that reason it's important for young leaders to expose themselves to some of the classic definitions of evangelical faith from past decades: books like Martyn Lloyd-Jones' *What is an Evangelical?* (reprint ed. of 1992), or John Stott's *Christ the Controversialist* (1970).

[81] See, for example, Tom Wolfe's summary of the post-'60s generation as perceived by McLuhan: 'They have the tribal habit of responding emotionally to the spoken word, they are "hot", they want to participate, to *touch*, to be involved.' (And, he adds, 'They can more easily be swayed by things like demagoguery.') (*McLuhan Hot and Cool*, ed. G.E.Stearn (1968), p.44.)

[82] This is a strong current in the secular postmodernity debates, represented for example by Alasdair MacIntyre in *After Virtue* (1984).

[83] Oliver Barclay describes the English church situation around 1910 like this: 'The whole protestant world seemed to have been swept away. That some old-fashioned Church of England parishes, the Brethren, isolated free churches and a few students in Cambridge should hold fast was of little consequence.' (*Whatever Happened to the Jesus Lane Lot?* (1977), p.72.)

[84] Lloyd-Jones, p.51, has some pungent comments on this topic, which are probably even truer now than when he wrote.

[85] Don Carson has a chapter in *The Gagging of God* (1996) titled 'On Drawing Lines, When Drawing Lines is Rude'.

[86] Gottfried Osei-Mensah, 'The Authoritative Word', *IFES Review* 1979-1.

[87] For a full study, see John Wenham, *Christ and the Bible* (1972), or Stott's *Christ the Controversialist*. Perhaps we should add that exploring this line of thought doesn't depend on our

personal starting-point being one of belief in the Bible's entire trustworthiness. Providing we begin by accepting that the Gospels give a generally reliable picture of the flavour of Jesus' teaching (such that the early Christians were willing to die for), then we will see that the unreserved way in which he uses and trusts Scripture (the old testament) is very obvious.

[88] The passages are all worth looking up to see how our Master works! Matthew 19:4-5 is especially interesting, since there Jesus clearly cites a comment by the narrator of Genesis as an utterance of God himself.

[89] We should notice the force of Jesus' commitment to biblical history here: 'As it *was* in the days of Noah, so it *will be* at the coming of the Son of Man'; the one would seem as historical as the other. Sodom, which might conceivably have 'remained until this day', will be judged alongside Capernaum, and it *'will be'* more bearable for Sodom; Jonah's audience *'will stand up'* alongside the current religious gurus and condemn them. (It is hard to see how that statement could be equated with something mythical like 'Father Christmas will stand up at the judgment' – or 'As were the days of Frodo the hobbit, so will be the coming of the Son of Man'!)

[90] None of this is meant to deny the place (or the difficulty) of careful interpretation; it is by no means always easy to hear what the Word, rather than our decade or background, is saying. It is what Scripture actually says, not what we misunderstand it to say, that God says. But that fundamental orientation is crucial.

[91] Jude 3. Douglas Johnson, the first general secretary of the British student movement, IVF (later UCCF), used this verse to summarize their vision in his title for their history: *Contending for the Faith* (1979).

[92] Galatians 2:11-14.

[93] For example, if a church (or seminary) doesn't affirm the full reliability of biblical history, its authority will be eroded for them; we can never be sure that the passage we're studying isn't 'the one that got away'. And so we inevitably start to think of parts of it (but which are they?) as a ragbag of traveller's tales. Christians taught in this way aren't going to spend time grappling with what God is saying through, say, Judges or 2

Kings. And so we are impoverished: and robbed of that vital sense of the God who acts.

[94] 1 Corinthians 15:1-4; and see 2 Timothy 1:13-14.

[95] As Chesterton suggests, we are like someone 'always expecting to meet Plato or Shakespeare tomorrow at breakfast'! (Quoted in Rebecca Manley Pippert, *Out of the Saltshaker* (1979), p.101.)

[96] She was using Alec Motyer's *The Message of Amos*, and the Lifebuilder guide on Hosea (*God's Persistent Love* by Dale and Sandy Larsen).

[97] Joshua 1:8, cf. Psalm 119:97: 'Oh, how I love your law! I meditate on it all day long.'

[98] David Ivaska comments on the specific value of memorization for 'storing up verses we can use to lead a person to Christ, to comfort someone troubled, to resist temptation, to claim his promises, and to praise his name'. (From a useful article in the IFES magazine *In Touch* titled 'Growth God's Way: Strengthening Your Group through Bible Study'.)

[99] 1 Timothy 3:2, 5:17. This multiplicity of input will be especially important in the coming decades as we face a culture shaped by post-modernist theory, with its fear of any 'single perspective' as 'authoritarian'. It is true that this aspect of post-modernism derives ultimately from its atheism, and hence its disbelief in any authority. But it is also true that no one perspective can supply all truth (or reflect all that is in the Word), and any claims otherwise are indeed suspect. God plans a plurality of input for his people, and we need to take that seriously.

[100] Samuel Escobar, 'Our Evangelical Heritage', *IFES Review* 1983-1.

[101] There is far more in these books than could be covered in the space we have (and than any one of us will ever know this side of glory!). So the incompleteness modelled here is deliberate. A pioneering spirituality doesn't expect to exhaust what is available!

[102] The Unicorn's call throughout the final chapters of C.S.Lewis, *The Last Battle* (1956).

5

What John Thought Were The Basics: Rereading 1 John

'Back to the basics' isn't a bad challenge for Christians. As we've seen, spiritual maturity pivots on our ability to keep a vision, continually renewed, of the 'basics' of the faith.

But then we need the best possible understanding of the question: What *are* those basics?

We can find one approach to that in Paul's letters, particularly Romans. Personally, I've always found them a lot easier than John's writings. Paul follows a logical line of argument – even if sometimes he gets thrilled about something, and shoots off at a tangent for a chapter or so. John's style is different: he meditates, circling round an idea, coming back at it from different angles. I've never found 1 John an easy book to grasp.

So recently it seemed a good idea to take a look at the book's opening, and see what the main themes were that John wanted to emphasize. So, Bible, pen, sheet of paper – and immediately there's a problem: where, how long, is the 'opening'? It's not obvious. I read the first page or so, looking for a break in the flow. One solution seemed to be to go as far as the couplets of 2:12, where John seems to begin a new, self-contained section.

Try it for yourself. You may notice different things from me. But I ended up noting down a list that seemed helpful (at least as a guide to prayer), of five 'basics according to St John'.....

Reality among us (1:1-7)

First, then (1:1-4): *It's happened: God's life has appeared among men!* John begins his letter with a declaration: 'That which was from the beginning, which we have heard, which we have seen with our eyes, which our hands have touched... this we proclaim.'

There's a sense of amazement here, of an emotional impact that John had never recovered from. The life at the centre of the universe, the Word that created all things – it became flesh among men, it walked among *us*, says John, we touched it... it became a man, our friend, eating bread with us, cooking fish for us... 'We have seen it and testify to it, and we proclaim to you the eternal life, which was with the Father and has appeared to us.' (And cf. 4:14.)

But then he goes on. The very life of God has come among us, he says, and that now has radical implications for our life together. 'We proclaim to you what we have seen and heard'– the astonishing thing we, tangibly, experienced – 'so that... you may have fellowship with us' (v3). True fellowship is created, or will be energized, as we grasp these realities; and as we realize that, relating together in God's Church, we are touching that eternal 'life' itself. We don't relate merely as human beings socializing with each other, says John. Instead, 'our fellowship is with the Father and with his Son'(v3)!

With these words he declares the incredible uniqueness, among all human communities, of the Church. It isn't a human organization, nor just some kind of club. The chapel down the side street by the railway, the fellowship that meets next to the factory... They may look unimpressive – sometimes 'no beauty or majesty to attract us'[1] at all: little groups of odd people with odd ways. (Think of your own examples...) But hidden beneath that exterior, as we saw in Ephesians, is a supernatural organism that will outlast the planet, directly in touch with God. 'The Church,' says the Russian writer Vladimir Lossky, 'is the centre of the universe...

The history of the world is a history of the Church.'[2] There is much more to the Church than meets the eye; our fellowship together is nothing less than fellowship with God, and to relate to the least of our brothers is to relate to Christ.[3] (*Lord, please help me view my sisters and brothers in this way...*) That, says John, should really impact us. 'We write this to make our joy complete!' (v4).

But second (1:5-6): *That means genuine change.* 'This is the message we have heard from him and declare to you', says John, and obviously what's coming next will be fundamental to what he wants to say: 'God is light; in him is no darkness at all. If we claim to have fellowship with him yet walk in the darkness, we lie.' Obvious enough. But to John, these seem words that urgently need to be preached. Why?

John is not alone. Elsewhere in the Bible, we see James felt the need to say something similar: loveless faith that doesn't lead to changed actions is no faith at all. And Paul, in Romans 6, targets the idea that grace allows us as Christians to 'continue to sin'. No way, declare both Paul and John.

Do we need the same message? It isn't enough to 'accept Jesus into your heart' – or, rather, it isn't *real* to 'accept Jesus into your heart' – if no radical transformation (real repentance) is involved. If we claim otherwise, says John, if we claim to be born again but have darkness unchallenged in our hearts, we are lying. *Lord, please keep me aware of that...*

Through the door and on the way (1:8-2:2)

John's third opening theme follows from that: *We have a real problem, but also a real solution.*

'If we claim to be without sin, we deceive ourselves... If we claim we have not sinned, we make him out to be a liar,' he says. But God has a solution, for those committed to the Way of repentance and faith: 'If we walk in the light... the blood of Jesus cleanses us from all sin... If we confess our sins, he is faithful and just and will forgive us our sins and purify

us from all unrighteousness... My dear children, I write this
to you so that you will not sin. But if anybody does sin, we
have one who speaks to the Father in our defence – Jesus
Christ, the Righteous One. He is the atoning sacrifice for
our sins...' To those who face and confess their sins and set
out to walk in the light, God promises not only fellowship,
but certain forgiveness of sin.

John is going to make very clear that if we don't love our
brothers we aren't saved. But he is not preaching a gospel of
works, to be set falsely against Paul's gospel of new birth by
faith. For John, as clearly as for Paul, the vital thing is to
'have been born of God' (2:29, 3:9, 4:7, 5:1,4,18). And in
John, as in Paul, that 'new birth' is obtained by believing faith;
look at 5:13 (and, from John's Gospel, the parallel 20:31). The
'joy' John announces in 1:4 clearly presupposes a door that
we've stepped through into the 'life' of God. The importance
of this becomes clear when we watch what happens in
traditions that lost this sense of once-for-all salvation, and
replaced it with an uncertain progress through a good life and
the sacraments. All too often we feel a lack of joy, a sadness of
spirituality; a yearning uncertainty, a repeated pleading, 'Lord
Jesus Christ, have mercy'; a conscience still burdened, too
often, by a feeling of unremoved sin. (Writing these words I
see the face of a friend in Moscow, deeply devout yet unable
to speak of her faith: 'How can I witness when I have so many
sins?')

That is not the 'joy' John speaks of, as he delights in a
radiant certainty of new birth. The life *has* appeared, our
fellowship *is* with the Father, there *has been* a sacrifice that
took away our sins: 'I write these things so that you may
know that you *have* eternal life'(5:13). The 'life' that shines at
the heart of eternity is now ours, and ours forever! (*I praise
you, Lord!*)

Do I feel that certainty of free approach to God? John really
wants it for me, both as I approach God in prayer now, and
in the judgment later. 'Continue in him,' John says, 'so that

when he appears we may be confident and unashamed' (2:28).
'This is... how we set our hearts at rest in his presence... We
have confidence before God and receive from him anything
we ask, because we obey his commands' (3:19-23). 'Love is
made complete among us, so that we will have confidence in
the day of judgment'(4:17). And, close to the end of the letter:
'...You may know that you have eternal life. This is the
confidence we have in approaching God: that if we ask
anything according to his will, he hears us' (5:14). *Lord, please
help me grasp this, so that I can approach you freely and
confidently, as a child approaching my Father; and so that I may
play my part in releasing your goodness on earth by prayer...*

Signs of true life (2:3-11)

John's fourth opening theme, then: have we come through
that door, and are we living in a place of confidence before
God? *How can we know that we have* (the past tense is
important) *come to know him?* (2:3,5-6). It is the same challenge
that Paul throws at the Corinthians: 'Examine yourselves to
see whether you are in the faith' (2 Cor 13:5). John's aim in
writing his letter will clearly be (5:13) to give his readers a
solid basis for joyous assurance, as we live in the presence of
God.

But he does this in a manner we might not expect!

He will proceed in two ways. Objectively, his 'children'
can be sure of salvation because they have shown themselves
to be those who listen to the truth (4:6). 'If anyone
acknowledges that Jesus is the Son of God, God lives in him
and he in God. And so we know and rely on the love God
has for us' (4:15-16, cf. 2:23). If we believe in the Son we can
be certain of eternal life, says John (5:13); and if we confess
our sins, we can be sure he forgives our sins and speaks to the
Father in our defence (1:9-2:1). Here are objective facts, that
give us certainty of where we stand.

But that comes later. What John puts first, both here in this opening section, and through a series of remarks ('This is how we know...') throughout his letter, is something different, a more subjective basis for our assurance. '*We know that we have come to know him* if *we obey his commands... This is how we know we are in him: Whoever claims to live in him must walk as Jesus did*' (2:3, 5-6).

There is enough there (as we review how Jesus 'walked' in the Gospels) to keep us busy for a lifetime. But there is a fifth step. John has a particular concern in mind within this idea of 'walking as Jesus did'; it is the '*new command*' (2:8). What is this 'new command'? Surely John's mind is going back here to the Last Supper, and Jesus' words after Judas had stepped out into the night to betray him: 'A new command I give you: Love one another. As I have loved you, so you must love one another' (John 13:34; look also at 2 John 5).

This command wasn't just an idealistic instruction; it was to be the mark of Christ's new community. Jesus knew how his disciples bickered, but still he declares that his 'new command' would become visible fact: 'By this all men will know that you are my disciples, if you love one another'(13:35). Indeed, he planned for their transformed relationships to be the proof of spiritual reality: 'May they be brought to complete unity to let the world know that you sent me,' he prays (John 17:23). And John knows he has seen this coming into being: 'Its' (the new command's) 'truth is seen in him *and in you*, because... the true light *is* already shining'(2:8). So here is our assurance: 'Dear children, let us not love with words or tongue but with actions and in truth. *This* then is how we know that we belong to the truth, and how we set our hearts at rest' (3:18-20).

Very helpful! Our *love* is the proof of our reality, says John; if the Spirit is there, the fruit of the Spirit will be too.[4] 'This is how we know who the children of God are... Anyone who does not do what is right is not a child of God; nor is anyone who does not love his brother'(3:10). 'We know that we have passed from death to life, because we love our brothers'(3:14). IFES general secretary Lindsay Brown said in *In Touch* that it took five years after his conversion 'before I received a deep assurance of salvation. I must have asked Jesus to be my Saviour twenty times! Assurance came through 1 John 3: "We know we have passed from death to life, because we love the brethren." I could see this in my reactions to people who were very different from me. This was like a shaft of light to my soul!'

That might make us despair. ('I can't seem to love this person, it's the way I am; so I can't really be a Christian.') But our ability or inability to love isn't something timeless and unchangeable. Rather – as is plain from all John's efforts to exhort us to love[5] – it is something correctable. And the proof of our reality as believers is not that our love is perfect, but rather that we want it to grow. ('Naturally speaking I don't *like* this person at all. But God is changing me, and I have committed myself to that. I cannot handle this alone, but I have Christ's Spirit, and the Spirit's fruit is love (Rom 5:5). Anyone born of God loves. So I'll draw on his Spirit and go and through him do the actions of love today, no matter what my feelings say.')

John knows full well that we haven't arrived yet (2:1), and that the possibility exists here of our 'hearts condemning us'(3:20). But repentance was basic to our new birth; so assurance of new birth comes from seeing real repentance doing its work in us – a refusal to continue in sin, a desire to do the acts of love in faith, until God's promise is fulfilled and we have overcome the evil in our hearts (see 5:3-4). ('Blessed are those who *hunger and thirst* for righteousness,' said Jesus (Matt 5:6).) Those who are real are those drawing determinedly on the Spirit within (1 John 4:11-13, cf. 3:23-24) to go and live in loving obedience to the Word. (*Lord, in all my weakness and failure, I want that...*) As both Jesus and Paul insist, it is the fruit of obedience to the Words of radical love that prove our reality (Matt 7:15-23, 1 Cor 13:1-2).

Once again, John's message here isn't salvation by good works; in 5:13 it's those who 'believe' who have eternal life. Rather, the changed actions are (as in Eph 2:8-10) the inevitable sign and consequence of new birth, if we *have* come to know him (2:3). Nor is a finally-perfected Christian character the mark of salvation. John knows we will fall into sin; it is to those who 'walk in the light' that God promises ongoing forgiveness of sin, because they are still going to need it (1:7, 2:1). Rather, the sign that we've been 'born of God' is that we will not comfortably '*continue* to sin' (3:9). Real repentance must have involved, by definition, determination of spirit to do all we can to stop sinning. The sign of the believer is a desire to obey the Father, a longing for holiness, a horror at breaking his commandments, above all, love for the brothers. (Holiness, John demonstrates, is not holiness unless it is loving; love is not love unless it is holy (cf. 5:2-3).) New birth is a heart-transformation; so the sign of its reality is that our lives really are becoming transformed. 'This is how we know we are in him: Whoever claims to live in him must walk as Jesus did' (2:5-6).

So let us be clear, says John. 'I am writing you a "new command"', albeit 'one which you have had since the beginning': 'Anyone who claims to be in the light but hates his brother is still in the darkness' (2:9-11). This is the end-point of his argument in this opening section, to which he returns repeatedly in the rest of the Epistle. '*This* is the message you heard from the beginning: We should love one another' (3:11). 'He has given us this command: Whoever loves God must love his brother' (4:21). Here is the heart of the matter, says John: God has created a new community, and desires it to be irradiated totally by his love. He did that in the old testament too, of course (the entire old testament law can be summed up in loving your neighbour as yourself, says Paul (Rom 13:9)). But now there is a crucial difference: he has given us his new birth and his Spirit to make it happen. And if we are real, *believe* it, it's going to start happening, in us!

(Lord, I believe; please help my unbelief. And please give me a deepening repentance, an increasing hunger to live according to your love: in the details and choices and words of today's reality...)

Defining the basics (speed-read 2:12-5:21)

Here, then, we have John's gospel. Like Paul's (Acts 20:21) and Jesus' (Mark 1:15), it can be summarized in two terms: repentance (turning to God for a radically transformed life), and faith that truly believes. 'This is his command: to believe in the name of his Son, Jesus Christ, *and* to love one another as he commanded us' (3:23; cf. 4:11-16, 5:1). If we love one another, God lives in us (4:12); if we confess Jesus as God's Son, God lives in us (4:15). The two are one: to 'believe' the truth of the gospel means, for John, to love God, but to love the Father means to love the child as well (5:1).

There's a difficult balance in this unity, encapsulated in Paul's instructions about 'speaking the *truth* in *love*'.[6] Christians so easily fall into either a hard, critical separatism that emphasizes the belief of truth without caring very much about love (e.g. for fellow-believers on the opposite side of debates about tongues or election), or else a spineless, woolly-minded sentimentality, stressing love but not interested in truth or in 'contending for the faith' (Jude 3). John, in contrast, is uncompromising in both directions.

If we want a faith that will survive the tough conditions of the coming century we had better take note. Anyone who does not love his brother is not a child of God, he says (3:10). But on the other hand there is no casualness in John about truth and distinctiveness. The closing sentences of this Epistle of love are full of concern for what is 'true', and end with the plea, 'Dear children, keep yourselves from idols' (5:20-21). Likewise, John's passion for love in chapter 4 does not prevent him describing those who deviate from the fundamental gospel as 'the spirit of the antichrist' (4:3); they need to be recognized for what they are (4:1). He does not shrink from using the language of conflict (4:4); unity can only be based on truth. (Compare his phrase 'whom I love in the truth' that begins both 2 and 3 John.) Those whose doctrine was false had not been able to stay in the community; and John recognized that division was unavoidable, because their lack of continuance had shown they had not been real in the first place (2:22,19). Rather, they were shown to be representatives of a religion that is actually part of a world-system (4:5) which is, John says, in its entirety (the force of this is shocking and our minds may try to evade it) 'under the control of the evil one'(5:19).

Love, then, is imperative; but love for the world is totally incompatible with love for the Father (2:15). That does not of course mean hating the doctrinal deviants themselves; we are called to love the sinner while hating[7] the sin. But distinctiveness, John is saying, must be absolutely uncompromising.

Please help me, Lord, I'm liable to get this wrong on one side or the other. It wasn't an easy balance for John. 'Son of thunder', he was originally nicknamed, and the Gospels show us why. We see him wanting to call down fire on an unrepentant village; trying to close down the ministry of someone who was casting out demons in Jesus' name but was 'not one of us'; trying to cadge the positions of power in the new kingdom. 'Son of thunder' indeed.

But then John had heard and seen things that left him dumbfounded and eventually transformed. He had heard Jesus' teaching in the Sermon on the Mount – about going the second mile, about turning the other cheek, about not worshipping if there's unresolved tension with your brother, about loving your enemy; and he had absorbed Jesus' words that those who failed to put these things into practice were building on sand. And he had seen: seen Jesus display the 'full extent of his love' (John 13:1); seen him, knowing 'that he was come from God and was returning to God', knowing that from among his closest disciples one was about to betray him, one deny him and the rest desert him; John had seen him, knowing all that, take a towel and, instead of retaliating, wrap it around himself, and wash their smelly feet. John had heard the teaching that followed: 'I have set you an example that you should do as I have done for you... A new command I give you: Love one another.'

For John, there was something unbelievable here, something eternal. The *life* had appeared, as he begins the opening section of his letter by saying. The Christian community was henceforth in holy fellowship, not just with itself, but with unimaginable, supernatural, personalized Truth and Love and Power. But if that was so, that same life must be visible in the transformed relationships of the distinctive Christian community. If it was real at all, that supernatural love would pour out from the community into the world.

That, in our society, is difficult. 'Love' is sometimes invoked to justify some very surprising actions. Indeed, many people in our culture are left with only a cynical doubt as to whether the term has any meaning at all. Love's a slippery word, and we no longer know what it signifies. ('I've never been able to figure out what love means,' Joan Collins told an interviewer.) Nor, when we think we know, can we make it work. That is the tragedy we find running through the work of some of modernity's most famous novelists – Lawrence and Forster, for example.[8] There is a desperate need for communities that – *Lord, please do it in us!* – can both teach what love really is, and demonstrate its reality. ('Show me someone who knows how to live it,' sings Bob Dylan in *Slow Train Coming*.)

The gospel covers both. In the new testament's teaching (e.g. Matthew 5 or 1 Corinthians 13), in the life of Christ, and above all in his cross, love is defined: 'This is how we know what love is: Jesus Christ laid down his life for us' (1 John 3:16a, cf.4:9-10). We have *seen* God's love, the life *has* appeared, says John – 'and we ought to lay down our lives for our brothers' (3:16b). Unless the life of the love of God is flowing out through us, the life of the love of God is not in us. But in the Spirit, God gives us his power to make it happen. (We will learn more of this next chapter, as we explore Romans.)

So the Spirit of God empowers the Church of God to live the life of the Word of God. Repent and believe God for it, John says, and go out to 'walk as Jesus did' (2:6): demonstrating (as Stott puts it) a love so supernatural that the world will be compelled to admit its divine origin. (*Lord, I believe you have put this power for love within me, by your Spirit. Help me to hear your Spirit's uncomfortable challenge next time I act out of accord with it. Help me, please, to reach out for your grace, and then to live by the actions that express your nature and your life in this world; more and more...*)

So now might be the time to turn back to 2:12, and go section by section through the remainder of his letter. What seem to be the themes of John's next section? How are they to be turned into praise and into prayer, and action?...

Notes

[1] Compare Isaiah 53:2 (about the Messiah).

[2] Vladimir Lossky, *The Mystical Theology of the Eastern Church* (English tr. 1957), pp.111, 178.

[3] Compare Matthew 25:40.

[4] Perhaps the two most difficult 'This is how we know' verses are 3:24 and 4:13. Is John saying we know we are saved because we sense within us an inward voice from the Spirit acknowledging joyfully the truth that Jesus is the Son? That may be a theme of 5:6-10 (and we can compare Romans 8:15-16); and the context following 3:24 is concerned with what kind of witness the true Spirit of God gives. On the other hand, the context *preceding* 3:24 stresses that we should 'love one another': which suggests that 'This is how we know that he lives in us: We know it by the Spirit' might be repeating the message of all the other 'This is how we know' verses, that it is the love God puts in us for the rest of the family that proves we are his children. If the fruit of the Spirit isn't there, neither is the Spirit.

In fact we find a similar combination, moving from love to truth, in the context preceding and following the other such verse, 4:13;

so perhaps it's an illusory interpretative choice between truth and love - they belong together! Either way it is only the Spirit who can enable us to 'obey his commands... believe in the name of his Son, Jesus Christ, and love one another' (3:22-23). Either way, our assurance is that 'those who are led by' (and follow) 'the Spirit of God are sons of God' (Rom 8:14).

[5] And, indeed, from the fact that the two great commandments (Matthew 22:37-39) both begin, 'You shall love' – God, in the one case, and our neighbour in the other. It may not always be easy, but evidently, with the Spirit within us, love is something we can (and must!) choose to learn.

[6] Eph 4:15.

[7] Compare Jesus' words in Revelation 2:6.

[8] See for example Lawrence's *The Rainbow*, or the sad ending to Forster's *A Passage to India*.

6

Liberated for Glory:
Rereading Romans 6-8

Romans 6-8: A Rough Guide

Chapter 6:1-14	Dead and risen with Christ
Chapter 6:15-23	Offering ourselves to God
Chapter 7:1-6	Finished with the law
Chapter 7:7-25	Struggling with our weaknesses
Chapter 8:1-14	Living by the flesh or the Spirit
Chapter 8:14-23	God's children, bound for glory
Chapter 8:24-30	Pain, hope, and destiny
Chapter 8:31-39	Triumph guaranteed!

Romans 6-8 is another magnificent source for pioneering! If we had not called Ephesians 'the vision of the ultimate', we could well use the phrase here.

Romans is Paul's clearest expression of the gospel, of just how God's people live by faith (cf. 1:15-17). We probably have some feel for his first five chapters. Or at least for their basic ideas:[1]

- the horror of human lostness and alienation, with no future except God's wrath (chapter 1);

- no one is truly 'righteous'– we all, 'religious' Jews as much as Gentiles, are equally lost and fall short of God's holy glory (2:1-3:20);
- God's magnificent solution, forgiveness through faith in Jesus' death for us (3:21-31);
- the way that faith fulfils the old testament, so that even Abraham was justified through faith, not the sacrament of circumcision (chapter 4);
- and finally the glorious assertion that now, 'since we have been justified by faith, we have *peace with God*'– security, freedom from his judgment, assurance that he has done all we could ever need, and his love being poured into our hearts by the Holy Spirit. Jesus has put triumphantly right everything that went wrong from the very beginning (chapter 5).

Glory to you in the highest, Lord Christ! These are the most important ideas in the world; if we haven't mastered them we must, because for everyone around us they represent the difference between life and death. If our church is doing its job they will have been preached quite frequently. They comprise about five pages in our new testament – thirty minutes' reading? Doubtless we all need to reread them every couple of years. [2]

But that's chapters 1-5. Somewhere round chapter 6, my own grasp of Romans tends to falter... And that, since Romans is Paul's expression of the real basics, is a real pity: a hint to start 'pioneering'!

It's doubly a pity because, when we read it, we find Romans 6 seems to be one of the 'keys to the universe'. It promises us something enormous: 'sin shall not be your master' (v14). We need to grasp just what that means: *there is absolutely no wrongful or destructive behaviour that we cannot, as Christians, break free from.*

It's irritating when you have a vital key in your hands, you know it is the right key but you can't turn the lock...

Memories of first love

I recall first discovering Romans 6 as a student. It felt like dynamite.

'Sin shall not have dominion over you', it said (I was reading the AV in those days). 'Our old man is crucified with Christ, that the body of sin might be destroyed... Reckon ye also yourselves to be dead indeed unto sin... For he that is dead is freed from sin' (vv 6,7,11,14). Fantastic! We are risen with Christ, guaranteed victory in our lives. These weren't 'ought-to-bes'; on the authority of Scripture they were facts, realities, *now*. Triumph! For a while it was my favourite chapter.

And then, somehow, it lost its shine. I couldn't quite remember how it worked. Also, on rereading it I found Paul didn't say quite what I thought. It wasn't merely, you are dead with Christ therefore you're guaranteed victory; he then went on, 'Sin shall not have dominion over you, *for* you are not under law but under grace': whatever that meant (v14). Frankly, it felt like a backward step. Surely freedom from the law was something to do with my getting forgiven and saved and born again, not with my ongoing Christian life. Still, one has to be disciplined and, when a biblical writer doesn't say what we want, to try to adjust... But the gloss had gone off the passage. Like the Pink Floyd album from the same era, it didn't get thrown away, but it didn't get listened to so often either.

And somehow, at forty, 'freedom from sin' seems less of a passionate concern than it did at twenty. I wonder how older readers feel. Does the very phrase have a ring of earlier years, of deeper hunger for holiness, of passions and heights and depths that go with first love? Now we've identified an acceptable level of compromise that we feel we can reasonably account for at the judgment seat; and, well, anyway, somehow one doesn't think that way quite so often, what with everything else that's going on.

And yet we know holiness does matter. A fair proportion of the old testament seems given over to underlining brutally just how much it matters. 'Make every effort to... be holy', says Hebrews, writing, presumably, not just for under-20s: 'Without holiness no-one will see the Lord.' 'Everyone who has this hope in him purifies himself' (1 John 3:3). Hmmm. 'Freed from sin... Sin shall not have dominion over you': did Paul mean it?

...What *is* Romans 6 about?

Looking for the flow

Never mind the answer, what is the question? Paul promises us that (NIV again now) 'sin shall not be your master'. Why? What exactly have we been given here?

Part of our problem in answering this is structural: chopping the Bible into short chapters often hides the ideas. Chapter 6 may not stand alone. So let's now speed-read chapters 6-8: where are they going? How does their flow of thought answer our question? It's good to jot down what seem to be the main sections, and their themes. (As usual, even if we get them wrong we end up knowing the passage better.)

Try it. As we do, the first thing we see is that the great promise of v14 isn't the passage's only concern; Paul's letters are rich, multi-levelled things. As we look for the overall shape of these sections, it seems marked by four repeated questions, 'What shall we say, then?... By no means!', in 6:1-2, 6:15, 7:7 and 7:13. And judging by these, his topmost aim here is to answer an opponent who objects to this radical gospel that redeems Jews and Gentiles without their fulfilling the Jewish ceremonial law. (We encounter this 'heckler' elsewhere too, in 3:1-8 and 9:14,19-20.) That is the passage's first concern, and as we're looking for the 'flow' we need to recognize it. *En route*, however, Paul's mind goes to work on just how this gospel liberates us from sin.[3] As we try to grasp the 'flow' of his argument, we may well feel that...

▪ The astoundingly liberating promise in v14, 'Sin shall not be your master', is linked to 'because you are not under law'; but that remark leads, not so much into vv15-23 (where Paul is dealing with the issues from his heckler's objection in v15), but rather into the verses about being 'released from the law' in 7:1-6.

▪ Again, 7:7-25 responds to an objection to Paul's gospel; and so he resumes the topics of 7:6 ('We serve in the new way of the Spirit, not in the old way of the written code') when he comes to the famous words of 8:1-2: 'Therefore there is now no condemnation for those who are in Christ Jesus, because through Christ Jesus the law of the Spirit of life set me free from the law of sin and death.'

▪ Thence, we'll probably feel, the argument proceeds straight down to, say, 8:14. After that, the next three verses make a transition into the book's next major theme.

So now we can try to list the answers these passages give to our question. Why will 'sin not be your master'?

▪ Firstly, because we've died and risen with Christ (6:1-11).
▪ Then, because we ourselves deliberately 'offer the parts of our body to' Christ, not to sin (6:12-13, 15-22).
▪ Thirdly, 'because you are not under law, but under grace' (6:14, 7:1-6, 8:1-4).
▪ And finally, we'll be victorious because we 'are controlled not by the sinful nature but by the Spirit' (8:4-14).

(We should pause here to worship God for each of these!)

8:2, and 8:4, make it sound as if the last two of these ideas may be two sides of the same coin: the law is dealt with, and the Spirit takes over. Paul says the same in his closely-related letter to the Galatians: 'If you are led by the Spirit, you are not under law' (5:18).[4]

It is because the first of these is true - that is, the legal barrier to our full communion with God has been removed by the cross – that the second, the coming of the Spirit, becomes

possible. The two together will promise us triumph.
Thankyou, Lord!

Something died inside us... (6:1-14, 7:1-6, 8:1-14)

So now we have at least a possible picture of these chapters'
overall direction. We can focus in again: what is Romans 6
really giving us?

It's a challenging chapter to grasp. But it's surely worth
working at, if full liberation from our negative behaviour
patterns is indeed what it's offering. Let's roll up our sleeves...

Let's take the first of the themes we've noted, from 6:5,6.
We're *'united with Christ's death... Our old self was crucified
with Christ'*. This probably isn't how we would describe our
conversion, left to ourselves. From our point of view there
was a choice, a change of heart – but maybe we didn't even
notice it at the time. So why put it this way? Is Paul being
unduly colourful in his phrasing? Or was something going
on we didn't realize? What do these phrases mean?

Let's start at the chapter's beginning. Paul opens with the
challenge, 'Shall we go on sinning?' His response is simply
that we can't; and the reason is that we're dead (v2). What he
goes on to emphasize is that we're totally identified with
Christ's death for us: with his burial, and his resurrection
into new life (vv3-11). Paul illustrates this from the dramatic
sign of baptism (v3) – because, when we demonstrate our
repentance by descending into that grave-like water, we express
our union with Christ's death in the clearest possible way.
(For Paul, the inward reality and the lived-out expression were
inseparable. But he wants us to understand clearly what it is
we're expressing.)

We're dead, says Paul, and this means that sin has no more
power over us. Look at v6: 'We know that our old self was
crucified with him so that... we should no longer be slaves to
sin, because anyone who has died has been freed from sin.'
Verse 14 fills out his line of thought: 'Sin shall not be your

master' – why? – 'because you are not under law'. Our union with Christ – we who are members of his Body – means we are included in all the benefits of his death; and that death fulfilled the law. Chapter 7 confirms this: 'The law has authority over a man only as long as he lives... You also died to the law through the body of Christ' (vv1,4). When Christ died, the penalty of death for sin (6:23) was paid; and we, 'adopted' into Christ, 'embodied' now with him, receive all the benefits of that. Sin's most fatal mastery is broken; heaven is assured us. *(Thankyou, Lord!)*

Long-term we will triumph! That would be good news enough. Our being 'declared just' before God, and freed from his righteous hostility to sin, is the burning heart of Paul's gospel; it is the basis of our 'peace with God' (5:1). Nothing could be more important. As David Gooding has remarked, without the cross we would face living under God's curse from the start of each day. But because of the cross our sins are paid for; we are declared just forever, nothing now can separate us from the love of Christ (8:35). Our identification with Christ's costly death that brought us heaven must obviously make us want to live as his servants, and not – not even briefly – the slaves of sin (6:16-22). It is a massive motivation for the struggle for holiness. *(Lord, please help me to grasp it...)*

But is there something even greater here? Not being under law means not facing long-term damnation; but does it give any cause for confidence as we wrestle now with our negative behaviours? Something that doesn't just motivate us, and call us to 'struggle', but actually changes that struggle, offering us a guarantee (v14) of triumph? There is indeed a hint of something truly dramatic and supernatural that has occurred inside us.

Reread v6; surely it sounds more than just motivational.[5] Rather, it seems to say that something has actually died, been destroyed, inside us now: 'Our old self *was* crucified with him, so that the body of sin might be done away with, that we should no longer be slaves of sin.' Freedom from slavery seems to refer here (and compare vv17-18) to this life, not the next (cf. also 7:5, '*when we were* controlled by the sinful nature'); so the destruction of the 'body of sin' (whatever that means) must refer to this life too. Hence the joyous clarity of v14: sin not merely *ought not* to be our master, it *shall not*. Something has changed inside us, now. Paul is not just saying that our union with Christ should motivate us, but rather that in some way we *have actually died* with Christ, and therefore the sinful 'old self' has been rendered powerless, right here and now.

It's a strange idea, but it runs throughout the passage, and we need to pause to really take it in. 'We died with Christ' (v8). 'We have been united with him in his death' (v5). 'Count yourselves dead to sin but alive in Christ Jesus' (v11). Or as he puts it in Galatians: 'I have been crucified with Christ, and I no longer live, but Christ lives in me' (Gal 2:20).

And then comes the second half: we're called to grasp that we have in some measure come into the glory of the resurrection, here and now. 'If we have been united with him in his death, we shall certainly also be united with him in his resurrection' (6:5) might sound initially like a promise of heaven after death. But is it? When we look more closely, we find chapter 6 talks of 'resurrection', not merely as our future, but as something that was part of our new birth. Look at v11: 'Count yourselves dead to sin but alive to God in Christ Jesus' seems a parallel to v5, but it clearly refers to the present; compare v4, where the burial of baptism precedes our 'living in a new life', but that is clearly radical new life on earth, not new life in heaven. Paul knows this is a hard idea for us to grasp: there's a sense of stretching our minds, of a need for real mental effort, in 'We will certainly...' (v5), 'We believe that...' (v8), 'Count yourselves...' (v11). But it certainly sounds as if that remarkable phrase 'united with his resurrection' describes something real that has happened to us in this world, when we first 'died with' and became 'united with' Christ. (Or, as we saw in Ephesians, heaven has started already.)

Chapter 8 will clarify it for us. There Paul talks in visionary terms about the entire creation being liberated one day from its 'bondage to decay', into glorious new existence. But he then makes clear that it has started now; this new life is something the children of God *already* possess, through the Spirit (8:21,23). Resurrection will one day swamp the cosmos; but it has begun, here and now, in us! No wonder 'sin shall not be your master'. Paul expresses the same ideas elsewhere: 'You died, and your life is now hidden with Christ... you *have* been raised with Christ' (Col 3:3,1), 'having been buried with him in baptism, and raised with him through your faith' (Col 2:12). Being seated with Christ in heavenly places starts *now*, not when we die (Eph 2:6). Paul's past tenses are no mistake: 'Those he justified he also glorified' (Rom 8:30). *(Thankyou, Lord, that my old self has died with you; thankyou, Lord, for giving me the new life of resurrection!)*

It seems, then, that Romans 6 reveals something unseen but totally remarkable that occurred in each of us when we were (to use Jesus' thought-provoking phrase) 'born again'. Some fundamental part of our being actually died (6:6) and was replaced, at the moment when we became identified with Christ. It wasn't just a religious change of mind, nor even merely an act of faith. There was something very central within us ('our old self', 6:6) that couldn't be reformed or cleaned up; it simply had to be amputated, and it was. We died; our baptism was a real funeral!

This is drastic religion.[6] It is far more than a call for good behaviour. Our salvation leads to the creation within us of a radically new kind of being. *(Even within me, Father! Thankyou!)* 'If anyone is in Christ,' says Paul elsewhere, 'he *is* a new creation; the old *has* gone, the new *has* come!' (2 Cor 5:17). In Romans 8:10-11 the sense of radical transformation is equally explicit: 'If Christ is in you, your body is dead because of sin, yet your spirit is alive because of righteousness...

The Spirit of him who raised Jesus from the dead is living in you!'[7]

'The Spirit is living in you': that takes us one vital step further. From Romans 6 we learn that we will ultimately be free from sin because Christ's death has freed us from the law's penalty; and, at our innermost centre, something has died, to be replaced by new life. At the heart of our existence now is something that can triumph over sin.

Chapter 8 clarifies what that 'something' is: 'The mind of sinful man (man in the flesh) is death, but the mind controlled by the Spirit is life and peace' (v6). What happened when we died and rose with Christ was that the Holy Spirit came to live in that innermost citadel. He could not live there as long as we were alienated from God by our sin. But now the legal penalty is dealt with, there is 'no condemnation' (8:1), and because we are 'not under law'[8] we can be 'led by the Spirit' (cf. Gal 5:18). To be born again, Jesus says, is to be 'born of the Spirit' (John 3:6-8); the new life we were born into is the 'new way of the Spirit' (Rom 7:6).

'Led' along a 'new way'. What brings about our freedom from sin, then, is settling the issue of control: 'The sinful mind... does not submit to God's law, nor *can* it do so. Those controlled by the sinful nature *cannot* please God. You, however, *are controlled* not by the sinful nature but by the Spirit, if the Spirit of God lives in you' (8:7-9). So here is the next thing that empowers our victory in the battle for holiness. Sin shall not be our master, because the law's fulfilment has removed the barrier to God's presence and power: therefore now, at the heart of our being, we believers are controlled by the almighty Holy Spirit. *(Lord, I praise you, I welcome you!)*

(I remember feeling frustrated when first as a preacher I began to grapple with Romans 8. It didn't say what I wanted. Romans 1-5 gave us the gospel, I thought; this, so much later, should be about our ongoing seriousness of discipleship – about whether we believers choose to live by the flesh or the Spirit. It seemed a marvellous passage to preach for that, with its clear opposition between living according to the flesh and living according to the Spirit (8:4). But there was one snag: Paul isn't talking here primarily about the difference commitment makes, but more about the difference conversion makes. Frustrating! But that's just the point. If we're converted at all, then we have the Spirit (v9).[9] It is our birthright as believers that promises each of us victory over sin.)

Instant triumph? (7:7-25)

Fine. We are united with Christ; our 'old self' has died, the almighty Spirit has come to live within us. But what do we do with all this?

First, it is clear that victory may be our birthright, but we're scarcely stepping straight into our inheritance. Romans 7 builds on Romans 6 – and it portrays an all too familiar picture of someone struggling with sin, and frequently losing: 'What I want to do I do not do; but what I hate I do' (v15).

Scholars have argued as to whether this is set before conversion (the plight of the merely 'religious' person), or after it. But many of us will recognize it from bitter post-conversion experience.[10] Its relevance there seems confirmed by the way Paul speaks at the chapter's end: I know in Christ I have final deliverance, he says, but then he goes on, meanwhile I am caught between God's law in my mind and the forceful tendency to sin elsewhere in my personality (vv24-25). 'What a wretched man I am,' says Paul. 'Who will rescue me from this body of death?'

'Body of death': remarks like that cause panic among certain kinds of theologians, in their anxiety to avoid any 'hellenistic' denial of the body and of the physical world. Maybe we've overreacted, however. As we read these chapters, it is difficult to avoid a recurrent note where Paul locates sin, for the Christian, in the body as against the spirit. 'The sinful passions... were at work in our bodies' (7:5). Paul sees a fatal tendency 'at work in the members of my body, waging war against the law of my mind and making me a prisoner of the law of sin at work within my members... Who will rescue me from this body of death?' (7:23-24). 'If by the Spirit you put to death the misdeeds of the body, you will live' (8:13). 'If Christ is in you, your body is dead because of sin, yet your spirit is alive' (8:10). Now, Paul is certainly not preaching an ascetic, body-denying, world-denying spirituality. But his point is perhaps closer (for once) to Freud: our physical nature has in it all kinds of drives and reactions, unhealed scars and hidden compulsions, derived deterministically from our genes, our history and our environment, that lead us with dire inevitability into behaviour we hate.

So now Paul announces liberating news: in our spirit, our innermost personality[11], the divine transformation has established its bridgehead. It takes place at an invisible level; you can't see the results of new birth in our physical condition, for example. But from then on, salvation begins to spread through our entire, physically-embodied personality – our thoughts, our values, our dreams, our ambitions, our affections, our emotional scars.[12] Indeed it seems unwise to insist that our physical bodies will remain untouched. (The more 'charismatic' our theology, the more strongly and 'holistically' we will put that!) Ultimately, says Paul, the 'rescue' he longed for in 7:24 will come, and our ageing mortal body, precious as it is to God, will be given total new life (8:11,23): though that has to wait till death or the second coming.

In other words, the biblical idea of salvation has three dimensions. In its most vital (and usual) sense it is past; our most fundamental being is permanently 'saved' (Acts 2:21, 16:31, Rom 10:9, Eph 2:8, etc). But the new testament also speaks of it sometimes as a continuous process (Phil 2:12, 1 Tim 4:16): salvation spreading through our personality. There is a lot to be done, and it won't be completed in this world. Finally, we look towards 'salvation' as future (Rom 13:11, Heb 9:28): finally the process will be complete, and all that we are will be swept up into salvation, with our bodies too receiving 'redemption' into glory (Rom 8:23, Eph 1:14).

We know this process in ordinary life. When we buy a house, it becomes, legally, ours: as we become, in our identification with his death at conversion, legally Christ's. We can go and live in it, as he comes to live in us. But the place is appallingly badly decorated; the wallpaper is a lurid shade of purple throughout, the bathroom stinks, the fittings are all in shabby disrepair. It may take us years to sort it all out. And so it is here. Once and for all we are legally made Christ's. Nor does he leave his 'house' empty: once and for all, he and his salvation have taken up residence in us. ('Christ is in you!' (Rom 8:10).) But for that transformation to work right through us is going to take time, and a great deal of skilful reconstruction. *(Thankyou, Lord, for your patience and your skill! Again I surrender myself to your rule, for your transformation: in the events of today, and for all the days to come.)*

Colossians 3 is one passage where Paul makes the process particularly clear. On the one hand, says Paul, 'you*have* taken off your old self with its practices, and *have* put on the new self, which is being renewed in knowledge in the image of its Creator' (vv9-10). That's definite, settled. On the other hand, that newness has to be deliberately spread through the personality; so in the selfsame paragraph he instructs them, 'Put to death, therefore, what *belongs* to your earthly nature – sexual impurity... lust... greed' (vv5,8). The citadel is secured, but the battle isn't over yet.

Seeking the steps forward

So: what do Romans 6-8 tell us about forwarding that transformation?

How shall we answer this question? One way is simply to reread these chapters, and list the practical 'instructions' Paul gives us.

As we do so, we notice how few there actually are: maybe as few as three. The crucial thing is what God *has* done! And then our response begins with that deliberate mental stance of repentance that is indispensable if real conversion has happened: the recognition, 'How can we live in sin any longer?'(6:2).

'*Count yourselves dead to sin but alive to God*' is Paul's first actual instruction (6:11). That is: grasp the vision of new birth as the fundamental reality of your life; develop a deep awareness that you really are dead and finished with an entire old way of living; choose a mindset that consciously, continually, yields itself to God. *(Lord, these are what I want. Please help me.)*

What Paul calls us to here is absolute, all-embracing surrender. '*Do not let sin reign in your mortal body... Do not offer the parts of your body to sin... but rather offer yourselves to God...offer the parts of your body to him*' (6:13). This second command comes immediately before that clear promise that sin will not have mastery over us (6:14), implying that it is basic to our victory. This makes sense: when we've 'offered ourselves' consciously to God, surrender to sin will be less likely in the minutes that follow! (As a student I was much struck by a tract advocating the discipline of consciously giving ourselves to God, five or six times each day. These verses imply that this isn't a bad idea.) When Paul returns to this theme later in Romans, he will start from the same point: 'I urge you, brothers, in view of God's mercy, to offer your bodies as living sacrifices' (12:1). *(So Lord, I do. I pause at this moment to give myself afresh, my body, mind, emotions and spirit, to you.)*

So here are the first practical steps; and we find that Paul devotes the second half of chapter 6 to deepening our grasp of this conscious 'offering'. The way he now rephrases his instruction gives a sense of our deliberately submitting to discipline: '*Offer the parts of your body in slavery to righteousness leading to holiness*' (v19). It's not surprising. In any skill, from judo to playing the saxophone, a period of submission to constructive disciplines is essential; only thus can we reach that freedom which instinctively 'does the right thing'. Holiness, Paul wants us to know, involves that same deliberate commitment to progress. *(Lord: please do not stop stirring up in me that desire!)* This conscious longing for holiness is crucial; we may not be as holy as we would like to be, says Tozer, but we are certainly as holy as we truly want to be.

But that's not the end. If we stopped here, we would not have progressed much beyond seeing the need for our own effort, the 'old way of the written code' (7:6). And then we might well end up trapped in the frustrations portrayed in 7:14-25: 'I myself in my mind am a slave to God's law'– so far so good – 'but in the sinful nature a slave to the law of sin.' We can't handle this in our own strength. 'After beginning with the Spirit', we can't expect to 'attain our goal by human effort' (Gal 3:3); we will still 'live by faith', or not at all.

So now we begin to see the point of what we find in chapter 7, Paul's long discussion of the value of the 'law' of God. The 'law' is basic to our transformation, he says, because it forces us to grasp our profound need for God's deliverance. The most helpful expositions I've encountered of this were by Leif Andersen from the Danish IFES student movement. Leif pointed out how bizarre are the things Paul says about the law, which till then I'd ignored as inexplicable. Our 'sinful passions' are actually *'aroused by the law'* (v5), says Paul; sin 'deceived me, seizing the *opportunity provided by the commandment'* (v8).

What is this about? Well, we may already have seen its meaning in evangelism. The need for forgiveness may not be where our witness starts; but, in the end, our friends aren't ready for Christ until they have grasped that need. But people are so very lost that they can't see it. How then are their eyes to be opened to their profound 'bentness', their deep need for forgiveness? Perhaps by experiencing how God's law reveals the sin in us – or even 'arouses' it! Forbidden fruit, we know, is attractive precisely because it is forbidden ('naughty but nice'); and that shows us that our nature doesn't just sin by accident. Rather it contains something so dark, so at enmity with God, that God's forbidding something becomes an 'opportunity', a reason to do it. So we desperately need deliverance. We see, then, how 'the commandment is good' (v12); the 'brutality of the law comes from God's compassionate heart', as Leif argues – it is God's way to show us our urgent need for forgiveness and rescue.[13] Such awareness will lead to conversion that will last. Indeed, Leif continues, encountering this law, seeing how much we needed forgiveness, will increase our subsequent love for Jesus. 'He who has been forgiven little loves little,' as Christ told us (Luke 7:47). It is as we grasp the seriousness of what Christ had to do for us – as we grasp the seriousness of sin, grasp the full force of the 'law' God revealed in the old testament[14] – that adoration wells up in our hearts.

So now, Paul announces joyously, we are finished with that law's enormous penalty; only Christ could have rescued us – and he has done so forever (Rom 7:4). But this same experience of our need is basic if we want the 'rescue' to extend through our personality. We are busy people... and we act as if we can get by without grappling with our need of supernatural power for transformation. We have to be helped to face reality; there is something deeply, stubbornly ugly in us, that we cannot master alone. 'I do not understand what I do,' says Paul here at some length. 'For what I want to do I do not do, but what I hate I do... I know that nothing good lives in me, that is, in my sinful nature. For I have the desire to do what is good, but I cannot carry it out. For what I do is not the good I want to do; no, the evil I do not want to do – that is what I keep on doing' (vv15,18,19). *(Lord, help me to face up to this...)*

When we have finally grasped this, we will be ready for chapter 8. We are born again, yes; but for salvation to spread within us, we need God as much as ever!

This is why those ongoing acts of surrender in chapter 6 were not just to the fulfilment of abstract commands. Rather, first, we 'offer ourselves' (6:13) to a deepening relationship with God – devoted surrender to the Person who has come to live in us, and who alone can now move us onward. Without this, transformation will grind to a halt. 'It is God who works in you to will and to act according to his good pleasure' (Phil 2:13).

So now we can read on into chapter 8. And we'll probably be struck by its repeated emphasis on 'the Spirit... the Spirit' – replacing that frustrated 'I... I... I' that recurs, helplessly, throughout chapter 7. Victory over sin – changing all that lurid purple wallpaper! – comes through active faith in the Spirit's power, not my own.

What we must learn, then, is the vital art of 'living according to the Spirit', and not 'according to the sinful nature' (8:4-5). As Paul says elsewhere: 'Live by the Spirit, and' – then – 'you will not gratify the desires of the sinful nature... The one who sows to please the Spirit, will from the Spirit reap eternal life' (Gal 5:16, 6:8).[15] *(Lord, thankyou: help me learn, and long, to 'please the Spirit'...)*

And this will guarantee us victory. Paul knew, as chapter 7 demonstrates, the ongoing difficulty of holiness. But he is clear that, if we are believers at all, we are destined (8:29), overall, to live lives that can finally be described as 'controlled by the Spirit' (8:9,14). That is why he is sure that sin will not ultimately master us. Scripture is plain that genuine new life will be accompanied by the Spirit's fruits. (This is 'Sin shall not be your master' again, but phrased the positive way round.) Those who are forgiven, Jesus taught, are those who, ultimately, take steps to forgive others (Matthew 6:15); those who go to heaven will be those who lived lives marked overall by practical social concern for the least of their brothers (Matthew 25). 'We know that we have passed from death to life, because we love our brothers. Anyone who does not love remains in death' (1 John 3:14). Luther phrased it precisely: We are justified by faith alone, but faith is never alone. Real new birth brings with it real internal change. Indeed there are steps we must deliberately take, choices for holiness we must consciously battle for. (Paul's words in v13, 'Brothers... if you live according to the sinful nature, you will die' leave no doubt of their seriousness.[16]) But the person indwelt and continually filled by the Spirit has received, 'built in', both the wisdom to make right choices, and the power to follow them through. Our task, then, is to learn, more and more, to 'live by the Spirit'...

God's agenda (12:1-13:14)

So this profound *'obligation'* becomes Paul's third instruction in these chapters: *'not to... live according to the sinful nature, but... by the Spirit put to death the misdeeds of the body'* (8:12-13).

How are we to obey it? Because it is evidently fundamental to our liberation.

Let's speed-read forward. Don't we find Paul's answer when he returns to his more personal theme in chapter 12? (That is after a joyous digression about the universal glory the Spirit is leading us into (8:15-39), and the unfailing wisdom of God's Word and strategy in bringing us all there (chs 9-11). It's worth wondering why he puts these first.) In 12:1-2 Paul comes back to the issue of how we live. He presents us with a vital choice of lifestyle; and it seems to develop chapter 8's challenge to live by the Spirit, not the flesh.

First he urges us, 'in view of God's mercy, to offer your bodies as living sacrifices' (12:1). Surely we recognize here Paul's two instructions from chapter 6. 'Offering your bodies' was the heart of 6:16-19; being a 'living sacrifice' matches 'counting ourselves dead' with Christ in 6:11– cultivating a mindset grounded on the 'cross through which the world has been crucified to me and I to the world'.[17]

Paul then helps us a step further, with the twin commands of 12:2: 'Do not conform any longer to the pattern of this world; *but* be transformed by the renewing of your minds.' So being a 'living sacrifice' means, first, breaking free from the fleshly 'patterns' of the 'world' (or 'age') around us. These, 1 John told us bluntly, involve 'the cravings of sinful man, the lust of his eyes, and the boasting of what he has and does', and loving them is totally incompatible with loving God.[18] It is as we repudiate these that we can 'please the Spirit'.[19] This combination is true 'worship', says Paul (Rom 12:1); and this is how we can 'be transformed'.

We have two aspects, then: continually turning away from the fleshly norms surrounding us, and instead seeking the spread of the Spirit's control to 'renew our minds'. *(Father, please help me find my way forward practically in each of these...)* 'Control' is the issue here: how far do we choose to be moulded by media reinforcing the norms of 'this age', and how far are we shaped by the Spirit's 'media' and Word?[20] It's a never-ending choice; Cranfield translates these verses 'Stop allowing yourselves to be conformed to this age, but continue to let yourselves be transformed'.[21]

Paul moves on to define this 'renewing of our minds' very practically. If we now list the themes of chapters 12 and 13, we'll find a series of 'Do nots' liberating us from the 'patterns of this world': from egoism; individualism; insincerity; lovelessness; lack of zeal; unwillingness to share; cursing; pride; conceit; revenge; lawlessness; dishonesty; drunkenness; immorality; dissension; jealousy. *(Lord, I need you to show me which of these, currently, are the issues for my life with you...)* 'If by the Spirit you put to death the misdeeds of the body, you will live', Paul has told us (8:13); and here are those 'misdeeds of the body', here is God's agenda for our transformation. Paul gives us no sense of therapeutic tolerance in this passage. We are called to a deliberate 'amputation' of sin! As Jesus said, 'If your right eye causes you to sin, gouge it out... If your right hand causes you to sin, cut it off' (Matt 5:29-30).

To paraphrase Andrew Jukes, Christ's death for us doesn't mean our own 'flesh' can safely evade the cross; instead, it makes its being 'put to death' unavoidable.[22] *(Christ who died: please teach me to be serious about this 'putting to death' of sin...)*

But the important thing is that we're not left to handle all this in our own strength. That is clear from 13:14, the section's closing verse. The secret is to 'clothe ourselves with the Lord Jesus Christ', and then we won't be thinking 'how to gratify the desires of the sinful nature'. Paul doesn't want his instructions to come in legalistic isolation.[23] Rather, he's building here on everything he has said about our 'union with Christ' in new birth, after which Christ lives within us and we are, at root, 'controlled by the Spirit'. What we must do is grounded in what God is doing. '*Since* we live by the Spirit' (after our new birth and the death it involved), '*let us keep in step* with the Spirit' (Gal 5:24-25); those essential right actions are the '*fruit* of the Spirit' inside us, by whom we need to live, and otherwise they wouldn't happen at all (Gal 3:3, 5:16,22). '*Continue to work out* your salvation with fear and trembling, *for it is God who works in you* to will and to act according to his good pleasure' (Phil 2:13).

As we grasp these things, we realize how much of the new testament exists to help us with this twofold agenda; to live not 'according to the flesh' but 'according to the Spirit'; not to 'conform to this age', but to grow 'transformed', radical; to 'count ourselves dead' to an entire world-system, committing our energies to the resurrection world. We think of Jesus' words: 'Do not store up for yourselves treasure on earth... Store up for yourselves treasure in heaven... For where your treasure is, there your heart will be also' (Matt 6:19-21). Or his teaching about identifying with the cross: 'If anyone would come after me, he must ... take up his cross and follow me. For whoever wants to save his life will lose it, but whoever loses his life for me will find it' (Matt 16:24-25). We recall, too, his long series of contrasts between 'this-agely' and 'transformed' behaviour: 'You have heard that it was said...

But I say to you...' (Matt 5:21-6:21). (*Lord, thankyou; please help me understand what these mean now for me, make each of them into growing realities, by your Spirit...*) We've seen in 1 Peter the stark choice between being 'conformed' (the same word as here in Romans 12:2) to the 'evil desires' of our surroundings (1:14), or 'setting our hope fully' on the alternative world (1:13).[24] The Word brings us back to these vital choices, over and over again. And, especially important, we have watched Paul pointing to this Word as the central power[25] for our being 'transformed' (2 Cor 3:14-18 – again the same term as here in Romans 12:2). As we grow soaked in the Spirit's Word, we feed the relationship that gives us the power to choose: power for transformation, power for freedom.

So here it is: our way forward, uniting many of the themes we've explored. 'By the Spirit put to death the misdeeds of the body', says Paul's third imperative; we break free into changed lifestyle as our minds are 'transformed' by the Spirit's power within, and salvation spreads out through all that we are, setting us free, choice by choice, to live like Jesus. It all comes back to those twin principles, repentance and faith, that were central to our conversion. We are called to grow in *repentance*: counting ourselves dead to the old world and risen with Christ, living by that death, turning from sin, and keeping our minds now 'set on what the Spirit desires'. We're called to grow, by the Spirit's strength, in *faith*, knowing Christ's death has set us free, rejoicing in his Spirit at the heart of our being (8:15-16), and trusting that 'He who began a good work in you will carry it on to completion' (Phil 1:6). And on the basis of these we continually 'offer ourselves to God', feeding, focusing on, deepening this union with Christ; 'so that, *just as* Christ was raised from the dead through the glory of the Father, we too may live a new life' (Rom 6:4).

And so there comes from God a threefold cure. First, we've been set free from the law's penalty for our past sins: liberated once and for all, by the death of Christ, which we joined in by 'dying with him' in new birth. Therefore, secondly, 'Christ is in you'; his Spirit now controls the citadel of our innermost being, and he promises that salvation will spread onward through our personalities, as we 'offer ourselves to God' rather than to sin. And, long-term, we are guaranteed total triumph, either when we die or when Christ returns: the 'redemption of our bodies', when we are finally swept free of all evil and decay, and our whole being is flooded with the glory of God. It is that confidence that makes Paul conclude, 'You did not receive a spirit that makes you a slave again to fear' (Rom 8:15), a spirit of ineffective moralism. Rather, he exults, we are on the way to unimaginable victory. The Spirit within us is the 'first fruits' of dazzling glory (8:23); he is the guarantee that we are passed far beyond all condemnation (8:1-2, 33-34), locked now by divine predestination into an infinitely loving masterplan, one from which nothing can ever separate us (8:29,39).....

Hallelujah! We need a new section for that...

'More than we can ask or imagine' (8:14-23)

'Sin shall not be your master.' *Thankyou, Father!* But there is more. Holiness is not merely negative, merely an absence of sin[26]; it is for a purpose. The best is yet to come, says Paul, in what (for me at least) is among the Word's most glorious sections...

'Those who are led by the Spirit are the sons of God', writes Paul as he moves us onward (8:14). 'Led' in the sense of being controlled, empowered for holiness: that is the point of the first half of chapter 8. But 'led' where? The Spirit's leading is not merely a leading *from*, it is a leading *to*.

The point of this is our sonship. We are now the earthly habitations of the Spirit, and that means we have become something remarkable – something Paul can only describe as 'God's children'. We use this extraordinary phrase so often that we miss its point. We need to stop and think: What does it mean?

First, it is relational. Mere rule-keeping human religion could never accomplish this. Paul recalls the sense of servitude, and hence fear, that marks legalistic religion where there is no assurance of forgiveness and new birth (8:15); and he contrasts that with the 'glorious freedom' flowing from the confidence of having become 'children of God' (8:21).[27] Deep within us, the Spirit cries out with our own spirits to God as our Father (or 'Abba', *Daddy*'[28]– a term for a 'close', loving God, one no legalist would dare to use[29]). This itself is a sign of his life within us; we can't truly cry out to Christ as Lord and to God as our Father except by the Spirit.[30]

But secondly, as God's children, we are his heirs: 'heirs of God and co-heirs with Christ' (v17). Now this really is something: joint-heirs with the 'heir of all things' (Hebrews 1:2) – 'that we may also share in his glory!'[31] Our modern imaginations may give way at this point, but we need to stretch them to grasp just where we are being 'led'. 'How will he not, along with Christ, graciously give us all things?' (Rom 8:32). Indeed, we are actually going to share Christ's throne (Rev 3:21)! 'No eye has seen, no ear has heard, no mind has conceived, what God has prepared for those who love him' (1 Cor 2:9). (*I do believe it, Father. And I worship you. Thankyou!*)

In short, says Paul, 'the sufferings of this present time'– and Paul knew plenty about these: floggings, prison, stoning, betrayal, five times the 'forty lashes minus one'[32]– 'are *not worth comparing* with the glory that will be revealed in us!' Indeed, the very creation itself is 'eagerly' waiting[33] for Christ's 'co-heirs'– us! – to be revealed as its fulfilment and consummation.

The whole creation, not merely humanity. Now what is this about?

Suddenly the horizons open up. Paul sets out in full the astonishing cosmic panorama that we saw hinted at in 1 Peter.

Since the Fall, our created world has been 'subjected to frustration' (Rom 8:20), to pointlessness and entropy. We live in a deterministic 'bondage to decay' (v21); 'Things fall apart,' in Yeats' famous words. There is no beauty that does not fade, no achievement that doesn't crumble, no glory that can endure. Ecclesiastes 1 records this pattern in its classic expression, mirroring the pessimistic insights of Eastern religion: 'Everything is meaningless. What does man gain from his labour?...The sun rises and the sun sets, and hurries back to where it rises. The wind blows to the south and turns to the north; round and round it goes, ever returning on its course. All streams flow into the sea, yet the sea is never full...All things are wearisome, more than one can say...What has been done will be done again; there is nothing new under the sun.' Nothing new, nothing lasts, nothing gained. Since the Fall, this has been a cosmos locked into tragedy, decay and futility: cut off by human rebellion from the loving purposefulness of God.

But now God has introduced an alternative order: the possibility of grace. In what we call the 'natural' universe, you start off with something, and you end up with nothing. Where the 'kingdom' of grace comes, you start off with nothing but you end up with something glorious: light where there was darkness,[34] joy instead of tragedy, love instead of hatred, resurrection instead of death. Cornish poet Jack Clemo calls it 'God's jazz breaking in upon the mournful music of the spheres'.[35] The entropic law of our universe is that 'the amount of disorder in a system always tends to increase'; can we imagine what a 'new heaven and new earth' could be like, where truly 'grace reigns'[36] – where instead of entropy there is ever-increasing beauty, 'from glory to glory', always moving 'further up and further in' through the creativity of God?

At any rate the entropic system is now broken; the alternative order is here; but its bridgehead is *us!* 'The creation itself will be liberated from its bondage to decay and brought into the *glorious freedom of the children of God*' (v21). We,

God's children, are 'marching to a different drummer'; our hearts have been liberated from the 'bondage to decay'. Clemo rephrases the gospel like this: humanly we are locked into a fate of unspeakable tragedy, but because of the cross we *need not fulfil it*.[37] God's children embody the *'firstfruits'* of the new universe of grace and of the Spirit (v23), that which one day the entire harvest will be like[38], free from futility, 'imperishable': 'Outwardly we are wasting away, yet inwardly we are being renewed day by day' (2 Cor 4:16). In the fullest possible sense, the law of the Spirit of life through Christ Jesus has set us free from the law of sin and death.[39] The Spirit within us now is a guarantee of the future, both for ourselves and for the whole creation. And the day will come when Christ returns, when transformation spreads out to the 'redemption of our bodies' (v23), indeed when the glory sweeps out from its present foothold and transforms the entire cosmos (v21). It's a vision worth thinking hard and dreaming hard about, on the bus, walking in the park, until it grips our imaginations: this is where we're going, in the light of which we should live now.

'In this hope we were saved'(v24). *Thankyou, Lord!*

Visions of horror and glory (8:22-30)

So the creation's suffering is not meaningless. 'The whole creation has been groaning as in the pains of childbirth right up to the present time' - and as John Lennox puts it, if these are the labour pains, what a colossal 'birth' must be coming!

But there is another, darker side. We the 'sons of God' may be the 'firstfruits' of the kingdom; but firstfruits isn't the same as harvest.[40] The 'whole creation' is 'groaning' (v22), and we have not been evacuated safely out of it; 'we ourselves' share in that 'groaning' of a desperately broken world (v23). We're called to hope, but as Paul says, if it's hope, then evidently it isn't something we already have (vv24-25).

'Blessed are those who mourn,' said Jesus (Matt 5:4). Anyone who can be at ease in our horror-strewn, violent culture and starving, poisoned planet either has no idea of what's going on or no sense of the love and compassion of God. And some of us are caught in a still more terrible way in the tragedy of 'exile', of a world still awaiting full redemption: cancer of someone dear to us, multiple sclerosis, children mangled in a car-crash. Even as I write this section comes an interruption, friends telling of a relative who miscarried then found that her husband had been adulterous. Christ came down to share our anguish and be trapped (*Lord, I worship you*) in this 'groaning' world's horror too, so that it might be changed forever; and we, says Paul, are 'co-heirs' with that same self-giving 'Christ – *if* indeed we *share in his sufferings*, in order that we may also share in his glory' (v17). There is a terrible reality here. We've noted that child-like word 'Abba', 'Daddy', that describes our relationship with God; but outside this chapter (and its Galatians parallel), its only new testament appearance is when Christ is in agony in Gethsemane. It is hard, but somehow the experience of that Abba-relationship seems profoundly bound up with the experience of our suffering.

God has been there, in Gethsemane, and still is there with us. Let no one say God cannot suffer; when we are in agony 'the Spirit himself' also is crying out in pain, as he 'intercedes for us with groans that words cannot express' (v26). He is there; and he shares our agony, in a way that goes far beyond what can be verbalized.[41]

It is stupid to try to 'explain' that black mystery of suffering that left Christ himself screaming, 'My God, my God, why?' I have been through nothing that gives me the right to speak of it. Yet there are hints here, faint candles in a darkness that will only make full sense when the 'old order' of tragedy has 'passed away' and there is finally 'no more crying or pain' (Rev 21:4).

There is, writes Paul, a meaning in what happens to us; and unlike us the Spirit can see where it is leading. He 'intercedes for us... in accordance with God's will' (Rom 8:26-27). Somehow there remains a 'will', a 'purpose', within even the darkest agonies that have flowed from our recurrent human rebellions;[42] somehow suffering is not alone, but suffering and glory will go together (cf. vv17-18). 'We do not want you to grieve like' (that is, in the same way as) 'the rest of men, who have no hope', Paul told Thessalonica;[43] for the believer, whatever else is true, there is not the meaninglessness that marks suffering outside Christ. Paul wrote three chapters earlier, as someone who knew agony first-hand, 'We rejoice in the hope of the glory of God. Not only so, but we also rejoice in our sufferings, because we know that suffering produces perseverance; perseverance, character; and character, hope' (5:2-4). And then he continued: 'And hope does not disappoint us, because God has poured out his love into our hearts' (5:5). Our security – our only security – is in that love of God; chapter 8 goes to great lengths to affirm that nothing, no suffering, can separate us from it (vv 35-39). Because we believe in this love, we can believe in a 'purpose' which will justify hope for us too.

But now Paul moves on. The astounding verses 28 to 30 will spell that purpose out, revealing a loving, almighty divine strategy at work beneath all the horror of a broken cosmos. We must dare to believe in it ('the righteous will live by faith'); as the saying goes, what we have seen of God in Jesus will enable us to trust him for what we cannot yet see.

Paul spells out here a massive promise from God: 'We know that in all things God works for the good of those who love him.'[44] 'In *all* things': here is God's response to Ecclesiastes' account of the pointlessness of life lived only in 'this-worldly' terms. 'In all things': in the end, says Paul, nothing will be without meaning. Paul cannot be saying that all that happens will be good (let alone pleasant). Some things that happen to us (as to Jesus) are utterly destructive, reflecting our fallen universe, or even satanic in their origin (e.g. Job 1). But even in the most anarchic occurrences, God's infinitely creative grace is somewhere at work. (Cf. v37: '*In* all these things we are more than conquerors.') Destiny, wrote the brilliant novelist Conrad in *Heart of Darkness*, is a 'mysterious arrangement of merciless logic for a futile purpose'.[45]   In contrast Paul offers a triumphant certainty: always, somehow, the Spirit is interceding (v27), and the Father has a way forward. (*Lord, I worship you...*) 'In all things' summons us to patient, imaginative trust – or as Paul says in 1 Thess 5:18: 'Give thanks in all circumstances; for *this* is God's will for you in Christ Jesus.'

At the same time, this is not an inevitable fate that has no respect for the individual. 'In all things God works for the good of *those who love him*.' Paul is not saying that everything will work out ideally for everybody. Those who choose to live apart from God remain in the old alienated, entropic system, in 'bondage to decay' and tragedy (v21). The new order, the subversive purposes of the kingdom where 'in all things God works for good', is for those who respond to God's invitation to join it, who '*love him*'. (*Lord, thankyou; help me, in all things, to be one who truly loves and trusts you...*)

And our love is far more than recompensed by the loving destiny God has for us. Verses 29-30 define it. The point of our justification is not merely the cancelling of our past sins; the purpose is our glorification.

Surely v29 is one of the most astounding verses in the whole Bible; it offers a truly staggering thought. (*Lord, please open my mind, help me grasp this.*) We see here the goal and consummation of our entire existence. Our 'predestination' is not just to be saved,[46] nor merely to be moral, or nice, or good. It is nothing less than to be 'conformed to the likeness of his Son', to have 'Christ formed in us' as Galatians says (4:19[47]), to be 'transformed into his likeness with ever-increasing glory, which comes from the Lord who is the Spirit' (2 Cor 3:18).

What can this mean? Surely – or, amongst other things – that all the love of Jesus, all the peace and gentleness and joy and power for good of Jesus, will one day flow out fully through us, just as they do through him. (We need to pause here to try and imagine that being true of ourselves as individuals.) Already, as we 'grow in him', we are learning to share his power to bring about good in this world by 'praying in Jesus' name'; but the day will come when we totally 'share his throne', share all his authority for goodness, because we have grown completely like him. The long process will be complete; heaven will finally have spread right through our personalities. 1 John 3 presents the same vision: 'Dear friends, now we are children of God, and what we will be has not yet been made known. But we know that when he appears, *we shall be like him*, for we shall see him as he is!'

It is good news. The Father's aim isn't just to clone us and make us 'moral'! (Wouldn't that sound safe, religious, dull and colourless?) Indeed, even the thought of 'conforming to his likeness' might conjure up fears of standardization. We do sometimes speak of Christians 'dying to self' in a way that sounds as if God might be into cloning – in defiance of all the evidence of his creational style. But that is a vast misunderstanding. It is sin, and its consequences, that obliterate human individuality (drug addiction is an obvious example). But the more we 'put off the old nature' and grow like Christ, the more truly individual we become. (Surely we see this in the Christ-like people we know?) Christ is God, is infinite; so there is space for us each to grow 'conformed to Christ' in infinitely diverse and individual expressions.

'Transformed into Christ's likeness' – 'attaining to the *whole* measure of the fullness of Christ' (Eph 4:13) – 'Christ formed in you': all this, once we really reflect on its meaning, becomes astonishing. Yet God has predestined nothing less for us (Rom 8:29). Now we see the point of that odd preposition in v18, where Paul spoke of the 'glory that will be revealed *in* us'. Not *to* us, as if we were to be mere

spectators. 'He comes to be glorified *in* his holy people...
that you might share in the glory of our Lord Jesus Christ.'[48]
What brighter glory – by definition – could he possibly grant
us than to be 'conformed to the likeness of his Son'? 'He who
did not spare his own Son, but gave him up for us all – how
will he not also, along with him, graciously give us all
things?'(v32). (*Thankyou, Father!*) 'Those he justified, he also
glorified'(v30): God is a God who delights to share all his
glory with us, from top to bottom. Millions of years will not
be enough to exhaust it.

Here is the goal of history. And here we see the twistedness
of Satan's lie back at the start in Eden, when he tempted the
first human beings to grasp at 'being like God'[49] – as though
'participating in the divine nature'[50] was something God
wanted to clutch to himself. In fact 'being *like* God' was
precisely God's plan for us, though not in a spirit of alienated
self-aggrandizement. God's nature is to share his glory and
power and likeness, not to use it to domineer, as Jesus showed
us (cf. Matthew 20:25-28). Hence the bizarre phrasing of God's
intention here: we're to be conformed to his likeness so that
Jesus might be the 'first-born among many brothers'(v29).
We're not just to be his 'servants', not even 'worshippers' or
'friends', but Jesus' 'brothers'. (It's one of those moments
when we feel, 'Had I written the Bible I would never have
said that.') In John 17 Jesus prayed to his Father, 'I have
given them the glory that you gave me', even though his
disciples were no more than a rabble about to abandon or
deny him.[51] And at the end of history Jesus' Bride will indeed
shine with the glory of God (Rev 21:11). As Ephesians says,
what God's love has planned for us is far more than we can
ask or imagine. (*Thankyou, Father!*)

God's purpose in all that happens to us, then, is to 'conform
us to the likeness of his Son', to enable us to share in the glory
of Jesus. All that Adam lost will be restored. In the situations
that befall us in this broken cosmos, we sometimes cannot
imagine how to pray; but somewhere beneath it all, God

knows what he is doing. His foreknowledge is not merely a matter of knowing who will respond to his grace and accept his salvation. He is the master dramatist (Ephesians speaks of us as his 'workmanship'), and he foresees everything that happens in our lives. Every friendship, every suffering, every sermon heard, every book read: he knows what we will experience in each of them, and weaves all this together with unimaginable skill so that, in the end, each of us will be like Jesus. Or he is like the master sculptor, chipping away at a block of stone. If the stone could speak, it might cry out at the chisel; but with each chip that flies off the block, from unprepossessing material a glorious likeness is brought into being.....

I worship you, Lord, because you know what you are doing: our destiny is glorious, and gloriously safe in your loving hands!

'Fixed in the certainty of love unchanging'[52] (8:30-39)

'So what shall we say to these things?' Surely, that we 'rejoice in the hope of the glory of God!'(5:2).

An enormous sense of assurance flows through these chapters. It was there in the flow of Romans' first section: all of us, pagan or religious, have fallen short of God's glory, so he has designed a way of salvation where everything is 'by grace and guaranteed' (4:16), because he sees to it all. And that good news led into the triumphant opening of 5:1: 'Therefore, since we have been justified by faith' – since there is nothing left now that could depend on our strength or achievement – 'we have *peace* with God!'[53] Romans 5 is one of the Bible's great chapters on assurance, and on God's undeserved love for us (5:7-11). Then, as we've seen, chapters 6-8 build on that sense of assurance: our new birth makes all the difference in the world, guarantees that sin shall not be our master, guarantees us glory. At new birth we have stepped 'into Christ'[54]; we have thereby opted into a destiny, like passengers stepping onto an express train, and now that train will most surely carry us to our destination. Those God knew about beforehand, he has also destined to be made like Jesus (8:29)! Of course there is another side. We can still sin, we can make the process very hard for ourselves, we can go the very long way round; and some of us do. But if we have truly repented, then the ultimate direction is certain: 'In all things God works for the good of those who love him' (8:28). 'He who began a good work in you *will carry it through to completion until the day of Christ*' (Phil 1:6).

That is the theme that will close this part of Romans: 'Nothing will be able to separate us from the love of God.' As we come to the end of this densely nutritious section we do well to ask: how do these verses complete what was happening earlier in the chapter? Knowing how it finishes, how can we express Paul's series of ideas, his flow of thought, to bring out the unity it surely had in his mind?

As we reflect, the answer becomes clear. Paul's vision of our utter security as chapter 8 closes flows with glorious logic from the way it started: it is the end-point, the final fruition, of the 'law of the Spirit of life' (8:2). Just as the 'law of sin and death' meant that our rebellion led inevitably to destruction (6:23), so with equal certainty the work of the Spirit leads us from forgiveness to glory. 'Those who are led by the Spirit of God are sons of God' (8:14); this is where he is leading us, and he will not fail. The Spirit of Christ is the one who will stand alongside us even in our darkest moments (8:23,26); but he is also already the 'firstfruits' of glory within us (v23), the guarantee that, while the present may be tough, the future is certain. He knows how to pray (v27) according to the divine purpose by which, ultimately, everything will serve to make us like Christ (v29). And he himself will see that purpose through: we are 'being transformed into (Christ's) likeness,' says Paul elsewhere, 'with ever-increasing glory, which comes from the Lord who is the Spirit.'[55]

So Paul uses these final verses to underline that glorious assurance, in at least four ways.

First, *God is for us* (v31). What an astonishing statement! Too many of us still labour under a notion of God as ultimately forbidding, unfriendly, critical, harsh.[56] When I was young, for example, I really doubted whether I had made it into the kingdom. I'd heard the gospel phrased so many ways: you must believe; you must repent; you must admit, and believe, and confess, A-B-C; you must trust in Jesus...And it wasn't very bright of me, but I used to wonder: maybe I could have repented but not confessed, or admitted but not trusted, and on the decisive last day salvation would slip between my fingers... Until in the end it clicked: the issue is the love of God for me. God is scarcely going to sit in heaven noting my slip and enforcing my exclusion; my salvation has cost him too much for that. That enormous love is the point here. *God is for us.* With all his care, all his power. No foe can hope to oppose us successfully, not in the long term.

Paul's second point is the proof of that. 'He who did not spare his own Son'– and none of us have more than the slightest notion of what that means:[57] that a Being so far above us, a Father so utterly identified with immortal, unfathomable love, should be sundered from his perfect Son and see him exposed to infinite agony for us – 'He who did not spare his own Son... how will he not also, along with him, graciously give us all things?' Ephesians 1:3 said the same: God has already 'blessed us in the heavenly realms with every spiritual blessing in Christ'. If his grace extended to giving us Jesus, even to the point of Calvary, then this is love unlimited; nothing else will be withheld. As we've just seen, our destiny is to be given absolutely everything that is good in God's universe: we are co-heirs with the 'heir of all things', and we will share in all his nature and all his glory.

Thirdly, there is no one left to accuse or condemn us; because God is the prime figure in all these issues, and he is with us, not against us. Indeed vv32-34 resolve a question that may have struck us back in vv26-27: why does Paul speak there of 'He who searches our hearts'? Surely because it underlines our security in the divine purposes. God is not destining us for glory because he has fortunately underrated some sin or inadequacy in us. Rather, it is 'he who searches our hearts' who stands with us, intercedes for us (v34 reintroduces this theme from v27), and sees us through to glory. He knows the worst about us, and has paid for it, and now it is forgotten. *(Thankyou, Lord!)* Here again we sense how Paul's certainty builds on all he showed us since chapter 6. Indeed the 'power of sin is the law'[58], it is the law's penalty that could 'separate us from the love of Christ' – and that law has been conclusively dealt with. So there can be no accuser, no condemnation. Nothing can separate us from the love, and the power, of Jesus.

Paul's last point is one we may well need in ordinary life. Don't 'trouble or hardship or danger' make us doubt whether we're quite so securely 'in the love of God'?[59] If we're the 'King's kids', these things shouldn't happen to us? Again the flow of the whole chapter culminates here. Suffering and glory go together, and in this world we are not kept permanently out of trouble, any more than Jesus was: 'For your sake we face death all the day long.' Trouble and hardship will come (cf. John 16:33); it is *'in'* all these things' (compare the 'in' of v28), not by being kept safely out of them, that we are 'more than conquerors'. Conquerors have to be soldiers; and God promises we will be 'more than conquerors'– 'more', perhaps because he not only takes us through the storms, but in his infinite wisdom he even uses the storms.

And so come the sublime final verses. 'I am convinced that neither death nor life, neither angels nor demons'– in some ministries or countries we may need that assurance– 'neither the present nor the future, nor any powers, neither height nor depth, nor anything else in all creation, will be able to separate us from the love of God that is in Christ Jesus our Lord.' *Hallelujah!* The doctrine of eternal security is a much-debated one. Is it true that once we are really born again – that is, not a casual wave of the hand to 'accept Jesus', but a true repentance of heart – then we can never be lost? Or is it possible for a believer to commit spiritual suicide, consciously to reject salvation, to step outside the love of Christ? Scripture isn't totally clear, and this author has changed his mind on the question at least twice! But these verses do sound like an extremely secure guarantee. That death cannot separate us from Christ seems plain; but that *life* cannot, is even more encouraging. Nor can anything in the present; nor anything– any deception, any pressure, any breakdown – in the future. Surely that is about as secure as we could be. And the reason is that it is grounded in what matters most of all: we cannot be separated from that colossal love we could never have earned or deserved, the '*love of God that is in Christ Jesus our Lord...*'

Again: *Hallelujah! Lord, thankyou for your astonishing, and invincible, love. Please help me be one through whom this gospel flows continually out into the world...*

Notes
[1] Of course a book's 'basic ideas' may not be the same as the author's most pressing personal concerns when he wrote. Doesn't the argument of Romans seem to come to summation in the call for unity of 15:5-13 (following on chapter 14's extended plea for mutual tolerance) – with a sense of Paul's task having been completed by 15:15 ('I have written boldly to you'), and what follows being a series of 'PSs'? (His aid project (15:25-27) is a very practical way of sealing this same unity.) If so, doesn't it suggest that Paul's pressing concern in writing Romans was to bind together Jews and Gentiles in unified praise (15:6-7), breaking down the age-long division, as the mission to the world went forward? Thus chapters 1-3 present both Gentiles and Jews needing the same salvation; chapters 9-11 show them both headed for the same glory. But God used this occasion also to give us a brilliant presentation of the gospel's fundamentals.

[2] John Stott's Romans commentary in the *Bible Speaks Today* series is, as usual with Stott, a classic, clear, thought-provoking guide, the kind every young Christian should work through in their first five years in the faith. Subsequently other perspectives can be

refreshing. Recently I found working through these chapters with
C.E.B.Cranfield's *Romans: A Shorter Commentary* (1985) a real
reawakening to the glories of the gospel.

[3] So, as with Mark, we are only exploring one or two aspects of
these passages here, albeit fairly central ones. But that's why we
're-read': as we return to these multi-levelled books at different
periods in life, with different questions and needs, God has new
slants on them to show us.

[4] Cf. also how the same pair of ideas appear in the shift of thought
from the law in Galatians 3:23-24 (which revisits ideas from Romans
7) to the Spirit in 4:4-7 (revisiting Romans 8). In many ways
Galatians parallels Romans, and we shall use it frequently in this
chapter as a source of helpful 'sidelights'. If we're studying Romans,
it's a good idea to speed-read Galatians' five pages too.

[5] 6:12-13 (like 8:12-13) clearly are specifically motivational. We
need this; we have a part to play in the process! But it seems there
is more going on in chapter 6 than that.

[6] One notices the academic commentaries often fight shy of
anything so dramatic, even at the price of distorting the exegesis.
As I noted earlier, I have personally found Cranfield's *Romans: A
Shorter Commentary* wonderfully helpful. But the difficulties he
gets into by arguing that 'dying with Christ' has four distinguishable
senses here (pp.128-29) suggests something is amiss. Does anyone
use the same words for four different things in so short a passage?
It surely makes more sense to see one fundamental reality.

[7] Or as Ephesians puts it, as unredeemed sinners we were actually
'dead', in the most vital sense of that term; and what God's grace
had to do was nothing less than raise us from the dead (2:1,5-6).

[8] It is probably of use to observe that Paul is not writing a
systematic study here of the old testament law in all its uses. The
law still has value for us as a source of teaching and principles; that
is why it is in our Bibles, and Paul certainly uses it that way
elsewhere (e.g. 1 Cor 9:8ff or 14:20ff).

[9] This is an important point to emphasize, since it is denied by
some Pentecostal teachers, in flat contradiction of what Paul says
clearly here. David Wilkerson's splendid *The Cross and the
Switchblade* speaks strangely of 'receiving the Holy Ghost' as
something separate from new birth, as if we could receive one

member of the Trinity without receiving the others. (Being and staying *filled* with the Spirit is of course an entirely separate issue.)

¹⁰ And cf. Gal 5:17. But of course the passage does speak forcefully to the powerlessness of mere religion, as against true new birth into the life of the Spirit.

¹¹ It seems unwise for us to attempt to be too specific in relating Paul's uses of 'mind' and 'spirit' to our modern use of these terms.

¹² One tempting reading of v6 – 'The mind of sinful man is death, but the mind controlled by the Spirit is life and peace'– is in terms of stress management. It is obvious that joyous faith in God's loving sovereignty, and the resulting tendency not to 'worry about tomorrow' (Matt 6:25-34), lead towards 'life and peace'. The 'worries of this life' (Matt 13:22) not only 'choke the good seed' but many aspects of our psychological and physical health as well.

¹³ Isn't Jesus using the law this same way in Matthew 5:20? And cf. Romans 5:20: 'The law was added *so that the trespass might increase.* But where sin increased, grace increased all the more.' Until you understand sin, says Leif, the 'good news' 'will remain theory, it will never become *life* to you! Unless you experience the power of sin in your heart, you will never experience the power of grace in your heart.'

¹⁴ Hence the value of studying Exodus, Numbers or Jeremiah. I have sat in a UCCF staff conference and watched staff both male and female turned to tears of worship as they saw the cross more clearly, through hearing Ezekiel's words expounded on sin and judgment.

¹⁵ We find the same emphasis on preserving the relationship with the Spirit in the 'Do not grieve the Spirit' passage at the heart of Paul's instructions about behaviour in Eph 4:30.

¹⁶ Cf. Jesus' uncompromising challenge in Matt 5:30: 'It is better for you to lose one part of your body', if it causes us to sin, 'than for your whole body to go to hell!'

¹⁷ Galatians 6:14.

¹⁸ 1 John 2:15-17.

¹⁹ Compare James' unusually-phrased remarks on the same topic: 'Anyone who chooses to be a friend of the world becomes an enemy of God. Or do you think Scripture says without reason that the Spirit he caused to live in us envies intensely?'(4:4-5).

[20] The difference, of course, is that the Spirit's control leads ultimately to true freedom (2 Cor 3:17), whereas domination by the all-encompassing media of this age is ultimately a brainwashing: sometimes consciously so. (Neo-Marxists would call it 'hegemony'.)

[21] Cranfield, p.296.

[22] Andrew Jukes, *The Law of the Offerings* (n.d.), pp.197-98. Jukes is an evangelical mystic from the nineteenth century whose books, while clearly of their time, are enormously profound and deserve to be far better known.

[23] Perhaps we can say the 'instructions' are God's agenda in the sense of showing us where we need to get to; only through Christ can we get there. The same is true of the old testament law as a whole: it unpacks what it means to live by love (13:8,10) – while showing us that only Christ can enable us to do it.

[24] In 1 Peter 3:21-22, as in Romans 6, all this links up with the meaning of baptism.

[25] Note too that in Colossians 3, when Paul again guides his readers what to 'rid yourselves of' from 'your earthly nature' and what instead to 'clothe yourselves with', he then speaks of our 'new self' being *'renewed in knowledge in the image of its Creator'*; and he concludes the section, 'Let the Word of Christ dwell in you richly' (vv10,16). So our absorption of the Word is vital to our being 'renewed in knowledge', in increasing transformation into God's image.

[26] The secular world attaches a negative meaning to 'holiness'. A challenge for us is to recapture its positive sense in our own imaginations: that glowing glory of purity that reflects the majesty of God.

[27] Cf. 2 Cor 3:17: 'Where the Spirit of the Lord is, there is freedom.' It is not anarchy, because it is set within the context of sonship, Christ's Lordship and the indwelling of the Spirit. True freedom can only exist within such a context.

[28] Some of us from broken families may have to work deliberately at learning to praise God through this concept. It may be a profoundly healing experience – and very important for the health of our own children.

[29] Cf. the marvellous moment in *The Secret Diary of Adrian Plass* (1987), p.64: 'He knows a different God to the one I do. His God's *nice!*'

[30] Cf. 1 Cor 12:3.

[31] Cranfield (p.18) helpfully presents this verse as the response to 3:23, where we all 'fall short of the glory of God'.

[32] Cf. 2 Cor 11:23-29.

[33] There is a hint here of a holistic notion of the environment different from that of our mechanistic Western worldview, and closer to those of, say, Australian Aboriginals or Native Americans. This is not without political implications.

[34] Cf. 2 Cor 4:6.

[35] Jack Clemo, *The Invading Gospel* (1972), p.67. Clemo himself knew blindness and deafness, and his triumphant book contains some outstanding Christian perspectives on the meaning of suffering.

[36] Cf. Rom 5:21. Abraham's story in 4:19-21 is among other things the story of this new kingdom breaking miraculously into one family's despair: of a 'God who gives life to the dead and calls things that are not as though they were' (v17), the God of a whole new order.

[37] 'Surrender the self that would fulfil that fate and the fate itself collapses,' Clemo continues. 'You become a new creature with a new destiny' (p.116).

[38] Cf. Jam 1:18: 'He chose to give us birth through the Word of truth, that we might be a kind of firstfruits of all he created.' (Note again the linkage of the Word in James and the Spirit in Paul.)

[39] But it is only because of the cross that we are liberated from the 'law of sin and death' (8:2). Paul's most lyrical account of how 'we will be changed... the perishable must clothe itself with the imperishable' comes in 1 Corinthians 15:42-58; but at its close he suddenly remarks – almost jarringly, to my ears at least – 'The sting of death is sin, and the power of sin is the law.' As in Romans 6, it is only because the penalty of the law has been dealt with at the cross that all this becomes possible.

[40] Or as v19 puts it, we the 'sons of God' are not yet fully 'revealed'. Cf. 1 John 3:2: 'Dear friends, now we are children of God, and what we will be has not yet been made known.'

[41] A friend who was sexually violated told me that the one thing which made sense for her in the following hours came from someone who said, 'Jesus is crying now too.'

[42] Even the creation's 'subjection to frustration' had meaning (v20): for example, we have learned things about the love and humility of God that could never have been revealed were it not for the Fall, our lostness, and the astounding and unimaginable act of self-abasement and rescue that God performed at the cross. (It isn't the resurrection that is hard to believe in Christianity; as Peter says, 'It was impossible for death to keep its hold on' God incarnate (Acts 2:24). It is the cross that is the really staggering part of the Easter story: that the God with so many galaxies at his disposal should submit himself to suffer like this. That is astonishing love. It is unsurprising that Muslims still find it the toughest part of Christian belief.)

[43] 1 Thess 4:13.

[44] The Greek could also be read as 'In all things he works', that is, the Spirit, in view of v27. An attraction of this reading is that then these verses develop the themes of the first part of chapter 8, with regard to how and where we are being 'led by the Spirit' (cf. v14).

[45] Cf. American novelist Theodore Dreiser: 'As I see him, the unutterably infinitesimal individual weaves among the mysteries a floss-like and wholly meaningless course – if course it be. In short, I catch no meaning from all I have seen, and pass quite as I came, confused and dismayed.' (Quoted in Clark Pinnock, *What's the Point?*(1972), p.8.)

[46] Likewise in Eph 1:4, where predestination is not about heaven or hell (as we sometimes think) but about holiness.

[47] It is noteworthy that Paul reuses the childbirth image from Rom 8:22 in this context in Gal 4:19.

[48] 2 Thess 1:10, 2:14.

[49] Genesis 3:5.

[50] 2 Peter 1:4.

[51] The past tense is striking in John 17:22, as it is in Rom 8:30. Nee comments, 'We look around and see breakdown everywhere, and we wonder, "What is the Church coming to?" I tell you, she is not "coming to" anything; she has arrived. God reached His end in Christ before the foundation of the world, and we move forward with Him on the basis of what already is. As we move in the light of that eternal fact, we witness its progressive manifestation... The only possibility of spiritual progress lies in our discovering the truth

as God sees it; the truth concerning Christ, the truth concerning ourselves in Christ, the truth concerning the Church the Body of Christ... God sees the Church utterly pure, utterly perfect. To know today the ultimate glory in heaven is the one sure way of living in the power of that glory on earth.' Nee's whole treatment is well worth reading. (*What Shall This Man Do?* (1961), pp.161-63.)

[52] The quotation is from T.S.Eliot's *The Elder Statesman*.

[53] Gooding observes that the foundation of our assurance in God's love in 5:1 is firstly his justice rather than his mercy. That is, assurance will be an increasing problem if we lose the sense of the 'legal', of what it means that Christ has 'paid for' our sins.

[54] As we noted at the end of our section on Ephesians, Paul emphasizes that everything that matters in salvation is available to us because we are 'in Christ'.

[55] 2 Cor 3:18.

[56] Often it has to do with our experiences of our own fathers. It is a huge responsibility to father children, because we define for them the meaning of the word 'Father' in a way that will shape their approach to the most crucial relationship of all.

[57] Perhaps the story of David and the death of Absalom has its uses here, in helping us understand a tiny bit of what fatherhood is – and might mean to God. 'O my son Absalom! My son, my son Absalom! If only I had died instead of you - O Absalom, my son, my son!' (2 Samuel 18:33).

[58] This phrase is from the similar argument in 1 Cor 15:50-57, where Paul declares that, because sin and the law are dealt with, resurrection and full transformation are guaranteed.

[59] The same question shapes chapters 9-11, but on the level of national, not individual, suffering and predestination. If the Jewish nation, the very heirs of the promises, can drift away from Christ, what does that say about a security that is based on God's Word? Paul responds with the two affirmations that shape chapter 9. First, 'It is not as though God's Word has failed' (v6ff); rather, his promises shape history, and ultimately Israel's national history has truly been shaped by those promises rather than human actions (e.g. Abraham's unwise efforts in conceiving Ishmael, or Jacob's deceptions). Second, Paul's reply to 'Is God unjust?'– that horrified reaction from his Pharisee opponents to his sidelining of Israel's human merits. 'Not at all!' (v14ff), he replies; God is not unjust, indeed

the golden calf incident shows Israel retaining their national place in God's purposes only through his merciful compassion that transcends their merits – or errors. Paul then explains Israel's situation in detail, leading us to the triumphant reaffirmation of God's trustworthiness at the end of ch.11: 'God's gifts and God's call are irrevocable' (11:29). This is vital for Paul's Jewish readers who are often in his mind in this Epistle (eg 4:1,7:1). But as Leif Andersen observes, it is also a deeply emotional issue – both for Paul himself and for us. 'The greater the love, the greater the sorrow. Paul's leap of joy' (chapter 8) 'releases the saddest outburst in the whole letter' in 9:2. The deeper our joy at the glory of ch.8, the greater our grief for our neighbours still outside Christ. In this world, glory and grief continue to go together – if we have learned to weep over its lost cities as Jesus did over unrepentant Jerusalem: 'If you, even you, had only known what would bring you peace' (Luke 19:41-42, 13:34)

7

Eleven Reasons to Reread Revelation

How could we omit Revelation from our pioneering! Yet the book has an alarming reputation.

There is a whole group of commentators whose discussions make it sound very daunting. The back-covers of their works are full of ominous comments about 'abstruse symbolism', 'bizarre imagery,' and the like. There has been a different group who saw Revelation as a fairly straightforward guide to the last years of human history; but they are out of fashion, and they had their problems too. The result is to leave many of us feeling that Revelation will be a hard book to tackle.

Yet we cannot believe it was meant to be incomprehensible. Certainly, if God designed the Bible to give us sustenance for seventy years of discipleship, some sections may be operating on 'time-release'; they release their nourishment only in response to an acquaintance deepened over the years. Nevertheless, 2 Timothy 3:16 remains true: '*All* Scripture', Revelation included, 'is useful for teaching, rebuking, correcting, and training in righteousness.' So to neglect Revelation is to live out a lack of faith in the revealing power of the Spirit – particularly as this is the one book in the Bible that comes specifically with a promise of blessing for those who read it (1:3)!

So a pioneering spirituality cannot neglect Revelation; because what we will receive from Revelation we will not receive anywhere else. *Lord, I trust you. Please help me understand this book, at least a little...*

So why should we make the effort? For at least eleven reasons!

Because of what it teaches us about Jesus (Chapter 1)

Revelation is not a puzzle or a horoscope. Above all, Revelation, throughout, is the 'revelation of Jesus Christ' (1:1). We learn much about Jesus from the Gospels, as we watch his life, his actions and teaching, and above all his death and resurrection on earth. But we also need to absorb the supernatural vision that Revelation 1:12ff gives us, that makes John fall at his feet as though dead (v17).

We don't need to understand every detail, but we do need to let that dazzling holy purity soak deep into our imaginations. Those eyes like blazing fire, that we encounter either in surrender or in judgment; those feet burning as he walks the earth, amid his churches; that sword from his mouth that is the piercing Word of God... Here is an overwhelming force of life that leaves the Apostle (who lent back so easily against this same Christ's shoulder at the Last Supper) devastated on the ground. Our Christianity is incomplete if we have never understood why.

And then that Christ places his right hand on John (v17; imagine how that would feel) and he says: 'Do not be afraid.' He does not waste these words on those who do not need them. And what he adds (v18), we can turn straight into acts of adoration:

Lord, I worship you that you are the First and the Last; thank you that you, preeminently, are the Living One; thank you that you the Living One, astonishingly, became dead; thank you that you are alive for ever and ever, and have the keys of death and hades....

The vision of Christ's glory is what equips John to hear God's Word for his culture. But this is only the beginning. Right through the book, Revelation keeps on showing us more of the glory of Jesus. (The phrase 'the Lamb' occurs twenty-six times.) Amid all the puzzling symbols, we need to keep anchored (and responsive) to that.

Because of what it teaches us about local churches (Chapters 2-3)

Revelation 2 and 3 are a series of letters from the Lord to a range of local churches. They are described clearly and honestly. God, we see over and over again, knows – and values – their actions. Some score highly on faithfulness and discernment of false teachers, but, crucially, they have lost their first love (2:2,4). Others score highly on love, but are disastrously weak on the truth (2:19-20). If we reflect on each letter, we learn how the Lord feels about the condition of these ordinary congregations, and what the consequence of their particular approach is liable to be.

The Ephesian church is a fascinating example, because it has received five messages in the course of the new testament: Ephesians, 1 and 2 Timothy (Timothy was based in Ephesus), this letter, and Paul's address in Acts 20. And here, as elsewhere in the new testament[1], we sense 'second-generationitis' set in; the sclerosis that can happen once the days of pioneering enthusiasm (and pioneering blunders) are over.[2] It seems Ephesus had finally learned the lessons about wrong doctrine that Paul had impressed so tearfully on their elders[3] and on Timothy[4]; we don't know what struggles they had passed through, but finally they had 'tested those who claim to be apostles but are not, and found them false' (Rev 2:2). A heritage to be proud of! And the Lord had seen their 'deeds, your hard work and your perseverance.... You have persevered and endured hardships for my name, and have not grown weary' (vv2,3). And now... and now, with all that, their witness was on the edge of being terminated (v5).

It is painful to read. For some of us it comes very close to home. We feel we have worked hard, laboured, persevered. And the Lord is not uninterested in these things; over and over again in these chapters he will say, 'I know your deeds' (2:2,19, 3:1,8,15). But somewhere along the line, Ephesus had lost the passion (v4). We recognize it all too clearly: among all our labours in God's service, a tiredness comes that leaves no strength to pray, to love, to worship. And our service grows weary, mechanical; the light is going out. The Lord issues a trumpet call to face up to the issue ('Remember', v5): we need to recognize the importance of the problem, and seek seriously for the Spirit to rekindle that 'first love' for Jesus. Collectively, too, 'lampstands' do most certainly get 'removed' (v5). There are all kinds of movements that once burnt with the fire of love for Christ but have no spiritual impact now, though tragically the purely human structure carries on regardless.[5]   Truth held without the 'first love' can soon extinguish all light; such churches can bring shame rather than glory to the gospel. And the 'removal of the lampstand' can happen to people who have worked so very hard for God's honour (vv2-3)...

Father, I thank you for your Word; please help me, help us in our own congregation, to grasp and work on the lessons of Ephesus. (And those in the letters that follow ...)

But after the seven letters, Revelation changes gear. An astounding and inspiring vision of glory is now in store for us. We need to pioneer on in the book...

Because of what it teaches us about heaven (Chapters 4-5)[6]

Revelation 4 and 5 take us to heaven. We need that. As we've noted earlier, Paul regards our 'hope' of heaven as a spiritual 'helmet', protecting our thinking (1 Thess 5:8); we've seen, too, how Peter presents a direct alternative between being dominated by unclean desires and being gripped by this longing for the eternal world of heaven.

This time, we get to see heaven for ourselves. And of course these chapters are strange. They ought to be. Of course they strain our understanding to its limit. That's what we should expect! But where understanding fails, worship and love continue. Read them and let the wonder and the glory sweep past you and into you.

We can leave aside what is (as yet) out of our reach, and worship God now for what is plain. There is a throne at the heart of heaven (4:2); one Lord, who has set his glory in eternity, exalted above the universe. *I love and praise you, Lord!* That throne is expressed through a rainbow (v3)– and we recall God gave us the rainbow as a sign of his mercy (Genesis 9:12-16). *Thankyou that, even in this book of judgment, your reign is expressed primarily through loving mercy!*

There are created beings there. We don't know much about them, but thank God that he has a place for created individuals right by his throne. And he honours them – he gives them thrones (v4). Again, that says a lot about the reign of heaven, marked as it is by the love that Christ embodied ('To him who overcomes I will give the right to *sit with me on my throne!*,' he says to the weakest of the seven churches (3:21). *I worship you, Lord!*) So does the presence of seven lamps before the throne, 'the sevenfold Spirit of God' (v5).[7] Light reveals; God reigns by light and revelation, not by darkness and secrecy. Presumably the lamps of the Spirit reveal the universe to the throne, and the throne to the universe. We recall that in John 16:8-10 likewise the Spirit reveals human sin for what it is, and divine righteousness for what that is. And it is by that same Spirit that we too are involved in the ongoing revelation of that reign (Acts 1:6-8).

There are 'living creatures' here too; utterly preoccupied with the divine holiness, furnished with innumerable eyes to feast endlessly on that glory (vv6-8). 'Living creatures': *life* is what marks them out, and they praise the God who '*lives* for ever and ever'; life and holiness go together. We've heard that denied; we've heard it said that holiness goes with a life-denying asceticism. Not so. Sin goes with decay; holiness goes with abundant, overwhelming life. *(Again, I glorify you,*

Lord!) Even if God had never revealed himself through the cross, still that endlessly life-giving holiness would be eternally worthy of our praise.

Because of what it teaches us about worship
(Chapters 4-5 again)

Obviously a book that is above all the 'Revelation of Jesus Christ' will give us many clues about how we respond to that revelation. ('I, John, am the one who heard and saw these things. And when I had seen them, I fell down to worship', we read in the last chapter. He had understood.) Why not go through the many outbursts of praise in the book, and see what they teach about worship?

For example, we can reflect on each of the three terms in 1:5, and then turn them into praise: *Thankyou, Lord Christ, that you are the faithful witness... the firstborn from the dead... the ruler of the kings of the earth!* John too responds in deliberate worship in 1:6 – and then suddenly seems swept up into joy in 1:7; sometimes that happens to us too! Or we can turn to chapters 4 and 5, with their threefold base for the adoration of God. First, for who he *is* - his eternal nature and holiness (4:8); then, for what he *does* - his glory as our sovereign Creator and Planner (4:11); and again for what he *has done* - his glory as Redeemer and builder of the global Church (5:9). *Father, please help me begin to learn to worship you for all that you are!*

And look at the symphony of praise in chapter 5: the four living creatures and the twenty-four elders sing their 'new song' to the Lamb (v9) (*our* prayers are at the centre of this, v8). Then comes the second movement (v11): millions upon millions of angels join the chorus of praise in a 'loud voice'. In a third movement, John hears `every creature in heaven and earth' join in (v13): leading to the climactic moment (v14) when the living creatures say, 'Amen', and the elders fall down and worship.

Hallelujah! One day we shall see this with our own eyes!

Because of what it tells us about suffering
(Chapters 5-6)

In chapters 5 and 6 we read of a sealed book no one can understand. Chapter 6 reveals it as the book of human suffering: of imperialism, war, famine, economic injustice, plague, religious persecution and – perhaps hardest of all – the silence of heaven, in the seventh seal (8:1). John 'wept and wept' because no one could open the book and explain it.

But it turns out that there is someone who can – the Lamb who was slain! Only he can open the book: for only he has been to the deepest heart of the darkness, and there redeemed us and made us a people for God (5:9-10). *(Lord Jesus, I worship you...)* Here is something enormously important for us to absorb.

Only here, only in the crucified Christ, can we find the ultimate answer to human suffering.

Because of what it tells us about judgment
(Chapters 7-11)

Does Revelation teach us the permanent principles hidden but active in every phase of history? Or does it show us a final, climactic period of history, when everything is at last 'revealed' as it truly is (cf. 15:4)?

Probably both. We are given three sequences of seven judgments – seven seals, seven trumpets, seven bowls – not overlapping entirely, but all apparently culminating in a climax of 'earthquake, thunder and hail' (6:12-17, 11:15-19, 16:17-21) that seems to mark the End.[8] In Revelation we are brought face to face with tough realities: that human sin and rebellion result in horrendous consequences; that these are not accidents, but that as one evil after another impacts the human race it is because it 'was given' them (a repeated phrase[9]) to do this. In 'judgment', then, the evils normally restrained by God are let loose (e.g. 9:1-2,14, probably 7:1-3), as a consequence of human sin. *(I worship you, Lord; you are Judge, and your judgments are righteous. And I thank you for Jesus who 'redeemed us from wrath'...)* But even when evil seems rampant, God remains sovereign.

Because of what it tells us about spiritual warfare (Chapter 12)

Revelation reveals. Behind the outward human events of war and persecution, we are shown demonic forces at work (9:14-16, 12:17, chapter 13, 16:14). Chapter 12 (possibly sweeping sublimely back to prehistoric times and Satan's fall, and probably taking in the time of the Incarnation) presents the 'dragon', the devil, seeking to devour the child who will share the throne of God, then failing and being driven out of heaven *(Hallelujah!)*, to unleash a brief period of unparalleled evil on earth (v12) – the days of the antichrist.[10]

There are many fascinating things here which we don't have space to go into. Some verses may not yield their secrets in our first or even fifth reading of Revelation. But we can set them aside for now; what is clear is that, whatever the details mean, this chapter teaches us how satanic onslaught is to be resisted by the 'overcomers', the people of God. 'They overcame him by the blood of the Lamb, and by the word of their testimony; they did not love their lives so much as to shrink from death.'

This central verse isn't entirely easy. But perhaps we may think of it like this. First, what does it mean to overcome? The victors here resemble those of 20:4, who suffered and did not give way and are vindicated triumphantly in the aftermath. (Compare Hebrews 11:35: they 'were tortured and refused to be released, so that they might gain a better resurrection'.) God's glory turns out triumphant even at those times when evil might most surely seem to have conquered the 'saints' (Rev 11:7-10, 13:7); and this is the pattern of the cross.

And so we overcome Satan *'by the blood of the Lamb'*, which has reconciled us to the all-wise God who will guarantee that anything we experience of 'becoming like him in his death' leads to our becoming like him in his resurrection.[11] But it also is that cross which guarantees us freedom from all Satan's accusations (12:10, Rom 8:33-34). And therefore it has the dramatic effect that Paul points to in Colossians 2:15: Christ's death has liberated us, once and for all, from all that the power of darkness can do.

Then, the 'overcomers' triumphed *'by the word of their testimony'* (they 'hold to the testimony of Jesus', vv17, cf. 20:4). We know from Romans 10:9-10 that the benefits of the cross become particularly real for us through our own act of confession of Christ. So perhaps here: does not the deliberate, insistent affirmation of the authority of Christ seem to have a powerful effect in times of fear or temptation or spiritual attack?[12] Is that why the 'loud voice' of 12:10 is all-important: *'Now'*, the time when Satan's power seems to be running rampant, is in fact the day of the 'power and kingdom of our God'?[13] And of 'the authority of his Christ', because in the 'blood of the Lamb and the testimony of Jesus' there is something the very worst of the power of darkness can never overthrow; and this awareness is our saving anchor throughout the toughest of possible times?

And, finally, *'They did not love their lives so much as to shrink from death'*: and that made them unconquerable.[14] Satan was left with little he could do. In its turn this triumphant freedom is obviously grounded in a profound faith in the heaven that has been the theme of earlier sections of Revelation (and compare Hebrews 10:34); we again encounter the reality that the hope of heaven is our essential 'anchor for the soul, firm and secure' throughout all spiritual warfare (Heb 6:19).

Lord, I worship you that at Calvary you showed yourself the faithful one – and the triumphant one. And Lord, you are the Almighty; please help me, Father, to grow in my faith in the blood of the Lamb; my devotion to the testimony of Jesus; and my liberation from the 'desires of this world' (1 John 2:17)...

Because of what it may teach us about future persecution (Chapter 13)

Here Christians disagree. Certainly the principle of the antichrist has been at work throughout the centuries (2 Thessalonians 2:7). But probably Revelation 13 also presents a final evil figure in whom one day will be consummated, unrestrained, all that Satan has been seeking to accomplish in the worst dictators – the Antiochus Epiphanes, the Neros, the Hitlers and Stalins – throughout the long spirals of human history. Satan, the 'dragon', is embarked upon a climactic assault on 'those who hold to the testimony of Jesus', and this is how he does it (12:17-13:1). Here at last he brings forth a tyrant (the 'beast', 'the Animal') with total power, who can demand blasphemous worship as the condition for being free to buy or sell at all (13:17)[15], and slaughters all who refuse (13:15). In this time of 'revelation' the choice is clear: in your forehead you carry either the mark of the Animal or the name of the Lamb (13:16-14:1).

Must we 'arm our minds' (and train ourselves and our children) for the possibility of having to live faithfully – true 'radicals' – through such a situation? Christians disagree. But, with the Great Commission now apparently so close to completion, the very uncertainty should make us prepare our hearts. Both in Russia and China, something like it happened in the very recent past. 'I have been greatly stirred by reading Revelation,' wrote the great pioneer missionary C.T.Studd, founder of WEC. 'The chief lesson I learned is that as Christ died for the world, so also must we, His Body, do the same. The tortures and deaths inflicted on Christians will evidently be of such a nature that no human being could endure them unless he was indwelt by God's Spirit. So the test will be a perfect one and only those come through as victors who can do the impossible, endure the unendurable, being specially enabled and indwelt by the Spirit of God. Thus shall God be perfectly justified in His anger and judgment when He comes to deal with a world which tortured and killed his Son Who came to save it, and did the same to His Body, the true Church who followed His only Son. Who indeed shall be able to stand? Holy-Ghost-possessed men, women and children and none else!'[16]

Many Christians will disagree with Studd. They remind us that the second coming will occur suddenly, when we least expect it (Matt 24:44); and since the Revelation persecutions would so clearly herald the End, they argue that the Church as we know it must already have been removed unexpectedly, by the events described in 1 Thessalonians 4:15-18. These, they suggest, may come on us at any moment; and only then, with all true Christian influence and restraint (the preservative 'salt of the earth') removed, will all hell break loose (2 Thess 2:6-8).[17]

It may be so. But Scripture is ambiguous (perhaps because both possibilities are spiritually beneficial for us). At least we need to be forearmed for the possibility that the Nazi annihilation of the Jews will not remain history's ultimate expression of evil, but that there is a worldwide persecution to come which will surpass it in horror, and of which the Church will bear the brunt.[18]

Lord Christ, do not bring us to the time of trial, but deliver us from evil; and if it does fall to us to face persecution, as it has to so many of our brothers and sisters, please give us grace at the time we need it (Heb 4:16), and your strength to be faithful in our utter weakness; so that if the 'day of evil' comes, we may be able to stand our ground, and having done everything, to stand' (Eph 6:13)...

Because of what it teaches us about 'civilized' religious and economic structures and systems (Chapters 17:1-19:5)

Part of Satan's final push concerns the emergence of a vast religious-economic system that Revelation refers to as 'Babylon'. Reggae fans may recognize the use of 'Babylon' to describe Western civilization; as we read chapters 17 and 18 we may wonder if, one day at least, the reggae musicians will be right. Even today we feel discomfort as, time and again, we see evil coming from the soulless machinery of our godless economic systems in their blindness and heartlessness: knowing no ethics but profit, destroying the physical environment, defiling the moral environment, grinding down the poor throughout the world. *(Lord, teach me to be perceptively holy, help me know how to be radical...)* Revelation shows us our discomfort may be justified; the devil can be underneath our supposedly 'free', but so evidently fallen, 'market system'.(18: 11-20)[19]

If that is so, then history's final battle may not be between the Christian gospel and communism, or the Christian gospel and Islam. The final, most dangerous foe of Christian truth may be what has been termed 'McWorld': the seamless global dominance of our own apostate Western system, denying all gods except money, pleasure and power. Or in the terms of Matthew 6:24, the final conflict may be between the two old adversaries, God and Mammon.

At any rate, we see here the emergence of an opposition that shapes the last six chapters of Revelation. On the one hand, we read, 'Come' (17:1) and see the godless system, the 'great city' with its sins 'piled up to heaven'(18:5,10), Babylon, the Great Prostitute. On the other hand, 'Come' (21:9-10) and see the 'holy city' 'coming down out of heaven', New Jerusalem, the Bride. We may even wonder if this is the climax of something going on right through the Bible; maybe as far back as Genesis 11 and 12 – the long alternative between the powers of Babel/Babylon (the city built on human pride, 'reaching to the heavens' by brute human strength, Gen 11:4), and God's people on their faith-full way to his promised heavenly 'city that is to come' (Gen 12:1-2, Heb 11:8-10,13-16, 13:14, Gal 4:26, Col 3:1-3).[20] *(Please help me get my loyalty right, Father!)* There may be horizons beyond horizons here...

Because of what it teaches us about the second coming and final judgment (Chapters 19:6-20:15)

There will be an End. We need to grasp this. One day the Lamb, the King, will be revealed for every eye to see. One day the long, ruinous experiment of rebellious human independence will be put to a merciful end. God himself will say 'Enough'. 'The Lord himself will come down from heaven' (1 Thess 4:16) – to judge the dead, to reward his people, to destroy those who destroy the earth (Rev 11:18). Many Christians see Revelation 20 as depicting a time directly after Christ's overthrow of the Animal at the second coming (19:11-21), when for a thousand years this world is freed from Satan's works and becomes what it was made for:[21] a paradise where the lion lies down with the lamb, and the earth is full of the knowledge of the Lord as the waters cover the sea (cf. Isaiah 11). (All heaven breaks loose!) Others interpret the chapter differently, as a picture of the Church's reign since Christ's victory at Calvary. Either possibility offers us tremendous encouragement. *Triumphant Jesus, I worship you!*

What is not in dispute is the reality of ultimate judgment at the chapter's close. Here is the stark alternative: heaven or hell. 'If anyone's name was not found written in the book of life, he was thrown into the lake of fire' (v15).

That, above all, we need to remember. *Lord, it's a fact my mind flees from. But I do believe your Word. And this is what you died for. May it shape how I relate to everyone around me...*

Because of what it tells us about the Church and about eternity (Chapters 21-22)

Revelation finishes with God's glorious new community, the New Jerusalem, finally revealed as it truly is: coming down out of heaven, 'the holy city... the Bride, the wife of the Lamb' (21:2,9). And we know what, or who, that Bride is: it is *us*! *(Thankyou, Lord!)* The promise hinted at by Paul in Ephesians 5:23-32 and 2 Corinthians 11:2 – that mysterious glory underlying his whole understanding of human sex and marriage – is now amply fulfilled. This is what history was for: this is what it was all about – the raising up, purifying and glorifying of the Church, to be, throughout the long years of eternity, the constant companion, beloved and lover, of the Lamb. The Bride 'shone with the glory of God' (21:11): sanctification is complete, Christlikeness and 'conformity to his likeness' are now, at last, a dazzling reality (cf. Rom 8:28-30, 2 Thess 1:10, 2:14). This is what was foreshadowed, sometimes encouragingly, often so brokenly, in the community of our local churches, chapels and tin tabernacles. Now, in Revelation, ultimate reality is revealed.

So the Bible's story comes to magnificent completion. We watch the return at last to Eden, to the tree of life (22:2): not now just with one couple, but an entire city. This time there will never be a 'curse' (22:3). No more death, no more mourning, no more crying, no more pain (21:4): instead, the healing of the nations (22:2), and the servants of the Lamb seeing his face, and reigning for ever and ever (22:4-5). *Hallelujah!* And the 'song of the great multitude' ('like the roar of rushing waters and like loud peals of thunder', 19:6), celebrating the triumph of the Lamb and his Bride, will be *our* song; because *we* shall be there!

'The Spirit and the Bride say, "Come!" And let him who hears say, "Come!" Whoever is thirsty, let him come... let him take of the free gift of the water of life!' (22:17).

It's all there. Read it! It isn't too bizarre or too obscure. We need it!

Notes

[1] Most obviously 2 Timothy (eg. 1:13-15), 2 Peter and 1 John; but we can also usefully read Hebrews in this light. The reality of 'second-generationitis' is the snag with the Orthodox claim to be the embodiment of new testament faith just because they are in substantial continuity with teaching that dominated large parts of the Church around the fourth or fifth century. An enormous amount of shift can take place in a spiritual movement's doctrine and priorities by its third generation, let alone in three hundred years (we would scarcely claim to be close to how the Puritans thought just because we happen to live within three hundred years of them, for example). Only the new testament gives an entirely trustworthy embodiment of the apostolic faith; any subsequent documents, while of real value, need always to be checked by their faithfulness to the sources.

[2] Phrasing it that way raises the question whether the pioneering days should ever be over. It is in most respects better to be in a pioneering 'Joshua situation' than a settled 'Judges situation'; the 'second generation' is a hard place to be, if sometimes unavoidable. Perhaps the solution is to find a way back as close to the pioneering frontier as possible.

[3] See Acts 20:28-31.

[4] 2 Timothy 1:13-14, 4:1-5.

[5] Compare Matthew 5:13: 'You are the salt of the earth. But if the salt loses its saltiness, how can it be made salty again? It is no longer good for anything, except to be thrown out and trampled by men.' (Jesus then proceeds immediately to compare the Church to a lamp, as in Revelation 2.)

[6] I want to express my particular gratitude to John Lennox for numerous insights into this section – and many others besides.

[7] I choose this translation (from NIV margin) over 'the seven spirits of God', partly because 1:4-5 seems to present the 'sevenfold Spirit' as part of the Trinity, and partly because of the integral connection between the 'sevenfold Spirit' and the Son in 5:6. We may not understand in what sense God's Spirit might be 'sevenfold', but nor should we necessarily expect to. (However: does Isaiah 11:2 give us some clues?)

[8] Rev 10:7 states that, when the seventh trumpet is sounded, the 'mystery of God will be accomplished', that is, completed; 15:1

speaks similarly about the bowls.

9 6:2,4 (twice),8, 7:2, 9:1,3,5, 13:5,7 (twice), 16:8.

10 We can and should read these sections as having application throughout history. But it also seems that Scripture is focusing our attention on a final and very specific 'short time' of crisis (cf. 12:12), described frequently in the three equivalent phrases of 1260 days, forty-two months, or three and a half times (years) – when for a brief period God allows humanity to experience the full consequences of its rebellion. Its brevity is drawn attention to by Jesus: mercifully 'those days will be shortened' because of their unequalled horror; 'If those days had not been cut short, no-one would survive' (Matt 24:21-22). There seems a repeated prioritization of this brief, carefully-numbered, and terrible period (Rev 11:2,3, 12:6,14, 13:5, Dan 7:25, 9:27, 12:7,11); it is the consummate time of 'revelation' climaxing human history, when all things are revealed as they really are – and also Satan's ultimate challenge to God and his people.

11 Cf. Phil 3:10-11. This is also the pattern of Romans 6:5-10, as we saw a few pages back.

12 Many evangelists would affirm that the public proclamation of Christ (in street proclamation, Jesus marches, etc) not only serves as evangelism but shifts the supernatural atmosphere that affects the fruitfulness of our evangelism.

13 It is possible that the specific 'testimony of Jesus' here is of his lordship over all earthly powers, in view of the demands of the satanic dictator in chapter 13. Paul (in a context (1 Tim 6) where he points to God as the 'blessed and only Ruler, the King of kings') speaks of 'Christ Jesus who while testifying before Pontius Pilate made the good confession'; which is (it seems) 'You would have no power over me if it were not given to you from above' (John 19:11).

14 Nigel Lee observes that suffering may be one of the few 'weapons' we have left in a postmodernity that has lost faith in words, truth and reason. And cf. Roger Forster and Paul Marston, *God's Strategy in Human History* (1989 edition), p.77, on the 'methods by which God works': 'The suffering and atoning death of Christ, and the suffering and death of the martyrs, will finally be too much for the forces of evil... The church is moving toward the "evil day" in the battle of the Lord. In this day we must withstand, and having done all must stand... Through this will come the final overthrow and

exhaustion of Satan and his power, in which the knowledge of God will fill the universe as the waters cover the sea.'
[15]The technology of an increasingly cashless, credit-card society could make this all very easy to begin with. The authorities would be very sorry: your credit line is currently cut off, your grocery, electricity and medical bills are not being paid, and you obviously cannot run up further expenditures. Eventually, since you cannot pay your local property taxes, you lose your house. And all because of your intransigence on a minor matter of worship! Life could become increasingly impossible for whole families, yet very cleanly and with no unpleasant violence or brutality. At least, that is how it might start.

[16] C.T.Studd, *Fool and Fanatic?*, ed. Jean Walker (1980), p.57.

[17] This is the view underlying Tim LaHaye's *Left Behind* novel series, that have topped the American secular bestseller lists for so astonishingly long. It should be said that there is a further group of interpreters who read these passages almost exclusively in terms of the underlying principles throughout history. To me, this approach is right in what it affirms but inadequate in what it denies. An example might be Michael Willcox's presentation of chapter 13 in his *Bible Speaks Today* commentary on Revelation (1975), pp.123-28, where there seems a yawning gulf between the brutal tone of vv14-17 and Willcox's exposition in terms of Christians 'reserving the right to criticise' the government in a liberal democracy. Whatever school of prophetic interpretation one belongs to, a denial that these passages also refer to a time of unparalleled crisis at the climax of history seems to neglect the whole flavour of the text. (Is there something in the English – as distinct from Celtic, French or Russian – nature that shuns apocalypse, and hankers after the hope that all things will rest within the bounds of moderation?)

[18] Roger Forster suggests that a major purpose of the entire book is to help us understand (and this is relevant to every era) what it means to be 'overcomers'. Certainly this is an emphasis at the start of the book, climaxing each of the seven letters in chs. 2-3, and at its close, in 21:7. 'He who stands firm to the end will be saved' (Matt 24:13, cf. Rev 2:26) – because 'standing firm' demonstrates that we are 'born of God' and have within us that true faith by which we are saved, as John himself says elsewhere: 'This is the

victory that has overcome the world, even our faith. Who is it that overcomes the world? Only he who believes that Jesus is the Son of God' (1 John 5:4-5).

[19] In that case we need to look out prayerfully, in various areas of our lives (our jobs; our media consumption; our investment), for the point where 18:4 may become relevant to us: 'Come out of her... so that you will not share in her sins.' This is not an easy issue, because sometimes we are called to be Christ's 'salt' resisting satanic dominance and bringing transformation into some very difficult places. But there can come a stage where involvement in a system is impossible without sin; it is (or should be) impossible to be a Christian mafioso, for example. And then we have to 'come out'.

[20] If this is correct, it sheds an interesting light on the old testament, where at least five books – 2 Chronicles, Isaiah, Jeremiah, Lamentations and Ezekiel – can be viewed as helping us understand the astonishing occurrence when the holy city of Jerusalem is apparently overthrown by Babylon. And Daniel, of course, teaches us how to live in Babylon, and to experience that ultimately God is sovereign even there.

[21] In other words, Satan doesn't win even in this world; on this planet, and not only by the coming of a new earth ('the first earth had passed away', Rev 21:1), the triumph of God will be made fully manifest. 'God didn't create the earth to simply screw it up like a piece of paper and throw it away', writes Roger Forster (explaining why he is 'staunchly pre-millenialist', in *Doing a New Thing?*, ed. Brian Hewitt (1995), p.126).

Epilogue:
And There Is So Much More...

I love the old testament!

It's true. There is so much glory in it. Agreed, some parts can be hard work. But once we realize how much is awaiting our discovery, we wonder why we didn't start reading it before.

'Your God is too small,' J.B.Phillips warned his readers a generation ago. It's often the case. We set out to share our faith, and realize we hardly know the God we're talking about. We meet suffering or temptation, and discover God is not present to us as a vivid reality.

When Jesus selected his disciples, he chose them to '*be with him*' (first!), and only then 'that he might send them out to preach' (Mark 3:14). Before God sent Moses to Egypt, he first led him to the burning bush for a dramatic revelation of his nature, expressed in his Name I AM WHO I AM (Exodus 3). God's way of making Isaiah into a prophet was likewise through an overwhelming vision of his divine majesty: only then was Isaiah ready to say, 'Here am I, send me' (Isaiah 6).

We desire to be God's prophetic people in the coming century. Where, then, shall we go for such a vision? The answer is obvious: to his self-revelation in the Bible – but the *whole* Bible. Of course the new testament is the place to start. But God has prepared for us a full diet, to give us a rounded picture of what he is like; and it's not for us to tell him we don't need what he wants to give us from Joshua, Exodus or Malachi! '*All* Scripture is God-breathed and useful...so that the man of God may be *thoroughly* equipped!'(2 Tim 3:16-17).

Welcome to the banquet!

It's tragic to meet believers who have been Christians for years and still have never read Genesis. (How can we grasp any book, the Bible included, unless we grasp its beginning and end?) For Genesis, above all, is the book of the basics. It has been marred by the long wrangles over evolution; but they are not what it's about. If we want to learn what God is like, Genesis 1 is a great place to start. If we want to know what it means to be human, chapter 2 shows us Adam as God's creature enjoying beauty, as explorer, worker, scientist, lover, poet. And if we want to be able to explain why God's world has gone so wrong, then we need chapter 3.

And what masterpieces of psychological and sociological realism these 'primitive myths' turn out to be. We watch temptation come to Eve in just the same ways as it comes to us: Did God *really* say...?'; 'You won't *really* die...'; 'God wouldn't judge you for so trivial a thing as a fruit.' And, underneath these, we see emerging the fundamental question that faces us all: will we worship God as God, submitting our lives to his definition of good and evil, or will we seek to 'be like God' ourselves, defining our own 'right' and 'wrong' (v 5)? Who rules – God or the human ego? And we watch how those first human beings snatch at an autonomy that shatters their relationship with the God who comes seeking them; and how then their other relationships disintegrate in turn – with each other (v 12), with nature (v 17); a breakdown spreading out into the general relational collapse (familial, sexual, racial) that ravages our world today.

By chapter 4 the process gets as far as the first murder. Cain is left separated from God's presence, radically alienated and lonely (4:14). The story seems a mirror of contemporary social reality as we watch him seeking to hide from his loneliness, starting a family, building a city. But human relationships don't ultimately work when that central relationship with God is gone. As the chapter moves on, human creativity – agriculture, music, use of metals – produces a more advanced culture (vv20-22); but it's all built on the wrong foundations, and slowly the earth becomes 'full of violence' (6:11), fit only for judgment and ecological catastrophe (7:23). A radical Christian analysis of our twenty-first century predicament could hardly do better than start from these profoundly realistic chapters.

Abraham's story that follows is equally fundamental. It always helps to see what the new testament chooses to emphasize about an old testament narrative; and in the new testament we see Abraham presented as the prototype of faith (Romans 4, Hebrews 11). Genesis depicts him venturing out from all his security, trusting God for his safety and his 'name' (12:1-2): unlike the egoists of Babel, anxious to build their own reputations and seeking security in their own tower (11:4), rather than obeying God's command to trust him and spread out across the earth (9:1-7). (It makes so much sense when we put it all together.) We watch as Abraham slowly learns the life of faith: grappling with the relative importance of possessions and relationships (12:14-16, 13:2,6-9, 14:22-23); struggling with uncertainty and the frustration of his deepest longings (15:2-3, 6-8); foolishly trying to bring about God's purpose by his own efforts (chapter 16); learning to wrestle with God in prayer (chapter 18); and, in a final lesson in faith, being challenged to sacrifice the very son on whom his dreams were centred (chapter 22). (Reminding us, perhaps, of another Father who, centuries later, went further, indeed went through to the very end with the sacrifice of *his* Son.)

And that's just the 'first course'. Exodus follows: the story of the way God sets his people free. There's the stunningly prophetic picture of Israel divinely delivered because, when judgment comes, they are sheltered under the blood of the lamb (chapter 12). But it doesn't end there; we watch how God prepares a people for himself, revealing his ways till, in the book's closing verses, he comes to live among them and the overpowering divine glory fills the tabernacle. (As Rene

Padilla says, there are two issues in Exodus: how to get the people out of Egypt, and how to get Egypt's effects out of the people. We can apply both of these – to both our individual salvation and transformation, and to our sociopolitical concerns.)

Leviticus is where it gets tough, if we're reading through from Genesis to Malachi in order. (There are other ways to do it: for example, to read one of the early books, then one of the later historical books, then one of the miscellaneous writings (Job through Song of Songs), then one of the prophets; then repeat the process.) Still, plenty of people find even Leviticus fascinating, once they've seen how the new testament uses it. Certainly speed-reading Leviticus drives home God's concern for the vital distinction (expressed in different ways for us today, of course) between what's holy and what's unclean. And that's maybe the old testament's least 'user-friendly' book!

There's so much more. What characterizes God's people when they're really going forward? Read Joshua. What's going wrong when they're stagnating, disintegrating? Read Judges. (Of course we might wonder if it's coincidence that 'Joshua' is the Hebrew for 'Jesus', 'God who saves'; and that, after the law-giver, Moses, can't bring the people into the Promised Land, someone called 'Joshua/Jesus' can and does. Then we might also wonder why the first story the book chooses to tell is about the prostitute Rahab – especially when we check the new testament's references to Rahab, and find they're concerned with justification by a living faith (Hebrews 11, James 2); which is, after all, where 'God's salvation' starts. Well, that may be another 'way in' to the book.)

Maybe we've just come into leadership, and are wondering what makes good leaders. 1 and 2 Samuel, and 1 Kings, give us a 'leadership manual', from the lives of Eli, Samuel, Saul, Jonathan, David, Solomon, Rehoboam and Jeroboam (including commando raids, love affairs, incest and the occult!). And they show us the flow of history; how God established his people in the promised land, and led them to build a temple revealing his glory to the nations; how, despite all his blessing, still they rebelled and ended up in slavery. We see, over and over again, that nothing short of a Saviour from heaven will suffice amid humanity's bentness.[2] But the lessons we learn from these narratives are also compellingly practical for discipleship today. And after all that we can study Nehemiah, and watch how God used one leader to rebuild his city in a time of defeat. (Read it alongside John White's *Excellence in Leadership*.)

There's so much here that we need for a rounded spirituality. Someone exposed to the titanic conflicts and questionings of Job is ready to be biblical rather than superficial when faced with others' suffering. The Psalms bring us face to face with God, giving us words for every intimate mood in our relations with him – joy, fear, despair, hope, thanksgiving. Proverbs is full of shrewd, practical wisdom; it's even been recommended as a management textbook! (Try it in the Living Bible.) Isaiah: glorious and indispensable – where else can we see the majesty of the living God as we do in sections like Isaiah 6 or Isaiah 40? How better to understand our rescue through the cross than via the astonishing prophecy of Isaiah 53? What more striking picture could there be of what the Spirit does than Isaiah 61; what more joyous celebration of God's gracious restoration than chapters 11-12 or 35 or 54-55; what stronger challenge to social righteousness than chapter 58? Jeremiah: we might not want a whole year with this book, but someone who has worked through Jeremiah has had burned into their soul the vital lessons that sin matters, that judgment is a reality, that God is a holy God we do not trifle with. And there's a vital reminder: Jeremiah would not have been fit to preach his fiery denunciations unless (like Jesus) he could also weep over Jerusalem, as he does, broken-heartedly, in Lamentations.

The minor prophets: negligible? Hardly! The book of Amos gave impetus to the evangelical rediscovery of social concern in recent years. (Chapter 25 of Leviticus, of all possible books, has been another basic text.) The American student movement InterVarsity have a multimedia show (fifty minutes long, with two dozen automated slide projectors) presenting God's challenge to today's society – the book they chose to base it on was Habakkuk. (The team spent a year with Habakkuk's three chapters before producing the show.) Read Habakkuk sometime to see the surprising context in which God first spoke those basic gospel words 'The just shall live by faith', and learn what it means to live by faith in a bleak time. And don't miss God's challenge to his materialistic people's priorities in Haggai; or Jonah, the tale of the reluctant missionary.

The ways forward

So how do we tackle an unfamiliar book? Some final suggestions....

▪ Decide that you *want* to know God, that you *want* to know his Word as a whole. And that, therefore, you'll set aside some time to study it in depth. (Our academic studies, or our ongoing business retraining, are important, and demand time: the results of our Bible study will be even more permanent and far-reaching.)

▪ Read it, turning what you read into prayer, and into worship. And reread it. In quantity, at least to begin with– three or four chapters a day. (At that rate we get through, say, 1 Kings in a week.) After getting a feel for the overall flow of the book, go back and study it in smaller sections and more detail. Write a one-page summary of the book; note down its general direction of thought, its main divisions and sections, and the themes and issues that are highlighted or repeated in each.[3] Check how the new testament uses it, and what it emphasizes about it.

▪ As you read, ask yourself, and ask God: Why is this passage in the Bible? What does it emphasize? What did it mean most for its original readers? What permanent principles does it present to me now? And: What does this teach me about you, Lord? about your salvation? about repentance and deepening discipleship, and faith? about people? Is there a sin for me to avoid, a promise to claim, a command to obey, an example to follow?

- Discuss the difficult passages with friends. Read books like IVP's excellent *The Bible Speaks Today* series, or CFP's *Focus on the Bible* commentaries. Take notes of your discoveries; use them as fuel for worship, and file them for reuse, along with the insights you get from books or Bible studies on the same passages. Keep exploring; there are many ways in to each book. Share (or preach!) what you've learned, with friends or co-workers, and learn from them too; set an example – make your fellowship a channel of life through which 'The Word of God increased and spread' (Acts 12:24).

This is spirituality. It will give us strength to live faithfully and radically for God in the challenging decades of the new millennium. It will make us people who genuinely '*know their God*'. And as we speak of him to others, they will sense he is not a stranger to us: that we have glimpsed his glory as we've studied his Word. So life flows out into the world.

Notes

[1] Thanks for the phrasing here to Rob Parsons.

[2] The structure of several old testament books seems to underline this lesson. In Genesis, Joseph rescues the Israelites from famine; but in the book's final verse he ends up in an Egyptian coffin, and the Bible's next book begins with him forgotten and Israel in slavery as a result. Judges tells of many God-gifted deliverers, but none can arrest the progress to the degradation of the final chapters. In 1 Samuel, a different solution, guidance by a king, is tried, with the appointment of an apparently ideal candidate, Saul; but in the book's last chapter, Saul is killed and Israel is overcome by the Philistines. David is then raised up as Israel's deliverer in 2 Samuel, but again the end of the book shows David's arrogance leading directly to the deaths of 70,000 of his people. Subsequent books show that

possession of the law, and the prophets, is not enough to keep Israel out of Babylon; and even after Babylon, the old testament closes with Malachi's warning that, as things stand, the coming of the Lord can only lead to judgment. The old testament reveals us as a race desperately in need of someone who can 'save his people from their sins', both in atonement and lasting empowerment for goodness; and that, of course, is just what is promised in the first page of Matthew.

[3] In IFES we have watched many groups of people 'turned on' to a new vision of the Bible through the 'manuscript method' pioneered by Paul Byer and others in InterVarsity-USA. Ideally this involves a group using wide-margin, double-spaced manuscripts of Bible books or shorter passages without chapter or verse divisions, which can be annotated freely and colourfully. (These can easily be created by downloading Bible passages from www.gospelcom.net, or by typing them out yourself – remove the verse numbers and add line numbers every five lines along the right-hand margin.) Participants read the passage through a few times and divide it up into sections themselves, giving headings to each section. Then they observe the 'Who? What? Where?' of each section, and highlight in different colours signs of the passage's 'flow of thought' – connections ('therefore', 'but'....) and contrasts, cause and effect, progressions, themes and words emphasized by repetition. Group members are also encouraged to record their questions and look out for things that appear strange or puzzling, and to observe the emotional and imaginative responses the passage evokes in them. Discoveries are shared and discussed in small groups; finally, connections are made between the different sections and the book's overall themes, and applications drawn out and turned into prayer. This has proved enormously fruitful in many cultures. Some aspects may sound difficult until it is watched in practice, but many churches are finding it very valuable; indeed Byer and Eric Miller have seen it work well among ordinary village people in the Indian subcontinent.

Acknowledgements

Not much of this book has been 'original'. Some acknowledgements are called for. But the snag with writing about the Bible is the glorious way it demonstrates the unity of Christ's Body! Quotations can be credited to individual books; but who could trace the sources of all (s)he has gathered from innumerable talks Sunday by Sunday, plus dozens of Bible study groups and conversations with friends? This writer was taught early on to record what he learned in a sermon or Bible study: for years in an old Bible, until the margins got overcrowded and illegible, and then, more usefully, in a loose-leaf file. The result in the preceding chapters is an indebtedness to a horde of people, hundreds certainly.

But some attempt at acknowledgement is essential. For myself the roots go back a long way: to being taught by my parents to read the Bible, as soon as I could read anything; to schooldays and especially an old head gardener, Albert Cheale, who would visit our school Christian Union and astonish and inspire us with his love of the Bible and its Author. Another huge debt is to John Lennox and Peter Elwood of Cardiff, who gathered students like myself in their homes on Sunday nights after church for thorough Bible exposition, followed by coffee and half an hour's questions. The liberating experience of a place where no question was out of bounds and most had answers, and of seeing how Scripture fits together magnificently as we worked through Genesis, Romans, 1 Corinthians or Hebrews, gave us deep confidence in the Word, and a desire to dig into, and share it. Many who attended those studies are now in Christian leadership. Would that many more university cities had such people. Their input, and that of David Gooding of Belfast, is no doubt evident in far more ways than I am aware of. Likewise the deep debts to many others: perhaps particularly to London church-planters Roger Forster and Roger Mitchell, working with whom has been a lasting education.

So any of us could go on. It is customary to say that none of the influences an author credits should be assumed to agree with what he wrote, nor responsible for his errors; that is certainly true in the above cases, which are theologically diverse. In writing about the Bible, however, one is conscious of compiling what God has already given his Church through others and confessing proudly our interdependence. It is in hope of taking a place, as all of us should, in the life-giving process Paul describes – the things we've heard, we're to pass on to faithful people, who will forward them on to yet others – that these enthusiasms and impressions are sent into the world, hopefully to be passed on again.

Christian Focus Publications publishes biblically-accurate books for adults and children. The books in the adult range are published in three imprints.

Christian Heritage contains classic writings from the past.

Christian Focus contains popular works including biographies, commentaries, doctrine, and Christian living.

Mentor focuses on books written at a level suitable for Bible College and seminary students, pastors, and others; the imprint includes commentaries, doctrinal studies, examination of current issues, and church history.

For a free catalogue of all our titles, please write to

Christian Focus Publications,
Geanies House, Fearn,
Ross-shire, IV20 1TW, Great Britain

For details of our titles visit us on our web site

http://www.christianfocus.com